Information
Sources
in Children's
Literature

INFORMATION SOURCES IN CHILDREN'S LITERATURE

A Practical Reference Guide
for Children's Librarians,
Elementary School Teachers,
and Students of Children's Literature

MARY MEACHAM

GREENWOOD PRESS
Westport, Connecticut
London, England

Contributions in Librarianship
and Information Science,
Number 24

Library of Congress Cataloging in Publication Data

Meacham, Mary, 1946-
    Information sources in children's literature.

    (Contributions in librarianship and information
science ; no. 24 ISSN 0084-9243)
    Bibliography: p.
    Includes index.
    1. Bibliography—Bibliography—Children's literature.
2. Children's literature—Bibliography. 3. Children's
literature—Book reviews—Periodicals—Bibliography.
4. Books and reading for children—Bibliography.
5. Libraries, Children's—Bibliography. I. Title.
II. Series.
Z1037.A1M4   028.52   77-91107
ISBN 0-313-20045-9

Library of Congress Catalog Card Number: 77-91107
ISBN: 0-313-20045-9
ISSN: 0084-9243

First published in 1978

Greenwood Press, Inc.
51 Riverside Avenue, Westport, Connecticut 06880

Printed in the United States of America

10   9   8   7   6   5   4   3   2   1

TO W. DAVID ZITTEL

Contents

Preface

For some time I have felt that a void exists in the knowledge of books and serial publications about children's literature among those who are interested and involved in this area. *Information Sources in Children's Literature* will be, I hope, a key to the vast resources available in dealing with the numerous questions, problems, and decisions in the area of children's trade books and other materials that librarians and teachers face daily in an ordinary elementary school library or children's section of a public library. Hopefully, it will help in deciding what children's resource materials to buy (and keep), and how to use them in answering reference questions posed by children or adults; it should help adults find out more about children's books and other media from preschool to approximately the sixth-grade level. Its scope is comprehensive, with much of it being a bibliography of bibliographies.

To some extent children's literature selection aids and reference sources are covered in courses on books and materials for children (and, rarely, in general library science reference courses), but the coverage is of necessity brief, since usually the whole range of children's books must be included in one survey course. Although many experienced librarians—in fact, many people who at a minimum have had a basic course in children's literature—will already be familiar with all or most of these titles, the purpose of this work is to supply a critical analysis of the characteristics and uses of the items included for the reader. Perhaps there will be a few new ideas or a saving of time for these people. For the inexperienced person or one with little or no background in children's literature, who nevertheless sometimes works *de facto* as a librarian or teacher, or with children, books, and nonprint media in some other capacity, I hope this book can serve as a guide. These people, in spite of their often great dedication and desire to help children, may find the operation of a children's library somewhat bewildering when they have had no specialized training. One hears reports of schools doing their library selection from a group of books brought in by a local bookstore, from a single publisher's catalog, or from pre-World War II selection aids. At least one school in a "progressive" system has a converted broom closet for its library—it is open one day every two weeks. The children's services in public libraries are sometimes little better: infrequent bookmobile service may be all that is available, and some small public libraries and branches of larger systems have only one librarian to provide all services to all patrons—children, young adults, and adults. This person, besides having to deal with a wide range of patrons, often does not have a master's degree in library science. Small public libraries have·not been able to pay enough to attract people with advanced degrees, and larger libraries and systems have often responded to tightening budgets by drastically reducing the staff of the children's section. This has also happened in school systems.

Some of these incidents may seem hardly credible (although I believe my sources to be reliable), but more sobering perhaps is this statement from *Library Manpower: A Study of Demand and Supply*, Bulletin 1852, United States Department of Labor, Bureau of Labor Statistics, 1972: "Probably no more than 40-50 percent of all librarians in the United States have a master's degree in librarianship" (p. 16). The study further states that nearly half of the 50 to 60 percent who do *not* have a master's degree work in school libraries or small public libraries where the degree is not required for employment; many if not most of these librarians are therefore working with children. Many states require a school librarian to have a certificate which usually includes a number of library science hours, in addition to a teaching certificate, either of which may require a course in children's literature. However, not all states actually *enforce* this requirement; one finds people with few if any library science hours working in school libraries. One southwestern state, for example, has only 67.5 full-time certified school librarians in the entire state, or an average of one certified school librarian for every 6,014 elementary school students! (*Summary of the Position Statement on Elementary Library/Media Programs in Oklahoma*, mimeographed material, February 10, 1977.) Public libraries vary widely in their requirements for librarians; usually, they need not require a master's degree if they do not wish to do so. A new publication by the American Association of School Libraries of the American Library Association, *Certification Model for Professional School Media Personnel*, attempts to set standards by which school media personnel may be evaluated in any state and may therefore have some effect on raising standards for school librarians.

Hopefully, this book will help some of these people, but one of the best things anyone who has not had a course in children's literature can do is to read a good children's literature textbook, such as *Children and Books*, by Zena Sutherland and May Hill Arbuthnot (Scott, Foresman College Division, 1900 East Lake Avenue, Glenview, Illinois 60025. 5th edition. 1977. $14), reading as many of the referenced children's books as possible at the same time. Students of children's literature may use *Information Sources in Children's Literature* as a help in understanding the body of reference material relating to children's books with which they are expected to familiarize themselves as part of a library science, English, education, and/or certification program.

There is never any substitute for the intelligent and concerned librarian or teacher who has children's best interests at heart. *Information Sources in Children's Literature* is meant not to encourage the abrogation of responsibility but rather to encourage the bringing together of children, books, and other media in an ever-expanding field. The joy of reading must never be sacrificed to more serious-sounding principles, no matter how admirable.

I especially wish to thank my husband, W. David Zittel, and Dr. Frances Laverne Carroll, professor of library science, University of Oklahoma, for their help, advice, encouragement, and patience in the preparation of this manuscript. Special thanks are also due the interlibrary loan department of the University of Oklahoma library for obtaining my numerous requests, and to the personnel of the library's social sciences floor for their cooperation.

I welcome users' comments and suggestions.

Introduction

Users of this guide will find that the selection aids are grouped by type in the internal arrangement. Perusal of the table of contents may therefore suggest an appropriate chapter if the name of a particular aid is not known. Every effort has been made to indicate clearly what kind of material is covered in each chapter section if the table of contents does not provide sufficient information. Users who need information about a specific title with which they are already familiar are referred to the index.

Chapter 1 deals with selecting books for children in a general sense, that is, building a basic collection. Two major, comprehensive book-selection tools and several supplementary aids are discussed.

Chapter 2 covers general periodical review sources which help keep a collection up-to-date, as well as some additional sources of reviews and news. This chapter also includes special tools in which to find book reviews for science books or basic science collections. Information about abstracts in children's literature and indexes to reviews, plus some yearly lists of best books, are also covered. The first two chapters are intended to help set up and maintain a comprehensive collection—a prerequisite for dealing with reference questions.

Chapter 3, the major reference section, provides help for special fields. It discusses guides to magazines, books on remedial reading, reference sources, international and foreign language books, publications for partially sighted and deaf children, multiethnic and nonsexist lists and readings, seasonal lists, audio-visual materials, folk literature (fairy tales), poetry, science fiction stories and series books, plays, biographies, history and historical fiction, paperback and inexpensive resources, miscellaneous works, and nonfiction. Topics differ in the type of material available; some have indexes to the material for use in answering specific questions; others have books telling how to select in each area and/or giving recommended books and materials. The best material on each will be included.

Chapter 4 considers an increasing number of books giving information about illustrators and authors of children's books. These may be suitable for child or adult use, depending on the book. A subsection refers to the major awards in children's literature.

Chapter 5, on using books with children, has bibliographies on curricula-related material, storytelling, and related activities, as well as sources for exhibits, fairs, and other promotional activities. The last part discusses books that help foster a love of children's books.

Chapter 6, on technical processes, is devoted to a few sources on ordering and simplified cataloging.

The appendixes contain a bibliography of books on how to run a library/media center and one of books about children's literature. There are also some guidelines for evaluating a children's book.

Since the purpose of *Information Sources in Children's Literature* is not to give a duplication of a course in children's literature, certain limitations have been imposed for reasons of size and usefulness. Books dealing primarily with the history of the development of children's literature, or with scholarly literary criticism, have generally been omitted. A list of such sources may be found in the bibliography. Likewise, aids dealing primarily with the books read by children of another country are only included in the bibliography. Publications about British children's books fall into this category since they are not, with a few exceptions, widely available in this country; furthermore, even though written in English, many are geared closely to a British orientation. *How to Find Out About Children's Literature,* by Alec Ellis (Pergamon Press, Inc., Maxwell House, Fairview Park, Elmsford, New York 10523. 252pp.), which to some extent provided the inspiration for this work, is a good source of information on British children's books. Individual biographies of famous authors or illustrators are beyond the scope of this work, as are books that deal with literary or artistic criticism of an individual's work, although *collective* works on both of these topics are included.

A few items were placed in the bibliography because they seemed to give promise of being useful, but could not be obtained for examination. Generally speaking, if a book was not available through the resources of a large university library, a medium-sized public library children's department, or via interlibrary loan, it was assumed to be unavailable to most children's librarians and not included. A few out-of-print titles were included if they seemed especially useful, in the hope that they will be reissued or that some children's libraries may already have copies or could obtain them via interlibrary loan at a nearby public library. In most cases, 1970 was the cut off date, to ensure up-to-date material, but exception was occasionally made for material published in the late 1960s. (Some material, of course, does not go out of date and so was included regardless of the copyright date.) A few titles went out of print only during the preparation of the manuscript. The end of 1976 was the later cut-off date for inclusion; if a new edition is expected in the near future this was noted in the text. However, some material published late in 1976 or early in 1977 was not available in time for evaluation and inclusion. Whenever possible, the fact that a new edition has just come out or is about to be issued is noted. No regional materials are included, and inclusion of all material was selective, based on the books and pamphlets that seemed to give the most promise of being helpful.

There are also some suggestions and references in the bibliography for those desiring to do further research, such as Virginia Haviland's *Children's Literature, A Guide to Reference Souces* (Library of Congress, 1966. Write to Superintendent of Documents, U.S. Government Printing Office, Washington, D.C. 20402. 341pp. $2.50. LC2.8:C43) and *First Supplement, 1966-69* (1972. 316pp. $3). For a collection of books about children's literature designed for the college or university where the course is taught and of children's books themselves, consult "Building a Children's Literature Collection" *(Choice* Bibliographical Essay, no. 3, Middletown, Connecticut *Choice,* 1975. 34pp.).

Unless otherwise indicated, the phrase "bibliographic information" may be assumed to consist of the following: name of author(s), editor, or compiler; title; illustrator; publishing company; date of publication; number of pages; information about illustrations; series or edition, if any; type(s) of binding; price; and suggested age or grade levels. Occasionally, the order of the information will vary slightly; suggested usage levels are sometimes at the end of the annotation rather than with the other bibliographic information, for example. A ten-digit number with or without designation ISBN (or SBN) stands for International Standard Book Number (or Standard Book Number), a distinctive number now assigned to virtually every new book. It is mainly useful for most children's librarians' purposes if requested on a book order form. Another seven-digit number, the Library of Congress (LC) Number, may also be given. This may be used to order sets of catalog cards from the Library of Congress. The term "illus" may mean either "illustrated by" or "illustrations," that is, the book has illustrations. The context should make clear which is meant. Prices, of course, change quickly; a recent annotation or review will probably have a current price, but costs and other ordering information should be verified in *Children's Books in Print* if there is any question of their being out-of-date or incomplete.

These symbols may be used separately or in combination in regard to binding; only a few aids will include any or all of these symbols:

Lib bdg or L.B. — library binding, a sturdy binding intended for library rather than home or individual child use, usually well worth obtaining when available. It may be either slightly more or slightly less expensive than a regular binding. (It is occasionally called PLB for publisher's library binding.) Note that a special *price* may be given to schools or libraries, such as a 40 percent discount, because they order in quantity. This would apply to whatever type of binding is ordered.

PB or Pab.—paperback binding, such as commonly seen in bookstores, department stores, and the like. Paperbacks can play an important part in library work, as long as they are not expected to last as long as hardback editions. (The paperback books put out by several well-known children's book clubs are only intended for individual child use, and are not suitable for library use because they will not stand up to it.) The symbol PB (or pb) is also used to mean a picture book; the context should make clear which is meant.

C.—cloth over boards, or cloth-bound, the sturdiest standard hardback binding, suitable for library use. (Library binding is the same as this but slightly sturdier.)

G.—bound with glue.

P.—paper over boards, a flimsier hardback binding; does not stand up well for library use. These kinds of children's books are often seen in grocery and variety stores.

Sm—Smythe sewn.

SS—side sewn.

The designation "unp." means "unpaged," which in turn merely indicates that the pages are not numbered, which is often the case in books for small children. References to the Dewey Decimal Classification System, the numbered arrangement of nonfiction books found in virtually all children's libraries, is abbreviated to DDC or DDS. The designation CIP means the book was "cataloged in publication," that is, before it was actually published. This is becoming a more common practice and means that printed catalog cards can be ordered at the same time or even before the books are ordered, instead of after the books are received, or that most of the cataloging can be done from this information, which is usually found on the verso (back) of the title page. The term "galley proof" refers to long pages of type which are set up before the book is ready for actual printing; occasionally, substantial changes are made in the galley proof, so the book itself may differ from the galley. One reviewing service (Kirkus) often uses galleys for reviewing; other journals or compilers of lists do so from time to time and will indicate when they do. Usually, an annotation or review which is only a sentence or two in length is descriptive only; value judgments generally require at least a paragraph.

"Children's librarian" is used to refer to any librarian who works directly with children and children's books and other media, whether in a public or private school library, public library children's section, or other setting. This will be understood to embrace the more recent term, "media center director," as a librarian may well be one who works with a variety of materials, not only books but audio-visual media as well. Similarly, "library" rather than "media center" is used. This decision was made partly to facilitate easy writing ("librarian" is easier to write or say than "media center director") and partly from a philosophical belief that a library or librarian can and should encompass more than only books. "Children's literature" or "children's books" generally are those for pre-school to about sixth-grade level. Fairly often, however, this range will extend to the eighth grade; this will be noted when it occurs. "Young adult" books are those for the junior high/senior high age and will occasionally be included to a limited extent with children's books in some of the tools. The division is not rigid and overlap often occurs. Textbooks are beyond the scope of this work; only children's trade (that is, library) books are considered, and no catalogs, selection aids, or guides to using books with children which deal solely with the books of a single publishing company are included.

Once purchased, the aids should serve as the basis upon which the library collection is built; notes such as which books the library owns (with their call numbers if desired), which books are on order, which should be ordered in the future, and any other pertinent or useful information can be helpful and may be made directly in the aids. These, if kept up-to-date, will give a good overview of the status of the library collection at a glance.

Information
Sources
in Children's
Literature

1

Building the Basic Collection

COMPREHENSIVE BOOK SELECTION AIDS

Over the years two main sources from which to build a basic collection of children's library books have emerged. They are *Children's Catalog* and *Elementary School Library Collection;* the latter, in addition to books, lists audio-visual material. In the opinion of the editors and compilers of these aids, they provide for a comprehensive collection; in other words, if a children's library purchased all the books and/or non-print media listed in these tools, the result would presumably be a complete basic collection of the best fiction and nonfiction for children from preschool to the sixth grade. This would amount to between five and seven thousand books in *Children's Catalog* and around eight thousand books and two thousand audio-visual items in *Elementary School Library Collection.* (Naturally, some of the books are duplicated.) These aids are also extremely useful for gathering material for lesson planning, for determining the merits of books already owned, and for making decisions relating to maintaining the collection, such as rebinding, weeding, or replacing. It may be important to note here, first, that public libraries often find themselves meeting curriculum needs, so that an aid designated for school libraries may be quite useful for public ones, and, second, that the line between curricular-related books and those read solely out of interest or for pleasure is a fine one and may be blurring more and more in recent years.

> *Children's Catalog,* 13th edition, edited by Barbara E. Dill. H.W. Wilson Company, 950 University Avenue, Bronx, New York 10452. 1976. 1408pp. $40. (Four annual supplements, 1977-1980 included.)

Children's Catalog, begun in 1909, is the older of the two aids. It has, in addition to the editor, two committees which assist in the selection and evaluation of titles. The advisory committee, consisting of children's librarians and instructors of children's literature, prepares a list of books

The **Commandos** of World War II. Carter, H.
940.54

Commencements
Drama
See pages in the following book:
Fisher, A. Holiday programs for boys and girls p340-49 (4-7)   812

Commerce. See Transportation

Commercial aviation. See Aeronautics, Commercial

Commercial fishing. Zim, H. S.   639

Commercial geography. See Geography, Commercial

Commercial products. See Manufactures

Commire, Anne
(ed.) Something about the author. See Something about the author   920.03

Committee on Reading Ladders for Human Relations. See National Council of Teachers of English. Committee on Reading Ladders for Human Relations

Commonsense cataloging. Piercy, E. J.   025.3

Communicable diseases. See Bacteriology; Germ theory of disease

Communication
Cahn, W. The story of writing (6-7)   411
Rinkoff, B. Red light says stop! (1-3)   001.54
See also pages in the following book:
Childcraft: the how and why library v12
011
See also Books and reading; Language and languages; Telecommunication
Bibliography
See pages in the following book:
National Council of Teachers of English. Adventuring with books p255-59   028.52
History
Adler, I. Communication (4-6)   301.16
Neal, H. E. Communication (5-7)   001.54

Communication. Adler, I.   301.16

Communication. Neal, H. E.   001.54

Communication among animals. See Animal communication

Communications relay satellites. See Artificial satellites in telecommunication

Community life
Pitt, V. Let's find out about the community (3-5)   301.34
See also Cities and towns

Compae Rabbit's ride
In Carter, D. S. ed. Greedy Mariani, and other folktales of the Antilles p41-45   398.2

The **companion.** Asbjørnsen, P. C.
In Asbjørnsen, P. C. Norwegian folk tales p84-96   398.2

Companions of the forest. Macdonnell, A.
In Sechrist, E. H. ed. It's time for story hour p206-12   372.6

The **Company** you keep
In DeRoin, N. ed. Jataka tales p45-47
398.2

Comparative anatomy. See Anatomy, Comparative

Comparative physiology. See Physiology, Comparative

Comparative religion. See Religions

Compass
Branley, F. M. North, south, east, and west (1-3)   538
See also pages in the following book:
Boy Scouts of America. Fieldbook p20-27
369.43

Compere, Janet
(illus.) Davidson, M. Louis Braille   92

The **complete** adventures of the Borrowers. Norton, M. See note under Norton, M. The Borrowers   Fic

The **complete** beginner's guide to bowling. Dolan, E. F.   794.6

The **complete** book of children's theater. Howard, V.   812

The **complete** book of dragons. Nesbit, E.   S C

Complete book of horses and horsemanship, C. W. Anderson's. Anderson, C. W.   636.1

The **complete** book of Indian crafts and lore. Hunt, W. B.   745.5

The **complete** fairy tales and stories. Andersen, H. C.   S C

Complete fairy tales, Perrault's. Perrault, C.
398.2

which are then voted on by consultants (children's librarians from all over the United States). A new edition is issued every five years, with smaller paperback supplements each of the intervening years to keep it up to date. Books for preschool to the sixth grade are included. (Two similar publications, *Junior High School Library Catalog* and *Senior High School Library Catalog*, have similar formats and complete the series for children and young adults; there are also two similar tools for adult books. Librarians and teachers who work with junior and senior high school students should consult the appropriate volume; some children's libraries will need *Junior High Catalog* as well as *Children's Catalog*.)

About half of *Children's Catalog* is an index at the back, with entries by author, illustrator, title, and subject, much like an ordinary card catalog in its arrangement. Some entries in the index, called analytics, consist of an author or title entry and then the words "In . . . "; this refers the user to a specific work in a longer collection. For example, a collection of short stories would have separate entries in the index for each author and title included in the collection. There will also be a main entry for such a collection; this consists of the word "Contents" and then a list of the titles it contains. Following a subject entry, that is, an entry by topic rather than by author or title, there may be the words "See pages in the following books" and an author, title, and page numbers. This is a subject analytic entry and refers to specific pages in a book which relate to the topic; the entire work, although probably written by one person, does not relate to the topic under consideration, so the user is referred only to the relevant pages. When there are several different titles for what is basically the same work, such as a folk tale, all the stories are brought together in one place under one title, called a uniform title.

Any book that is listed in *Children's Catalog* is recommended for purchase. Because an author or illustrator is included for one or more title, however, does not mean that all of his or her books are recommended, only those specifically listed. About five thousand books are included in each edition of *Children's Catalog;* the supplements for the intervening four years add about two thousand altogether. (There is no additional charge for the four supplements that are sent out automatically.)

After each entry in the index there is one of the following: F for Fiction, SC for Story Collection, E for Easy, or a Dewey Decimal Number. This refers both to the classification of the book and to the section of *Children's Catalog* where it may be found. The nonfiction books, arranged by Dewey Decimal Number, come first; they are listed alphabetically by author *within* each decimal division. Biography is found in the nonfiction section (920), first collective biography, that is, biographies about several people in one book, and then individual biographies. The latter are arranged alphabetically by the person *written about, not* by the author. Fiction, Story Collections (several short stories published together as one book), and Easy Books, those often known as picture books, follow; arrangement is alphabetical by author in each category. Nonfiction for young children is classified by Dewey Decimal Number in the nonfiction, not in the Easy Books.

Having looked up a book or group of books, turn to the main part (called the dictionary catalog or classified catalog) to find the actual entry for that title. Each actual entry consists of the bibliographic information as follows: author; title; name of illustrator (if any, and if different from author); publisher; copyright date; number of pages or unpaged (that is, pages not numbered); information on illustration (such as "col. illus" for colored illustrations, maps, charts, and so forth); price (with possibly a second price to indicate a library binding, paperback binding, and the like); grade levels for all but Easy Books (such as 3-6); Dewey Decimal Number if nonfiction, or F, SC, or E if fiction; the subject headings if applicable (these are numbered 1, 2, 3, and so on, and are useful in making catalog cards), and the International Standard Book Number for ordering purposes. If there is more than one ISBN, the first refers to the first edition listed, the second to the second edition listed, and so on.

Next is an annotation for the book; this is usually several short paragraphs in length. In many cases the annotation will actually be a part of a review which first appeared in a well-known reviewing tool; it is in quotation marks and the name of the source is given. Two or more sources may be quoted in the same annotation; occasionally, a publisher's review or the foreword or preface of the book itself may be quoted. Some annotations were written by the compilers of *Children's Catalog* and are not in quotation marks. Special features such as indexes are pointed out. Many annotations are a combination of several of the above and are on the whole clear and interesting to read, with their length making it possible to obtain a good idea of what the book is about for purchasing decisions. The bibliographic information is complete enough for ordering (with price verification elsewhere) and for cataloging, but the individual library, of course, will have to make the necessary adjustments in subject headings and classification numbers to conform to an already existing catalog. Some annotations for materials for the adult working with children and books and some for selection aids are also included. There is a list of publishers and their addresses.

For librarians in Roman Catholic elementary schools, there is a Catholic edition of *Children's Catalog.* The Catholic Library Association, 461 West Lancaster Avenue, Haverford, Pennsylvania 19041, may also have other lists of recommended books. It publishes a monthly journal of

CHILDREN'S CATALOG
THIRTEENTH EDITION, 1976

CLASSIFIED CATALOG

000   GENERALITIES

001.54   Communication

Neal, Harry Edward
Communication; from stone age to space age; illus. with photographs. [Rev. ed] Messner 1974 192p illus $6.25, lib. bdg. $5.79 (5-7)   001.54
1 Communication—History
ISBN 0-671-326511; 0-671-32652-X
First published 1960
This historical survey of human communications describes the development and functions of languages, alphabets, numbers, writing, printing, newspapers, radio, telegraph, various forms of telecommunication, visual arts, and music
Bibliography: p183-84. Sources of further information: p185

Rinkoff, Barbara
Red light says stop! Illus. by Judith Hoffman Corwin. Lothrop 1974 unp illus $4.75, lib. bdg. $4.32 (1-3)   001.54
1 Communication 2 Signs and symbols
ISBN 0-688-41588-1; 0-688-51588-6
"Bright colors and bold lines make the pictures in this communications primer attractive. And Ms. Rinkoff's text is easy for the beginning reader to handle. Investigated here are ways in which signals are used instead of speech or writing: a shrug of the shoulders means 'I don't know,' a slam of the door means 'I'm angry.' But we find the conclusions arbitrary: Couldn't a shrug mean one doesn't care? . . . The Morse code, the semaphore, Braille, sign language, smoke signals and drumbeats are all discussed, as well as other nonverbal messages." Pub W

articles and book reviews, *Catholic Library World,* which includes children's literature and librarianship.

> *Elementary School Library Collection, A Guide to Books and Other Media, Phases 1-2-3*, 9th edition, edited by Phyllis Van Orden. Bro-Dart Foundation, Inc., 1609 Memorial Avenue, Williamsport, Pennsylvania 17701. 1974. 778pp. $24.95. 9th edition *Supplement,* $17.95. 9th edition and *Supplement* combined price, $29.95.

The Elementary School Library Collection is similar in intent to *Children's Catalog.* It, too, provides a basic, core collection of recommended books for children's libraries, based on surveys of elementary school curricula, textbooks, and the like. (Nonetheless, public as well as school libraries find it useful.) The editor was assisted by a committee of nine children's literature specialists, a special consultant for Spanish-language materials, and two special consultants for fiction.

There are entries for about eight thousand books for children from kindergarten through the sixth grade, with selection based on the merits of the book and its probable appeal; these are divided into phases 1, 2, and 3. Phase 1 (Ph-1) consists of those books which are felt to be necessary for an "opening day" collection, even though coverage may be incomplete in some areas. They would ideally be supplemented as soon as possible by the phase 2 (Ph-2) books, and ultimately by the phase 3 (Ph-3) purchases. Furthermore, about two thousand audio-visual items are included, also divided into phases and interlisted with the books.

The three extensive indexes are divided by author, title, and subject rather than grouped together as in *Children's Catalog.* For easy usage, the author index always begins with a pink page, the title index with yellow, and the subject index with blue. References to the entries themselves in the classified catalog are by item number, which merely means that each entry has been given a designation of two letters and three numbers to use in looking up entries. This number is in the upper right corner of the entry.

The entries themselves are in the form of catalog cards. In addition to the usual bibliographic information (author, title, illustrator, publisher, date, number of pages, and information about illustrations), the following is found: an annotation, from one sentence to a short paragraph in length, usually written by the selection committee specifically for *Elementary School Collection;* subject headings; indication of phases (see above); interest and reading levels; a suggestion if more than one copy of the title should be purchased in phase 1 (indicated by 2c or 3c); and a price. A "B" means that special prebinding charges have been included in the price. An asterisk is used to denote titles new to the work since the

Elementary School Library Collection—index

cutoff date of the last revision in April 1973. This is useful for those libraries which have been using the earlier edition and want to add only those titles that are new to *Elementary School Library Collection.* (The supplement covers the period from April 1973-1975.) The letters and numbers in the upper right corner of each entry are the citation numbers for finding the entry from the index, mentioned above. Two sample entries near the front of this tool are explained very fully and should be consulted.

The combination interest and reading levels are an important feature. Letters are used to show the appeal to the child: N for preschool (even though the book's difficulty may be as high as the middle grades); N-P for kindergarten and the lower primary grades; P for grades one to three (although difficulty may be beyond third grade); P-I for upper primary; I for grades four to six; I-A for sixth grade; and A for mature sixth graders, with combination symbols sometimes used. Reading levels by grades are then fairly often added to the interest levels. Two well-known methods are used for computing reading levels, based on the number of syllables and sentences in the books. These are the Spache formula for grades one and two and the Fry graph for other grades. (An appendix further classifies four lists of books by first half of the first grade, second half of the first grade, first half of the second grade, and second half of the second grade. While all this results in a very specific designation of reading difficulty, it should be pointed out that it is not customary for children's library books to be this closely identified by difficulty level and may even be unnecessary and undesirable.) The combination interest/reading levels are sometimes hard to interpret, especially given the somewhat complicated nature of the interest levels.

If the entry is for an audio-visual item, this will be shown by a set of symbols. These are: CH for charts; MP for films, that is, movies (8mm. only); MPL for film loops (8mm. only); FS for filmstrips; FSS for sound filmstrips; GA for games; KIT for kits; MAP for maps; PIC for pictures; RD for recordings; SL for slides; RT for tape recordings; and TRA for transparencies. This designation is found before the Dewey Decimal Number in the upper left corner of the entry. For audio-visual entries, the name of the producer is given along with technical information about the item, such as number of frames in a filmstrip, length of a film in minutes, number of slides in a set, and so forth. Sets of audio-visual items may be listed as a group or separately depending on how closely related the items are. Interest levels only are given. Audio-visual material is not in a separate listing but interfiled with the books, except that there is an appendix of media for preschool children which lists by author and title all the N (preschool interest level) books and audio-visual items from the classified catalog itself. For the annotation and other information about

001.5   BV199
MCCAIN, MURRAY. Books! Designed and illus. by John Alcorn. Simon and
Schuster 1962. unp col illus.
    A "zany" exercise in reading about books, intended to motivate and perhaps
"titillate the reader."
    SUBJ: Books.
                                           Ph-3 I $1.34

001.6   BV200
BARNETT, LEO. Careers in computer programming, by Leo Barnett and Lou Ellen
Davis. Walck, H. Z. c1967. 117p illus. (Careers for tomorrow)
    Reading list: p109-11.
    Computers are used to track missiles, to monitor surgical operations, to
control traffic, to score multiple-choice tests, and to make possible many other
activities. While the emphasis in this study is on the careers in computer
programming, the reader is presented the history of computers, an explanation
of how they work and where they are used, and the opportunities available in
the computer field.
    SUBJ: Vocational guidance./ Programming (Electronic computers)
                                           Ph-3 A $3.38

001.6   BV201
COOK, JOSEPH J. The electronic brain; how it works. Putnam c1969. 71p illus.
(How it works)
    Glossary: p70.
    Diagrams and photos help tell the story of man's use of computers, beginning
with the earliest counting device, the abacus to present electronic giants which
can compute payrolls, help defend our nation against enemy attack, and guide
satellites. The section on binary arithmetic, the basic symbol form of the
electronic age is clearly presented.
    SUBJ: Computers.
                                         Ph-1 A-9 $3.69

001.6   BV202
DE ROSSI, CLAUDE J. Computers, tools for today; illus. by Margaret Fiddle.
Children's Press c1972. 87p illus.
    An introduction to computers, giving background and history, meaning of
terminology, how computers work, and uses and limitations of this important
tool.
    SUBJ: Computers.
                                         Ph-3 I-A-7 $3.56

001.6   BV203
JONES, WEYMAN. Computer: the mind stretcher; foreword by Christopher C.
Kraft; diagrams by Nicholas Costantino. Dial Press c1969. 120p illus.
    Glossary: p111-15.
    This understandable explanation of the way computers work gives numerous
specific examples and step-by-step diagrams to explain and clarify the
complex pattern of problem-solving used by the computer.
    SUBJ: Computers.
                                         Ph-1 A-8 $2.65

entries in this appendix the user must refer to the entry for that item in section 1, the classified catalog itself. Generally, an audio-visual adaptation of a children's book is not included unless the book itself is recommended.

The overall arrangement of the catalog is by Reference, Nonfictional (arranged by DDC and including biography), Fiction, Easy (that is, picture books and picture stories), Periodicals, and Professional Tools (those intended for the adult who works with children and books).

Elementary School Library Collection is frequently revised and a new edition published. Occasionally, a supplement is issued to bring it up to date between revisions, such as the current 1975 supplement which adds about one thousand titles. (Since the preparation of this book, a completely new edition of this aid appeared late in 1976.) Each time there is a revision all entries are reevaluated and reconsidered for inclusion. There is a directory of audio-visual publishers and one of publishers of periodicals in the front. While directories of book publishers are widely available, these two are not as easily found.

In spite of some obvious differences between *Children's Catalog* and *Elementary School Library Collection,* many of the same books are found in each. As enumerated above, each aid has some special features to commend it and some possible drawbacks. Many children's librarians have a fairly strong preference for one or the other. Any children's library, no matter how small, should have one, preferably both, and the fact that *Children's Catalog* is geared more toward public libraries and *Elementary School Library Collection* perhaps more toward school libraries is not the only determinant. Considering the merits of each, most children's libraries should probably, in spite of the cost, make an effort to purchase them; for books colisted, this provides a double recommendation. The expense will be amply repaid in a better collection and better service to the children and adults who use the library.

More information about selection policies, theories, and issues of selecting children's books can be found in *Issues in Children's Book Selection*, twenty-nine articles on the topic reprinted from *School Library Journal*, edited by Lilian Gerhardt. R. R. Bowker Company, P. O. Box 1807, Ann Arbor, Michigan 48106. 1973. 225p. $9.95.

OTHER GENERAL BIBLIOGRAPHIES

In addition to *Children's Catalog* and *Elementary School Library Collection*, there are several other general bibliographies of children's books which cover a wide range of books and some audio-visual material. These can be very useful, but are always best used in conjunction with one of the above to supplement a collection. It is unlikely that most children's libraries would need or want all of them; obviously, there will be a certain amount of duplication of titles. Inclusion of a book in several sources constitutes a strong recommendation for that book, of course, but it is usually not necessary to have more than one favorable annotation or review if the source is reputable. (The exception would be a situation in which library policy dictates otherwise, such as requiring three annotations or reviews for each book, or a case in which the librarian has some doubts about the proposed purchase and feels several recommendations are necessary.) A subsequent chapter will cover reviewing aids devoted solely to children's science books.

See the yearly lists in chapter 2 for annual selection lists; aids dealing with paperback books only are in chapter 3, as are selection aids for audio-visual material.

> *Books for Elementary School Libraries, An Initial Collection,* compiled and edited by Elizabeth D. Hodges. American Library Association, 50 East Huron Street, Chicago, Illinois 60611. 1969. 321 pp. OP.

Assisted by a group of consultants and an advisory-steering committee, Hodges has prepared a list of more than three thousand books with short annotations for each. The coverage is from kindergarten to eighth grade, and the books are mainly geared to the school curriculum. To this end, a number of curriculum guides from various schools were examined. The list is intended to establish a collection in a new school library during its first year, *not* to provide a minimum collection. In this it differs from the two aids above. It can also be used to supplement an existing collection, but three thousand books will not provide a large enough collection in itself: this number was chosen because it was felt that it would "give reasonably good support to the curriculum during the first year of the library's development" (preface, p.viii) and could be purchased and processed in one year.

As in other aids of this nature, the best books are included, both old and new. It does not include out-of-print books, and there are no audio-visual materials or magazines, but there are occasional books in foreign languages or for special situations (for example, the beginning or problem reader, the gifted child, and so forth). The compiler explains that preference has been given to the hardback rather than the paperback edition of a book whenever possible in order to give physical durability to a beginning collection, and that the collection may not be "balanced" in some areas; a book of mediocre quality was not included merely to provide coverage in a particular area. There are about one thousand books for kindergarten to third grade, one thousand for fourth to sixth grade,

2083   **Geography and History**

2083 **Riwkin-Brick, Anna.** Sia Lives on Kilimanjaro; photos. by Anna Riwkin-Brick; text by Astrid Lindgren. Macmillan, 1959. unp. $2.94 net. (P)
Excellent photographs tell most of the story of a little girl who follows her parents to a feast in honor of the king. A good introduction to life in Tanganyika.

WEST AFRICA

2084 **Buckley, Peter.** Okolo of Nigeria. Simon & Schuster, 1962. 125p. $3.95. (P-I)
Through easy text and excellent photographs the reader learns of life in Nigeria as a Nigerian boy struggles to get an education so that he can help his people adjust to the modern world.

2085 **Davis, Russell, and Ashabranner, Brent K.** Land in the Sun: The Story of West Africa; illus. by Robert William Hinds. Little, 1963. 92p. $4.50; lib. ed. $4.58 net. (I)
Life in the rain forests, the bush villages, and the cities of West Africa is described in interesting, well-illustrated text covering people, religion, art, industries, animals, and relations with America.

2086 **Forman, Brenda-Lu, and Forman, Harrison.** The Land and People of Nigeria. Lippincott, 1964. 160p. $3.25; lib. ed. $2.93 net. (I-U)
After sketching Nigeria's history and describing its geography and present-day conditions, the authors discuss the efforts of the new nation to maintain its independence and unify its people. Excellent photographs and maps and a pronunciation guide.

and another thousand for seventh and eighth grades.

Arrangement is by a modified form of the DDC, with nonfiction first, followed by Stories for Intermediate and Upper Grades (that is, fiction books for these grades) and Picture Books and Stories for Primary Grades. Each annotation is from one to three sentences long, after the usual bibliographic information has been given. Within each category, arrangement is by author's last name. Each entry has a number to be used with the index, which has authors, titles, and subjects listed together. A three-page section near the back of the book lists some professional books useful to the librarian and teacher.

Books for Elementary School Libraries should not be used as a substitute for *Children's Catalog* or *Elementary School Library Collection*. First, it is not intended as even a minimum collection, but rather as a starting point. Second, it was published in 1969 and is currently out of date and out of print, although many copies still exist in library collections. (A revision is being considered.) However, it will be useful for the librarian who is faced with beginning a collection or strengthening an already existing one. In the former case, it should be supplemented after the first year by one of the above. It was, of course, less expensive than *Children's Catalog* or *Elementary School Library Collection*, but its very close tie to the curriculum limits it somewhat.

> *Adventuring with Books, 2,400 Titles for Pre-K — Grade 8*, 2d edition, by Shelton L. Root. Citation Press, 50 West 44th Street, New York, New York 10036. 1973. 395 pp. $1.95pb.

Prepared in conjunction with a committee of the National Council of Teachers of English, *Adventuring with Books* is, as its title suggests, an annotated bibliography of about 2,400 books for children from preschool to eighth grade. According to the foreword, books were selected that "combine the qualities of entertaining reading with literary merit" (p.x). It concentrates therefore more on those books children are likely to enjoy than is customary with many of the aids.

The arrangement is simple, with picture books and fiction listed first, followed by a series of nonfiction titles by broad subject category rather than by DDC: Traditional Folk Literature; Biography; Poetry; Holidays; Religion and Holy Days; Social Studies; Biological Sciences; Physical Sciences; General Sciences; Sports and Hobbies; Arts, Crafts, Music, Drama, Dance; and Foreign Languages. Arrangement is alphabetical by the author's last name within each large category. Annotations of one to five sentences in length follow the bibliographic information. Some of these are rather brief and descriptive only; others are longer and capture much of the flavor of the particular book. Note that the section titled "Picture Books for Young Children" actually includes books for older

Richardson, Grace. *Apples Every Day.* Harper 1965. $3.50; 12 up.

The discovery of freedom is one of the motifs of this lively story about young people in a progressive boarding school.

Rinkoff, Barbara. *A Guy Can Be Wrong,* il. by Harold James. Crown 1970. $3.95; 8–12.

Carlos Martinez spends two weeks with a well-to-do suburban family during the summer. This easily read book tells of the tensions that arise between Carlos and the son of the house and their eventual acceptance of each other.

———. *Member of the Gang,* il. by Harold James. Crown 1968. $3.50; 9–13.

Allegiance to the gang is the only loyalty allowed, but Woodie Jackson slowly moves toward a better value system and learns that nothing comes easy. The urban slums loom in their effect on the characters.

Robertson, Keith. *Henry Reed's Journey,* il. by Robert McCloskey. Viking 1963. $3.50 (P—Grosset, $.60); 9–12.

The clear-eyed entrepreneur of *Henry Reed, Inc.* sees America on a cross-country trip with his friend Midge and her family and continues to expose the shortcomings of the adult world in his journal. Though somewhat less inventive than the first book, this sequel has irresistibly dry humor. Also in the series: *Henry Reed's Baby Sitting Service.*

———. *The Year of the Jeep,* il. by W. T. Mars. Viking 1968. $3.77; 9–12.

The excitement of planning and working for the realization of a great dream is explicit in this excellent book. As a secondary character Wang Ling is as real and believable as Cloud Shelby, the hero of the story.

Robinson, Joan. *Charley,* il. by Prudence Seward. Coward 1969. $4.95; 8–12.

Charley, believing herself unwanted by anyone, runs away to retain her self-respect. Her experiences are wholly believable. She emerges as one who has the grit to cope, while, at the same time, being able to use her imagination to its best advantage.

Robinson, Veronica. *David in Silence,* il. by Victor Ambrus. Lippincott 1966. $3.50; 9–12.

A moving story of a boy born deaf who is rejected from games by other boys at school. This novel has special value for helping children understand the problems of a deaf child and for helping deaf children understand how hard it is for other children to understand them.

boys and girls, occasionally as old as eleven or twelve, and some folk literature is here rather than in the folk literature category. Also, age rather than grade recommendations are used. There are separate author and title indexes but unfortunately no subject index: the table of contents serves, however, as a guide to broad subject areas. Paperback editions are indicated by a P. Prices will need to be updated in *Books in Print.*

Overall, *Adventuring with Books* is another tool that may supplement an already existing collection or be used in conjunction with a more comprehensive aid. It is useful for its emphasis on books children would enjoy, and is very inexpensive, but there are not enough titles nor sufficient depth in all subject areas for it to be used as the only selection aid. The books were, after all, selected for children's pleasure in reading them, and the editor stresses that a child should not be forced to read a particular book, even though to the adult recommending it, it may seem to be a good book for that child. A new edition, edited by Patricia Cianciolo, appeared in the spring of 1977.

> *Bibliography: Books for Children, 1974 Edition*, edited by Patricia Maloney Marcun and Joan Toussaint Lane. Association for Childhood Education International, 3615 Wisconsin Avenue, N. W., Washington, D.C. 20016. 1974. 112pp. $2.75pb.

This is a listing of nearly two thousand books for children from preschool to age fourteen. They were selected by teachers, librarians, administrators, professors, and parents, mostly but not entirely from those books which were recommended in other selection aids. Literary quality was the primary criterion for inclusion, and there are both very new and older books. Many of the latter were read to children as well as being read (or reread) by the compilers before being included, while some of the new books were so recent they were read in galley proof. There are both fiction and nonfiction titles.

One interesting feature in this publication is that the winners of ten well-known children's book awards are indicated in the annotations by symbols. These are: Australian Book of the Year (ABY); Canadian Book of the Year (CBY); Carnegie Medal (CM); Hans Christian Andersen Medal (HCA); John Newbery Medal (JNM); Kate Greenaway Medal (KGM); Laura Ingalls Wilder Award (LIW); Mildred L. Batchelder Award (MLB); National Book Award (NBA); and Randolph Caldecott Medal (RCM). An explanation of these awards and the organizations which confer them is given. The award symbol, if any, is combined with the usual bibliographic information; if the abbreviation for the award is listed after the author's or illustrator's name, the award was given for the whole body of the person's work. If it is shown after the suggested age level, it was given for an individual book.

McCloskey, Robert.
Two popular, humorous books about a boy in a small mid-American town. Il. by author. Viking. Ages 9-12.
HOMER PRICE. 1943. 149 pp. $4.25.
CENTERBURG TALES. 1951. 190 pp. $3.56.

McLean, Allan Campbell. **STORM OVER SKYE.** Il. by Shirley Hughes. Harcourt, 1957. 256 pp. $3.75.
Murder, mystery and sheep-stealing in ,an atmospheric Scottish tale; one of several suspenseful novels by the same author. Ages 10 up.

MacKenzie, Sir Compton. **THE STAIRS THAT KEPT GOING DOWN.** Il. by Kenneth Longtemps. Doubleday, 1973. 57 pp. $3.95.
Direct, dramatic tale of a 10-year-old boy who discovers a kidnappers' den in a London house and bravely rescues the victim. Ages 8-10.

Macken, Walter. **THE FLIGHT OF THE DOVES.** Macmillan, 1968. 200 pp. $4.95.
Two English children, fleeing from a villainous stepfather, finally reach haven in Ireland with their grandmother. Ages 10-12. F

Meader, Stephen Warren. **SPARKPLUG OF THE HORNETS.** Il. by Don Sibley. Harcourt, 1953. 245 pp. $4.25.
Gregory's afraid his small size will keep him from Hackersville High's basketball team, but it all works out. Ages 12-14. S

Miles, Miska. **MISSISSIPPI POSSUM.** Il. by John Schoenherr. Little, 1965. 41 pp. $3.95.
Simply told story of a black family's escape from a raging spring flood — with the possum Rose Mary befriends. Ages 6-9. A, NU

Montgomery, Rutherford. **KILDEE HOUSE.** Il. by Barbara Cooney. Doubleday, 1949. 209 pp $3.50.
Seeking quiet among giant redwoods, a man copes with ever multiplying animals, and a lively, feuding girl and boy. Ages 9-12. A, F

Morey, Walt. **KAVIK THE WOLF DOG.** Il. by Peter Parnall. Dutton, 1968. 192 pp. $4.50.
A plane crash, a boy-dog devotion, and a grueling trek through the Alaskan wilderness are the ingredients of this realistic novel. Ages 9 and up. A

the monster Manta Diablo, finding an enormous jewel. Ages 12 up.

Peck, Richard. **THROUGH A BRIEF DARKNESS.** Viking, 1973. 142 pp. $4.95.
An innocent young girl is caught in the intrigue about her gangster father in a fast moving story of suspense. Ages 11-14. F

Ransome, Arthur. **SWALLOWS AND AMAZONS.** Il. by Helene Carter. Lippincott, 1931. 343 pp. $6.95.
Two families of lively and imaginative English children camp and sail about a small island. Other books about the same inventive children may be out of print in the U.S., but available in British editions or in libraries. Ages 9-12.

Robinson, Joan G. **CHARLEY.** Il. by Prudence Seward. Coward, 1970. 190 pp. $5.95.
An unquenchable English tomboy, erroneously thinking her family doesn't care about her, runs away — to a new nest of troubles. Ages 9-11. F

Salten, Felix. **BAMBI: A LIFE IN THE WOODS.** Il. by Barbara Cooney. Simon, 1970. 191 pp. $5.95.
Detailed drawings in russet, brown, and black accent this new edition of the much loved fantasy-touched fawn-to-stag tale of talking forest creatures. Ages 8 up. A

Slote, Alfred. **MY FATHER, THE COACH.** Lippincott, 1972. 157 pp. $4.50.
Baseball, town politics, and valid victory for the unlikely underdogs! Ages 9-12. F, S

Smith, Emma. **NO WAY OF TELLING.** Atheneum, 1972. 256 pp. $5.25.
A suspenseful mystery in which a huge, mute intruder comes to Amy's quiet cottage during a blizzard, grabs food, then disappears. Ages 9-11.

Snyder, Zilpha K. **THE EGYPT GAME.** Il. by Alton Raible. Atheneum, 1967. 215 pp. $5.25 Lib. Ed.
Lively children, engrossed in their play on the theme of ancient Egypt, skirt dangerously near neighborhood tragedy. Ages 10-11. F

Sobol, Donald. **ENCYCLOPEDIA BROWN SAVES THE DAY.** Il. by Leonard Shortall. Nelson, 1970. 96 pp. $3.75, $3.95 Lib. Ed.

The work is divided into a section for Early Childhood (Picture and Picture-Story Books, and Reading in its Early Stages) and one for Middle and Older Children (Fiction, Folklore, and Nonfiction), with separate sections for Poetry and Verse, Religion, and Story and Miscellany Collections. Each section is further subdivided into much smaller units. The annotations are short, usually a few lines in length; some series of books are considered together as a unit and have group rather than individual annotations. In some cases additional titles for an author are listed but not annotated. There is no subject index, so the table of contents must be used for locating books by topic; it is detailed enough to make this feasible. There are title and author indexes. Note that range is given by ages rather than by grades. Another feature is the use of symbols to indicate the type of story for some of the fiction after the age range at the end of the annotation: A for Animal Story, F for Family Story, NU for Neighbors Unlimited, and S for Sports Story. Finally, a list of other ACEI publications about using media (book or audio-visual) with children is found at the back of the book. Many of these publications are modestly priced and can be ordered directly from ACEI; some would be most useful to the classroom teacher, some to the librarian.

While the *ACEI Bibliography* is too slight (only about two thousand entries with short annotations) to be used for anything other than a supplement to a more comprehensive selection tool, and lacks a subject index, its several special features make it potentially very valuable. The pages on reference books are discussed separately in Chapter 3 and are available as a pamphlet. The ACEI also publishes a work with a very similar title, *Bibliography of Books for Children*. The last edition, in 1974, was edited by Sylvia Sunderlin; it is revised every three years, so a new edition is now in process. It consists of the reviews from *Childhood Education*, an ACEI journal which includes articles about children and their education and reviews of children's books and other media. The similarity of title may cause some confusion.

> *Children's Books Too Good to Miss*, 6th edition, by May Hill Arbuthnot, et al. The Press of Case Western Reserve University, Cleveland, Ohio 44106. 1971. 97pp. $2.95pb.

May Hill Arbuthnot, who may well be called the dean of American children's literature, prepared this edition of *Children's Books Too Good to Miss* shortly before her death. Coauthors were Margaret Mary Clark, Ruth M. Hadlow, and Harriet G. Long. Arbuthnot explains in the foreword that the purpose of the book is to expose children to certain books that are indeed "too good to miss"—because of their appeal, because they have become part of our culture, or because of their inherent literary value. (Children must be free, however, to reject those that do not appeal.) She goes on to explain that the best of both the old and new books were selected for a total of about two hundred fifty books. To help determine inclusion, the compilers used as their first criteria: Was a book good literature, even *without* its illustrations? This rather startling method of evaluating even picture books was adopted to weed out those books that had a pedestrian text. To this end, many books were read aloud to adults or children without their illustrations. The books were also judged on whether or not they would help children develop, or give them laughter or beauty (p. xi). This involved considerable discussion of books with children and with adults who remembered the books from childhood. The third criteria used was the appeal of the books to children, even though this appeal might develop only after several readings or several years. Circulation records, teachers and storytellers, and standard bibliographies were all consulted to determine this. However, the result was not merely a list of the most popular books for children, since the other criteria mentioned, and the judgment of the compilers, all authorities in the children's literature field, were also used. The result is, in Arbuthnot's words, an "irreducible minimum" (p. xiii) of books every child shoud have a chance to meet, even if some are rejected.

There are five sections: For Children under 6; For Children 6, 7, and 8; For Children 9, 10, and 11; For Children 12, 13, and 14; and The Artist and Children's Books. Within each of the first four categories there is a broad division by type of book, with entries by title. Only fiction, folk literature, biography, and poetry are covered. The bibliographic information consists only of title, author, illustrator, and publishing company; a separate list in the back of the book serves as a combination title index and price list. (Price verification and more complete ordering information should be obtained elsewhere.) There is also an author-illustrator index. The annotations themselves are a paragraph in length and exceedingly well written. Winners of the Newbery and Caldecott Medals are indicated.

The last chapter, The Artist and Children's Books, consists of illustrations and annotations for eighteen contemporary children's books. The annotations mainly describe the illustrations (which unfortunately are not in their original color) and give a few facts about the illustrator and some remarks on his or her artistic style. Other well-known titles by the same illustrator are mentioned. One full page is devoted to each annotation and illustration; some are books that are already considered in one of the previous chapters. No cross-references are made to these, nor are they found in the title index, but they can be located in the author-illustrator index. The work as a whole does not have a subject index, but since nonfiction is not included and it is an easy book to browse through to find something that appeals, this is acceptable.

177. THE TWENTY-ONE BALLOONS   Viking
   William Pene Du Bois
   Illustrated by the author

Weary of teaching mathematics to the young, Professor Sherman equips a balloon and flies off in search of adventure. His journey ends suddenly when a hungry gull punctures the balloon and forces him down on the volcanic island of Krakatoa, rich in diamonds, unusual inhabitants, and explosive potentialities. A rare and imaginative pseudo-scientific tale told with great good humor and profusely illustrated by the author-artist. *Newbery Medal, 1948.*

178. JOHNNY TREMAIN   Houghton Mifflin
   Esther Forbes
   Illustrated by Lynd Ward

Revolutionary days in Boston found Johnny, a boy of thirteen, apprenticed to a silversmith. Accidentally maimed for life and unable to follow his trade, Johnny was caught up in the struggle for liberty. The author has a remarkable talent for transporting the reader to the scene; the wharves and streets of Boston, the Tea Party and what led up to it, and the fighting at Lexington and Concord are before the eyes as though the intervening years had been rolled aside. *Newbery Medal, 1944.*

179. MY SIDE OF THE MOUNTAIN   Dutton
   Jean George
   Illustrated by the author

An incredible story of a modern boy's life alone in the Catskill Mountains for one year. Making his home in the hollowed trunk of a hemlock tree, Sam Gribley learns to build a fire without matches, make a deerskin suit, and cook everything from frog soup to venison steak. This competent young "Thoreau's" descriptions of unforgettable experiences in the heart of nature make the book a delightful flight from civilization.

Children's Books Too Good to Miss, by May Hill Arbuthnot, Margaret Mary Clark, Harriet G. Long, and Ruth M. Hadlow. Published by the Press of Case Western Reserve University. 1971 edition.

Children's Books Too Good to Miss might be called a list of classics, a confusing term that means different things to different people. If the definition of a classic is a book that has stood the test of time (that is, ongoing popularity) and the test of critical appraisal (that is, literary distinction), then these are classic books. Librarians especially are familiar with the demand for "a classic" emanating from parent or child. Teachers may also sometimes feel the need to expose children to some classic literature from time to time. In any of these situations, *Children's Books Too Good to Miss* will provide a handy source. Its attractive format and small size make it useful for direct use with patrons (children and adults) as well as a good reference tool for the librarian. It can be used for all these reasons and also for buying books not already contained in a collection, to help those preparing storytelling or similar programs, or as a book to browse through. Also, many of the books are very popular with children, so it should prove very good for recommending books children will enjoy. It is slightly out of date (1971) but not seriously so. Its modest price and wide usefulness commend it, and its foreword alone is worth the purchase price.

> *Growing Up with Books*, compiled by Eleanor B. Widdoes. R. R. Bowker Company, 1180 Avenue of the Americas, New York, New York 10036 (Frieda M. Johnson, Bookseller Services). 1976. 32pp. $12.25 for 100 copies. (One copy free; send a self-addressed, stamped envelope.)

This is one of a series of three small pamphlets, about three by six inches, each consisting of two or three hundred very short annotations of books on various topics. (See *Growing Up with Paperbacks* and *Growing Up with Science Books* in the appropriate chapters.) Selection is based largely on reviews from *School Library Journal*, which is discussed in the next chapter, Keeping Up-to-Date, and from some other reviewing tools. Although the publishers of the books pay for part of the publication costs of the pamphlet, the fact that most of the books were favorably reviewed in a reputable journal removes what otherwise might be a stigma. *Growing Up with Books* is a listing of about two hundred books of general interest to children. The arrangement is by age: for the youngest, ages 3 to 5, ages 5 to 7, ages 7 to 10, ages 10 to 12, and ages 12 and Up. Each category has a number of sections designed to appeal to children's interests, and both fiction and nonfiction are included, although the emphasis is on fiction. There is no attempt to tie the books to any curricular needs. Each entry has only title, author, and price, followed by a sentence or two of description. These are written in a manner so as to be of interest to the patron (child or adult) as well as to the librarian or teacher.

Growing Up With Books series, published by R. R. Bowker Company.

Too small in number of books covered and length of annotations to do more than supplement an existing collection, the pamphlets' small size, attractive, colored covers, and inexpensive price make them quite useful for public relations—to give to an adult or child who wants a list of "good books." They can even be imprinted with the library's name and address for an additional charge of $4.80 per hundred and will have far more appeal than a mimeographed list, no matter how carefully compiled. One caution should be mentioned in using them: if the library does not own most of the books listed, it is better to wait until more have been purchased. The best list in the world is of little use if the books are not available, and users only become frustrated when they cannot find books that have been suggested or recommended. These pamphlets are updated approximately every year; the categories may differ slightly from year to year but are similar.

> *Picture Books for Children*, by Patricia Jean Cianciolo. American Library Association, 50 East Huron Street, Chicago, Illinois 60611. 1973. 159pp. $6.50pb.

In conjunction with the Picture Book Committee of the National Council of Teachers of English, which consists of children's librarians and instructors of children's literature, Cianciolo has prepared an annotated bibliography of about four hundred picture books for ages four to fourteen. They are divided into four categories: Me and My Family; Other People; The World I Live In, and the Imaginative World. In spite of its title, *Picture Books for Children* includes books for preschool to junior high age and for adults, such as parents, teachers and librarians, and students of children's literature. (It is not always desirable to use what are usually thought of as picture books much above the third grade; although some of the books in this compilation are recommended for as high as age sixteen or eighteen, they are not the usual children's picture book.) Thirty-five of the books have sample illustrations in black and white. All books included were selected for literary quality, artistic appropriateness, and relationship to the curriculum (introduction, p. 2); overall, however, the value of reading for its own enjoyment and rewards is stressed rather than necessarily curricula-related values. Most of the entries are for fairly new books, but some older titles, including classics, are included. For each there is simplified bibliographic information with broad age ranges and short annotations which consider both the text and illustrations; some of the books have an explanation of the style of artwork used, such as pen-and-ink or acrylic—since many of the titles are recent, newer styles and techniques in artwork are exemplified. Many of the books are fiction and poetry, but there is some nonfiction. Arrangement is alphabetical by author in each category.

Atwood, Ann   8-16
HAIKU: THE MOOD OF EARTH   YEARS
   Photos by the author. Scribner, 1971. $5.95
   An exquisitely beautiful and perceptive compilation of original haiku and photographs in full color establish the "connection between the moods of man and the moods of earth."

68

Baker, Betty   4-8
THE PIG WAR   YEARS
   Illus. by Robert Lopshire. Harper, 1969. $2.50
   A cleverly·told, interesting story of how the British and Americans warred over a pig long ago. An "I Can Read" history book, illustrated with line-and-wash drawings.

Barton, Byron   4-9
WHERE'S AL   YEARS
   Illus. by the author. Seabury Pr., 1972. $4.95
   Bright, colorful, and boldly simple pen-and-ink drawings, printed in four colors, combine with a minimum of words to tell an action-filled, satisfying story about Al, the puppy who chases after a stick, gets lost in the big city, and is reunited with his young owner.

Baskin, Hosea, Tobias, and Lisa   6-10
HOSIE'S ALPHABET   YEARS
   Illus. by Leonard Baskin. Viking, 1972. $4.95
   A sophisticated blend of mind-stretching and imagery-building captions and accomplished, expressionistic paintings of creatures make this a present-day masterpiece of graphic art and literature.

Behfel, Tages   9-18
I NEVER SAW ANOTHER BUTTERFLY   YEARS
   Illus. with children's drawings. McGraw-Hill, 1964. $3.95
   An anthology of poems and full-color drawings created by children confined in the Terezin Concentration Camp from 1942 to 1944, commenting on life in the camp or life in general. Also included is a biographical sketch for each child whose poem or

The index is by author and title; there is no subject index or arrangement except by the four large categories. A lengthy introduction explains some of the elements of a children's book and the possible values to be found therein, with many examples to explain the different points.

This is an interesting supplemental list, the more so because picture books are seen as being suitable for all ages. The sample illustrations add much even though they are not in their original color. If there is a need for more picture books in the library, this would be a good source to consult. Many are well-known titles, however, that will also have been listed in the basic collection tools already discussed.

There are also several other relatively short and generally inexpensive lists of recommended books for children, especially for the young child. They are usually in pamphlet format and may be updated from time to time by the organization which compiles them. Write directly for date and cost of the most current version of each:

Books for Beginning Readers, by the National Council of Teachers of English, 1111 Kenyon Road, Urbana, Illinois 61801.

Books for Pre-School, by the National Association for the Education of Young Children, 1834 Connecticut Avenue, N.W., Washington, D.C. 10009.

Books for You, by Jean A. Wilson. Simon and Schuster, 630 Fifth Avenue, New York, New York 10020.

Reading with Your Child through Age 5, by the Children's Book Committee of the Child Study Association. Child Study Press, 9 East 89th Street, New York, New York 10028.

In addition to the above sources, local state libraries, state departments of education, or large public libraries sometimes publish lists of recommended books for children's libraries. These often take the form of reviews of new books, usually those purchased by the library compiling the bibliography. Most of this material is either relatively inexpensive or free. The appropriate local, state, or regional agencies can provide specific information on what is available. (Large libraries, such as New York Public, Chicago Public, or Enoch Pratt in Baltimore, sometimes make this type of material available to librarians all over the country, but it should be used with the reservation that it may have been designed especially for the use of the library compiling it.) State agencies may publish lists more geared to local conditions; useful for enriching a collection, they should not be used, except in dire circumstances, as a substitute for the foregoing sources.

2

Keeping Up-to-Date;
Science Books;
Indexes and Abstracts

The aids described in the foregoing chapter, Building the Basic Collection, while indispensable in amassing a core collection of books, will not keep a collection up to date. There are approximately two thousand children's books published every year, plus a considerable number of audio-visual items, and the children's library will want to add a number of these titles regularly. Sometimes these will replace older books or other media because they are better written or more current, but more often they will simply be additions to an ever-expanding collection. The aids that follow all appear periodically and contain many reviews of recently published books and/or nonprint media. Whether or not the items reviewed are recommended for purchase, or with what reservations, must be determined on the basis of the individual publication. Some of the journals also contain articles about children's literature and reports of recent activities in children's library work.

For reviews of science or multiethnic books, consult the appropriate special categories.

MAJOR REVIEWING SOURCES

> *Booklist*, children's books edited by Betsy Hearne. American Library Association, 50 East Huron Street, Chicago, Illinois 60611 (Robert Nelson, Manager of Membership, Subscription and Order Services). Twice a month (1st and 15th) September to July, once in August. $24 per year.

Booklist is one of a number of reviewing aids published by the American Library Association. It is directed toward both public and school libraries, including adult patrons in the former. Therefore, young adult and adult as well as children's books and materials are reviewed.

Approximately the first half of each issue is devoted to adult and young adult books; the children's book reviews begin around the middle of each issue, and range from preschool to eighth or ninth grade. *All*

Booklist

Albert, Burton.
Codes for kids. Illus. by Dev Appleyard.
1976. 32p. col. illus. Albert Whitman, lib.
ed., $4.25 (0-8075-1239-7).

A Jungle Jumble, Popsticklers, Brainbusters,
Zigzaggers, and Jefferson's Nose are but a few
examples of the 29 codes explained and illustrated here. Each code offers a practice session
to test readers' wits, and an answer key checks
out the decoding. Easy-to-understand directions, brown-and-black line drawings, and
suggestions for using the codes make this fun
for perennial secret-clubbers. Gr. 3–5. BE.

001.54'36   Ciphers   [CIP]   76-25456

Banister, Manly Miles.
Wood block cutting & printing. Sterling,
$6.95; lib. ed., $6.39.

Useful for hobbyist and art student as well as
for librarians wanting background materials for
explanations of art forms found in picture
books. See also p.448.

Barry, James P.
The Great Lakes. Illus. with photos. by the
author. (A First book) 1976. 62p. illus. Watts,
lib. ed., $3.90 (0-531-00337-X).

An initial chapter traces the route of the *Red
Wing,* a freighter filled with grain, as it moves
from Duluth through the waterways, canals,
and locks of the Great Lakes to Port Cartier on
the Atlantic Ocean. Following this glimpse of
the modern scene, Barry backtracks, giving
brief information on the area's geologic begin-
nings, Indian tribes, and early French and British explorations. Returning to contemporary
times, the author generalizes on tourist attrac-
tions, summarizes the lakes' shipping industry,
and describes pollution problems. A plea for
better environmental care concludes the book,
illustrated with black-and-white photographs.
Gr. 4–6. BE.

977   Great Lakes || Great Lakes region   [CIP]   76-15641

Casey, Winifred Rosen.
Cruisin for a bruisin [by] Winifred Rosen.
1976. 150p. Knopf; dist. by Random,
paper-covered boards with cloth backbone,
$6.95 (0-394-83291-4).   **YA**

The sophisticated daughter of a well-to-do psy-
choanalyst grapples with the same problems
adolescents cope with everywhere—sex and
self-assurance. In a smooth first-person narrative, Winnie Simon does an impertinently funny job of presenting readers with a slice of her
life, mostly in terms of relationships: with John,
her first love; Diana, her beautiful but jealous
sister; her father, to whom she is unknowingly
similar; one of his patients, who uses her to find
out about his doctor; and her mother, who never really goes beyond her role in the book to
take on personality. The ending is abrupt, and
there isn't much depth to Winnie, but she's
mod and fun to read about, and her situation
may ring familiar to many other 13-year-olds.
Gr. 6–9. BH.
[CIP]   76-5488

Cobb, Vicki.
Magic . . . naturally! Science entertainments
& amusements. Illus. by Lance R. Miyamoto.
1976. 159p. illus. Lippincott, $5.95
(0-397-31631-3); paper, $2.95
(0-397-31632-1).

Thirty magic tricks with accompanying scientific explanations are arranged according to
phenomena of mechanics, fluids, energy,
chemistry, and perception. The emphasis is on
fun, however, with the information presented
to insure a true understanding of the "magic."
Each stunt describes what happens, explains
the setup and act, and gives tips for the perfor-
mance. For example, the "Intelligent Eggs"
trick relies on the principle of buoyancy and
depends on the audience's unawareness that
sugarwater will keep one egg afloat while plain
water will sink another. Useful in the classroom
as well as a boon to amateur magicians. By the
author of *Arts and Crafts You Can Eat (Booklist
70:1103 Je 1 74).* Younger magicians should
see Wyler, below. Gr. 5–7. BE.

793.8   Science—Experiments || Magic tricks   [CIP]
                                              76-13179

books reviewed are recommended for purchase. The reviews themselves are one paragraph long, usually about 150 words. They are mainly written by the staff of two full-time reviewers and an editor. ("Easy-reading" materials are evaluated by a special outside reviewer, as discussed in the following paragraph.) About fifty to seventy or more books are reviewed in each issue, plus the easy-reading books in one issue a month. For a particular type of book an asterisk denotes exceptional quality. Suggested grade levels are given (except for books for very young children, which have age ranges) as are DDC numbers and subject headings at the end of the reviews. The notation CIP after some of the entries means that the book was cataloged in publication by the Library of Congress, that is, the classification number, subject headings, and other bibliographic information were prepared while the book was in the process of being published. A number for ordering Library of Congress sets of printed catalog cards is at the lower right. Although these cards are prepared by the Library of Congress, the children's books are classified by Dewey Decimal Number, not by Library of Congress Number. Some books which are also suitable for young adults have the designation YA at the end of the review.

A special section in every other issue, on the fifteenth of the month, is titled Easy Reading, and evaluates those books which are known as beginning-to-read, easy-to-read, and high interest/low vocabulary; these are not texts, but books written rather specifically to fill a reading need for the child who is just beginning to read or who has difficulty reading. Because of the frequently poor quality of both text and illustrations in books of this nature, most of the journals have not usually reviewed them. *Booklist* attempts to raise the standards of this type of material by reviewing only those with good quality in both text and illustrations. Both reading level and interest level based on the Fry graph are given.

Sixteen millimeter films and filmstrips are reviewed in columns following the children's book reviews in each issue. Although not restricted to children's materials, they often include reviews of children's and young adult media. (A wide range by ages or grades is usually given for each item.) The long reviews in this section are generally favorable and recommended, except that in a review of a series part of the series may be unfavorably reviewed. Title, name of distributor, date, length, price, and rental price if available, are given. Also, from time to time there are reviews of 8mm film loops, slides, multimedia kits, children's recordings, and video-cassettes or audio-cassettes, usually one type in each issue.

A rather new feature, special reading lists of foreign language children's books, now appears in the issue on the first of the month. These list books published in a non-English language, but the annotations are in English and there is a translation of the titles. Lists of popular books, such as mysteries or sports stories, compiled retrospectively, and lists of

easy reading

The reviews in this column, prepared by Judith Goldberger, focus on easy-to-read books for beginning readers and older children with reading problems. Following the book's evaluation, which will indicate interest level, are grade levels designating the book's overall appeal and a specific reading level (R.L.) determined by application of the Fry Graph.

Behrens, June.
What I hear, in my school. Golden Gate Junior Books, Childrens Press, $4.95.
Some beginning readers will rise to the challenge made here to listen for and identify familiar school-day sounds. Gr. K–2. R.L. 1. See also p.471.

Blance, Ellen and **Cook, Ann.**
Lady monster has a plan. Quentin Blake drew the pictures. 1976. 37p. col. illus. Bowmar, paper, $1.25 (0-8372-2135-8).
†372.412 Primers || Reading (Elementary)   76-3908

Blance, Ellen and **Cook, Ann.**
Lady monster helps out. Quentin Blake drew the pictures. 1976. 36p. col. illus. Bowmar, paper, $1.25 (0-8372-2126-9).
†372.412 Primers || Reading (Elementary)   76-3912

Blance, Ellen and **Cook, Ann.**
Monster and the mural. Quentin Blake drew the pictures. 1976. 33p. col. illus. Bowmar, paper, $1.25 (0-8372-2124-2).
†372.412 Primers || Reading (Elementary)   76-3906

Blance, Ellen and **Cook, Ann.**
Monster, lady monster and the bike ride. Quentin Blake drew the pictures. 1976. 36p. col. illus. Bowmar, paper, $1.25 (0-8372-2125-0).
†372.412 Primers || Reading (Elementary)   76-3910

Blance, Ellen and **Cook, Ann.**
There's a monster in my reading program! 1976. 44p. illus. Bowmar, paper, $1.25 (0-8372-0707-0).
†372.412 Primers || Reading (Elementary)

As the accompanying guidebook for teachers informs us, the lively stories in the monster series are based on children's retellings of simple, adult-constructed ones. Thus, much of the young child's language and thought filters through in the final, adult-revised versions. Monster himself—giant, purple, kind, but unclever—is grist for any kid's mill as he bakes cookies, learns to ride a bike, or takes lessons in house building from Lady Monster. Throughout, little children cluster around Monster, as will readers. The authors' young helpers' attention to and love of detail is evident; a casual attitude toward tense and (occasionally) grammar will not confuse readers, and the vitality of an involved telling more than makes up for points of order. It's easy to see why Blake's ingenuous color pictures were inspirational. The guidebook, though claiming to be a panacea, does give many good suggestions for use. Staple bindings. Gr. 1–3. R.L.: *Plan* 3, *Helps Out* 3, *Mural* 2, *Cookie* 2, *Toy Sale* 3, *Pet* 3, *Job* 2, *Town* 3, *Beach* 2, *Circus* 4, *Hospital* 2, *Bike Ride* 3.

paperback reprints of children's books, are two other new features. Professional books for the adult working with children and books are reviewed from time to time. Usually, one of the latter three lists appears on the fifteenth of the month after the Easy Reading column. The *Notable Children's Book List,* selected each year by the Book Evaluation Committee of the Children's Service Division of the American Library Association, is published in *Booklist* in the spring, with annotations included. See this chapter, Yearly Lists, for more information. There is an index in each issue of *Booklist* and a cumulative one in August of each year.

Booklist is a well-known and well-regarded selection aid, used by both school and public libraries. As with all reviewing tools, however, the final judgment must rest with the librarian, even when all the books are recommended for purchase, as in *Booklist.* A separate publication, *Reference and Subscription Books Review,* which is found in the back of each issue of *Booklist,* will be considered in Chapter 3 with the reference books.

> *Bulletin of the Center for Children's Books,* edited by Zena Sutherland. University of Chicago Press, 5801 Ellis Avenue, Chicago, Ilinois 60637. Monthly, except August. $10.

Bulletin of the Center for Children's Books is a reviewing journal published for the University of Chicago Graduate Library School under the editorship of Zena Sutherland, who is the·coauthor of *Children and Books,* one of the best-known children's literature texts. Sutherland writes the reviews, assisted by an advisory committee of six members, which meets weekly to discuss the books and their reviews. About sixty to seventy-five fiction and nonfiction books for children and young adults are reviewed each month. The reviews are lengthy and detailed, often with specific examples or quotations. The *BCCB* is known for its outspoken and lively reviews. It uses a set of symbols to indicate recommendations. In addition to these categories, an asterisk is added to some reviews under the grade-level range to show books of special distinction. It should also be noted that some issues of *BCCB* have only one or two books in the NR category and sometimes none at all.

The bibliographic information for each entry includes: author, title, illustrator, publisher, date, Library of Congress card order numbers, number of pages, and price. If both a trade and library binding are available, prices for both are given. If the book is part of a series, a statement of the name of the series follows the illustration statement. Grade ranges are given at the left beneath the recommendation symbol. These are given by ages for preschool books. The arrangement of the entire publication is alphabetical by author with no division of fiction and nonfiction or other categories.

EXPLANATION OF CODE SYMBOLS USED
WITH ANNOTATIONS

*   Asterisks denote books of special distinction.

R   Recommended

Ad Additional book of acceptable quality for collections needing more material in the area.

M   Marginal book that is so slight in content or has so many weaknesses in style or format that it should be given careful consideration before purchase.

NR Not recommended.

SpC Subject matter or treatment will tend to limit the book to specialized collections.

SpR A book that will have appeal for the unusual reader only. Recommended for the special few who will read it.

Except for pre-school years, reading range is given for grade rather than for age of child.

*   *   *

Corey, Dorothy. *You Go Away;* pictures by Lois Axeman. Whitman, 1976. 75-33015. 29p. Trade ed. $3.75; Library ed. $2.81 net.

R
3-5
yrs.
Although simple enough for the beginning reader, this is primarily for reading aloud to preschool children. It iterates the idea that people who go away—whether it's a baby being tossed into the air, a little brother hiding under the bed, Daddy going off with a basket of laundry, or Mother leaving a child with a sitter at a sandbox —come back. The text moves from a brief distance and a brief time to longer times and distances, concluding with parents going off with luggage, "far away." Each time, reassuringly, "I come back," or "You come back," and in closing, "You will come back!" The pictures have ethnic variety, the text can help extend concepts of time and distance as well as helping children adjust to the realization that having a parent leave does not mean one is being abandoned.

Cornish, Sam. *Grandmother's Pictures;* illus. by Jeanne Johns. Bradbury, 1976. 75-33566. 31p. $4.95.

Ad
4-6
A prose poem is beautifully illustrated by soft, almost blurred pictures that look like selections from a family album—and, indeed, this is what the text refers to. Not a story, but a fragmentary musing, the reminiscing is done by a black boy who loves his grandmother but is awed by her, who cannot remember the father who died when the boy was very young, who is intrigued by finding associations with the past. The random nature of the boy's memories does not preclude the establishment of a vivid picture of an elderly woman's sometimes lonely life, but the verbal collage does falter when an irrelevant note is introduced. For example, the boy is describing articles in his grandmother's home, moves to another topic, then back to his grandmother: " . . . her wash hanging from the clothesline in the kitchen. One day I got into a fight with the boy upstairs because he said his father had the longest blackest car in the neighborhood and electric lights in every room. Pulling down the shades before she lit the oil lamp to read . . . did not keep any secrets from the neighbors."

Couffer, Jack. *African Summer;* by Jack and Mike Couffer; sketches by Charles Callahan. Putnam, 1976. 76-7917. 96p. $6.95.

R
6-
A record of a summer spent on an island in an East African lake is recorded alternately by Jack Couffer, there to film a television series, and by his thirteen-year-old son, who came along with his friend Charles. Some of the sequences describe filming episodes (some dangerous, some amusing) and others adventures with the wild creatures of Kenya or the tame performers, chiefly lions, brought in by the television crew. The writing styles are informal, the setting fascinating, and the double lure of filming and animals should capture readers.

Inside the back cover of each issue there is always a short list of sources of information about children's literature for the adult. These bibliographies and readings are sometimes especially compiled for the librarian, teacher, or parent, and provide excellent references. An index is published once a year as part of the July-August issue. The *BCCB* may be purchased in both microfilm and microfiche.

Bulletin of the Center for Children's Books is a good source of current book reviews. Its system of recommendations puts much of the responsibility for selection on the librarian, since the interpretation of categories is largely dependent on local conditions. Its practice of citing specific examples or quotations to illustrate a point, pointing out a book's strengths and weaknesses, and comparing the book to other books, all give more of a flavor of the book being reviewed than is found in some of the other journals. Furthermore, the style of the reviews appeals very much to some people. Although *BCCB* receives and considers for review almost every children's trade book published in the United States, only about six or seven hundred of the two thousand children's books published yearly are reviewed.

> *The Best in Children's Books, The University of Chicago Guide to Children's Literature, 1966-1972,* edited by Zena Sutherland. University of Chicago Press, 5801 Ellis Avenue, Chicago, Illinois 60637. 1973. 484pp. $12.50.

The editor of *Bulletin of the Center for Children's Books* (see above) has selected fourteen hundred reviews from those which appeared in the *Bulletin*. All received a recommended review in the *Bulletin* except for a few from the additional or special reader categories. The arrangement is alphabetical by author, which means that fiction and nonfiction are not divided. Suggested usage levels are by grade for school-age children and by age for preschool children, as in the *Bulletin,* with some materials graded as high as tenth grade. Overall, the book is an attempt to bring together the best books for the years indicated. No attempt was made to balance the collection in terms of subjects or grades, so this cannot be called a basic collection tool. A number of British children's books are included; addresses are given for the publishers in an appendix.

One special feature of this aid is that there are six indexes: title index; developmental values index (references to books that will help a child develop the appropriate value for her or his age, such as "devotion to a cause" or "imaginative powers"); curricular use index (references to units likely to be found in the elementary school curriculum); reading level index (arrangement is by progressive difficulty, from ages two to four to grades ten and up—the editor points out that the indicated age or grade ranges are suggestions only); subject index (arrangement is by topics similar to subject headings found in a card catalog rather than by curricular units), and type of literature index (arrangement is by type of children's literature, such as nursery rhymes or folk and fairy tales).

Since almost all the books in this aid received a Recommended review in the *Bulletin,* this is a selective list of good books (in the opinion of the editor and compiler) for the time period indicated, and its special indexes further increase its usefulness. However, all the selection of books, recommendations, and review writing were done basically by one person, so a wide diversity of opinion is not represented.

> *Children's Book Review Service,* edited by Ann L. Kalkhoff. 220 Berkeley Place #1D, Brooklyn, New York 11217. Monthly, with two special supplements in fall and spring. $30.

Children's Book Review Service, begun in 1971, makes a special attempt to review books that will appeal to today's children; most of the reviewers work directly with children and books and many are themselves members of minority groups. (The books reviewed are not necessarily about minority groups, however.) Overall, emphasis is on books that deal with contemporary social issues that children will want to read, but fantasy and nonfiction, not just realistic fiction, are also reviewed. Each entry has bibliographic information including the publication date by month and day (which may be a month or so in the future), Library of Congress Numbers, and suggested age (not grade) levels, usually in a wide range. If a library binding is available, this is shown in parentheses after the regular binding price. Many of the books were cataloged in publication by the Library of Congress and this is noted when it occurs. There are three sections of reviews: Picture Books (up to about age eight), Younger Readers (from around age five to ten or eleven), and Older Readers (age eight to around seventeen). About fifty books are reviewed in each monthly issue and a considerable number in two special issues in the fall and spring. The reviews themselves, according to the *Service,* tend not to focus on plot summaries or comparisons with other books, but on how well the books will appeal to children. Although there is no specific statement, set of symbols, or recommended/not recommended indication, more often than not the reviews are favorable. Each review is initialed and the list of reviewers in the back gives their full names and affiliations; they are school and public children's librarians, authors, illustrators, university instructors, and people in related fields from all over the country. The *Service* feels that many of the other reviewing journals do not adequately reflect the interests of contemporary children and that even those that use practicing librarians are not liberal enough in their orientation.

Children's Book Review Service

Children's Book Review Service Inc.

ANN L. KALKHOFF
PRESIDENT AND EDITOR

220 BERKELEY PLACE
BROOKLYN, N. Y. 11217
212-622-4036

| Volume 4 | July 1976 | No. 13 |

PICTURE BOOKS

Adams, Adrienne   THE EASTER EGG ARTISTS   Scribner's $6.95   4/19   Ages 2-7
LC 75-39301

The Abbotts rabbit family paints Easter eggs and portraits, cars, houses, airplanes and flagpoles. Orson Abbotts' growing talent and responsibility and his parents' satisfaction with him pleased my preschoolers who requested the story several times. The pictures are colorful, charming and full of wonderful designs — some rather like Pennsylvania Dutch stencils.   EM

Adoff, Arnold   BIG SISTER TELLS ME THAT I'M BLACK   Holt $4.95   5/6   Ages 3-6
LC 75-32249   CIP

Big sister builds a positive self concept about being a black child. The illustrations contribute to its text and togetherness.   MGR

Bornstein, Ruth   LITTLE GORILLA   Seabury $6.95   4/76   Ages 3-7   LC 75-25508   CIP

Children will identify with "little gorilla" as he grows up. Everybody in the jungle loves him from birth on, and when he grows big . . . they still love him. A good story for nursery group read-aloud time, this book is about as bland as bananas. Illustrations are warm and simple in earth tones of green, gray, orange, and brown to go with the jungle settings.   BSW

Breinburg, Petronella   SHAWN'S RED BIKE illus. by Errol Lloyd   Crowell $6.95   5/12
Ages 4-7   LC 75-40362   CIP

In this third book about Shawn, our hero saves for a new two-wheel bike. After its purchase Shawn discovers it is really too big for him, but he doesn't give up and at the end of the book you know he will keep trying till he can ride it. It's a real book about a real little boy who is growing up along with his many fans.   ALK

Clifton, Lucille   EVERETT ANDERSON'S FRIEND   Holt $5.95   4/29   Ages 4-8
LC 75-32251   CIP

Everett was eager to meet his new neighbors. What a disappointment to learn that it is a family of girls. However, Everett learns that, "Things have a way of balancing out."   MGR

Galdone, Paul   PUSS IN BOOTS   Seabury $6.95   4/76   Ages 4-9   LC 75-25505   CIP

This ageless tale of the clever cat and his gentle master delights us once again with the assurance that with wit and good intentions, the small and powerless can be victorious against formidable forces. Through his colorful and expressive illustrations, Paul Galdone has brought new dash to the characterization of Puss, and he has created a world of comic fantasy which will endear this classic to a new generation. JM

Children's Book Review Service offers a general service with a concentration on its avowed purposes of reviewing books about minorities, about current social issues, and those that are consciousness-raising. Note that its reviews are very current, sometimes even ahead of publication, although this is not as crucial for children's as for adult books. There is an index by author in each issue; the entire publication comes in a loose-leaf format suitable for a standard-size spiral binder.

Horn Book Magazine, edited by Ethel Heins. The Horn Book, Inc., 585 Boylston Street, Boston, Massachusetts 02116. Bimonthly. $12.

Horn Book has long enjoyed the reputation of being one of the most scholarly and literate publications in children's literature. Many children's librarians regard it highly and look forward to its arrival every two months. About half of each issue is devoted to articles about important topics and issues in children's literature (including editorials), discussions of exceptional books, the historical development of children's literature, or interviews with and critical appraisal of authors and illustrators of children's books, occasionally continued from one issue to another. *Horn Book* also regularly prints the complete texts of the Newbery and Caldecott Medal acceptance speeches, which usually deal with the author's or artist's views on children's books and their creation.

The reviews in *Horn Book* are written by the editor and members of an editorial staff of five or six people. Books reviewed are considered to be recommended for purchase, subject to the limitations of the review. Each review must be read and evaluated, as no set of symbols or other indication is used, and all reviews may be qualified by remarks within the review. About fifty books are reviewed in each issue and the reviews are frequently longer than in many other journals. Sample illustrations (in black and white) are included fairly often, another somewhat unusual feature. The reviewing section usually begins with a special long review of an exceptional book by the editor. The first section is titled Picture Books, followed by Stories for the Younger Reader (suggested for ages six through eight), Stories for the Intermediate Reader (suggested for ages nine through twelve), and Stories for Older Readers (suggested for age twelve through young adult). These categories are all primarily fiction, including folk tales; nonfiction is arranged by broad subject categories following Stories for Older Readers.

In addition to the children's books there are usually reviews of several books in the section Of Interest to Adults, the category which follows the nonfiction. Special lists of various types appear from time to time, such as lists of children's classics or books that have been reviewed in *Horn Book* which are now available in paperback, or Recommended New Edi-

STORIES FOR THE YOUNGER READERS

LILLIAN HOBAN, Author-Illustrator   *Arthur's Honey Bear* g
                                      64 pp. Harper 1974 2.95
                                      Library edition 3.43

Arthur decided to have a tag sale to dispose of his old toys. With
his sister Violet helping, he blithely attached prices to all of his
toys until he came to his beloved Honey Bear. Then, he tried several
delaying tactics to keep Honey Bear for himself. But the machinery
for the sale had been set in motion, and he finally had to yield to
Violet's offer to buy Honey Bear for " 'thirty-one cents, my color-
ing book, my crayons, and half a box of Cracker Jack with the prize
still in it.' " However, with the same resourcefulness that had en-
abled him to turn his cookie-making fiasco into a great triumph in
Arthur's Christmas Cookies, he found a way to honor his agreement
with Violet and still keep a close relationship with Honey Bear.
The little chimpanzees are completely captivating, childlike, and
convincing in motivations and actions; and Arthur's solution to a
problem that has been faced in some way or other by many a small
child is both logical and satisfying. A delightfully illustrated I Can
Read Book with flavor, suspense, a good plot, and a fresh situation.

                                                                  B.R.

GABRIELA MISTRAL   *The Elephant and His Secret/ El Elefante
y Su Secreto* g   40 pp. 8¼" x 10½" Atheneum 1974 5.25
A Margaret K. McElderry Book. Translated from the Spanish and
adapted by Doris Dana. Illustrated by Antonio Fransconi. The well-
designed title page, the uncrowded bilingual text, and the nine
doublespread woodcuts in effective black, white, orange, and purple
are a graphic delight. The text is based on a fable and embellished
with poetic details. It begins as a how story: The elephant got his
wrinkled, rough skin because he needed one, and found "a great
gray shadow that a huge mountain cast over the plain. . . . The
shadow hung a little loose and baggy at the seams since, after all,
it was the shadow of a very *big* mountain." The elephant was
pleased; but he needed eyes; suddenly, after he wished "harder than
he had ever wished in his life," two tiny eyes opened. Carrying a
secret whispered by the mountain, off went the elephant to win the
friendship of all the other animals. The secret came true (it was
the Second Deluge); and the story ends when the great elephant,
"trumpeting his arrival like a ship coming into port," carries all
the other animals safely to Ararat, "where Noah's Ark had landed
thousands of years before." v.h.

tions and Reissues (older well-thought-of books that have been issued in new editions or reissues of books that have been out of print). A few books are sometimes placed in an Also of Interest listing. These do not have full reviews but are considered worthy of mention.

Several other regular features of *Horn Book* are Views on Science Books, two or three pages of reviews of a few (usually four to six) recently published science books for children; Outlook Tower, reviews of five to ten adult books that may be of interest to high school or even younger readers; the Hunt Breakfast, brief snippets of news about authors, artists, awards, and goings-on in the children's book world in general; and Audio-Visual Aids, a new feature which reviews a few nonprint items. Reviewing of a few Spanish-language books has just begun and is expected to be a twice-yearly practice. Each issue of *Horn Book* is indexed in the back and there is a yearly index in December.

Horn Book reviews only about fifty children's books every two months, or around three hundred per year, so it is not by any means as extensive as some of the other journals, but many people rate it as highly as any reviewing aid and consider it essential. It may be read as much for its scholarly articles as for its reviews. Certainly it maintains as fine a reputation, for both its articles and reviews, as any journal in the field.

Horn Book also publishes a number of books, reprints of articles, and bibliographies of recommended books on various topics, some of which are discussed in other chapters of this book. Write directly for a current *Catalog of Horn Book Publications*. Prices range from $.25 to $20.

> *Horn Book Crier,* edited by Elizabeth S. Halbrooks. The Horn Book, Inc., 585 Boylston Street, Boston, Massachusetts 02116. Bimonthly. Free (send name and address for mailing list).

This is a broadsheet (that is, one piece of paper printed on both sides) which is similar to Hunt Breakfast in scope, although not a duplication of its material. It presents news of happenings in the children's book field, such as lectures, conferences, and speeches; lists availability of books, pamphlets, posters, and bibliographies about children's books; and fills occasional requests for information or for back issues of *Horn Book* from readers. To some extent, materials prepared by *Horn Book* are stressed.

> *Kirkus Reviews,* children's books edited by Sada Fretz. 200 Park Avenue South, New York, New York 10003. $150 (or $33 for libraries with book budgets of $4,000 or less yearly).

Kirkus Reviews is entirely a prepublication service. It comes out twice a month in loose-leaf format to be put in binders, is used by many bookstores for selection, and has an entire section devoted to children's and young adult books in each issue. The reviews are a paragraph long, are

KIRKUS CHOICE for 1976 follows reviews on p. 1309 (J-431)

PICTURE BOOKS

Musgrove, Margaret
ASHANTI TO ZULU:
African Traditions
Illus. by Leo & Diane Dillon
Dial $8.95;   PLB: $8.44
12/22   LC: 76-6610
SBN: 8037-0357-0;
PLB: 8037-0358-9

From Ashanti to Zulu, 26 African tribes appear in a sort of slide show alphabet, each one allotted a lavish painting over a paragraph of text, with words and pictures joined in a formal, vaguely deco-style frame. This prescribed format gives a superficial air of sameness to the pictures even though the Dillons are careful to depict differences in headdress, dwelling structure, etc., and it gives the pages a static, stilted look which the illustrators do nothing to allay. The text, higgledy-piggledy, simply supplies a cultural snippet on each tribe: a general characterization of the Jie, herders in Uganda whose "men . . . roam with their cattle while the women do the farming," but only a fashion report on the Masai and a crocodile legend from the Baule. Nor is any distinction made between a custom peculiar to the tribe and, for example, the Fanti one of "pouring libation" with palm wine. Of course, the intent of the presentation is no doubt less systematic description than appreciation, and the Dillons' paintings fairly glow with appreciation—and the expectation of a like response. (Their sheen in fact not only glows but often glares, though the tones remain subdued.) At the same time, in a reversal of the usual division of labor, the pictures are crammed with information: a man, woman, child, home, artifact, and animal is conscientiously worked into almost every tableau. With no selective focus there's an exhausting much to look at—too much to effect the distillation achieved in the Feelings' Swahili counting and alphabet books, though of course this is certain to attract much regard.

7–8

Stokes, Jack
LET'S BE
NATURE'S FRIEND
Illus. by the author
Walck $6.95
1/3   LC: 76-15087
SBN: 8098-0000-4

"If you're wondering how/ you can stop the pollution,/ Here are things you can do/ for an easy solution." Stokes' solution is not only easy but fatuous, as outlined in fourteen blandly didactic rhymes exhorting readers to recycle, plant trees, shun bug spray, fix drips, etc. They're all the sort of platitude that proliferated a few years ago when ecology became a fad; let's hope we've advanced since then, if only in sensibility.

4–5

written by the editorial staff, and often try to give some indication of the popularity the book can expect to enjoy (or lack); many reviews are very critical. The expected publication date, by month and day or by month only, is of course included, so orders can be sent ahead of time. Usually the reviews run anywhere from one to three months ahead of publication and occasionally the final book will have changed from the information originally supplied by the publisher. The children's books reviews are divided into Picture Books, Books to Read Aloud, Easy Reading, Younger Fiction, Younger Non-Fiction, and Young Adult categories. (Adult books are in a separate section.) Suggested age levels are given, although the designation "???" may sometimes be used. Asterisks seem to indicate a book of exceptional quality. About twelve hundred juvenile books, and the same number of adult books, are reviewed in the course of a year. There is an index in each issue as well as cumulative indexes throughout the year.

The reviews are very outspoken and interesting to read, but it should be pointed out that for children's books the necessity for reviewing before publication is not as great as for adult books, because children do not read from best-seller lists as do adults. A list of one hundred children's books especially for libraries appears in the January 1 issue for the year just ended. There are also a few books for parents and teachers in this list as well as from time to time throughout the year. A library that subscribes to *Kirkus* for the adult reviews may find the children's books reviews very useful; a children's library may certainly consider subscribing to it on the strength of its reviews, but not probably for the pre-publication aspect for children's books.

> *Media Review,* edited by Sharon Kathryn Walsh. University of Chicago Laboratory School, 1362 East 59th Street, Chicago, Illinois 60637. Monthly, except for combined July/August index issue. $8. Single copy $1.

A publication of the Center for Educational Media for Children and Young Adults, *Media Review* evaluates about forty children's films, film-strips, filmloops, and slides each month. Usually each issue begins with a short article or two on the topic which is the main concern of that issue — Multi-Ethnic, Ecology, or Values, for example. There are also general reviews in each issue as well as the reviews related to the topic of the month. Each review is lengthy—often a half page to a full page—and is written by a *Media Review* contributor, most of whom are teachers in the Chicago area. Librarians, university faculty members, guidance counselors, and so on, also sometimes contribute. Each item is assigned a rating at the end of the review as follows: Excellent, Very Good, Good, Fair, or Poor. (In the case of a series of related items, reviewed as a set, each one is discussed separately and individual ratings are assigned.) Suggested curricula areas or subjects are shown, and suggested grade levels, usually by a wide range, are given; these encompass preschool through high school, college, and adult. Each film is judged on its content, photography, and sound, and the reviews are generally very knowledgeable and show considerable depth. Often there are comments by students and/or teachers from the University of Chicago and its Laboratory School and from other schools in the Chicago area, both public and private, who viewed the film.

The arrangement is alphabetical in each of the two sections (topic for that month and general), and the bibliographic information consists of the title, producer, date of release, indication of sound or no sound, indication of black and white or color, type of media, length, guide to be used in conjunction with the audio-visual item (if any), distributor, and price (purchase price and rental fee, if any). The full names and addresses of producers, distributors, and publishers are in the back of each issue. Occasionally, a few books and articles relating to the use of media are reviewed.

Also of interest is the fact that the Center for Educational Media is in the process of creating an examination collection of nonprint media for children and young adults and plans to sponsor institutes and workshops relating to media.

Media Review is published by the same institution (University of Chicago) which publishes *Bulletin of the Center for Children's Books,* although not by the same department. The size and format are similar, and since *BCCB* reviews only books and *Media Review* only nonprint media, the two together could be considered as complementing each other and providing rather complete coverage. Their styles of coverage are not dissimilar. Certainly, *Media Review* is a major reviewing aid for audio-visual materials.

> *Previews,* edited by Phyllis Levy. R. R. Bowker Company, 1180 Avenue of the Americas, New York, New York 10036. Monthly, September to May. $7.50.

Previews is devoted solely to nonprint (audio-visual) media. It consists primarily of reviews of 16mm. films, filmstrips, transparencies, prints, slides, games, kits, and records and cassettes, the latter two in a separate section. The range includes children's, young adult, and adult material, arranged by topics, not by age groups, and closely tied to the curriculum. The reviews are written by media specialist/librarians, whose names and addresses appear at the end of the reviews. Materials reviewed are not necessarily recommended; each review must be read and judged individually. Each review includes the title, indication of color or black and

Early Childhood

Follow Through with Sights and Sounds (Series from *The World I See . . . The World I Hear* Series). cassette. automatic & manual. color. 4 strips with 4 cassettes. 48 fr., 8 min. ea. with tchr's. guide. Prod: Knowledge Aid. Dist: United Learning, 6633 W. Howard St., Niles, Ill. 60648. 1975. #1050. $52.50 ser. Includes: *There Is No School on Saturday; Monday Is a School Day; A Rainy Day at Home; Looking and Listening Games.* Gr PreS-3

These filmstrips are designed for use with preschool and primary children and special education classes in teaching eye, ear, and hand coordination, auditory and visual association, and auditory and visual discrimination. The extensive teacher's guide is essential to the effective use of the series. It details the objectives of the program, gives pre-screening and follow-up discussions and activities, and contains the entire scripts. In *Monday Is a School Day* the familiar setting of walking to school is used to highlight auditory environment, communication skills, sound discrimination, and a few safety lessons. Expansion of the environment by a trip to the zoo is the theme of *There Is No School on Saturday.* The concepts of scale and size, perspective, and the volume and sources of sounds are emphasized. *A Rainy Day at Home* focuses on the sights and sounds at home with reference to the sequence of sounds, the logical order of a task, and the identification of textures and moods. The final strip, *Looking and Listening Games,* differs from the others in that there is no story line. Its purpose is to reinforce the program through noncompetitive games. Each strip ends with three silent study frames for sparking discussion. This well photographed and moderated series has applications not only in language arts, but also in creative art, health and safety, mathematics, and science. Recommended for school libraries as valuable supplementary material for early childhood education.— *Carol Nauth Euller, Library Media Specialist, DeWitt Road Elementary School, Webster, N.Y.*

white, length in minutes, name and address of producer and distributor, date, purchase price, rental fee, suggested usage levels, and preview service if available. This refers to the practice of some companies of allowing the prospective purchaser to borrow the item for a brief time to examine it and make a determination whether to purchase the item. Some reviews have small illustrations from the items, and there are also special articles and bibliographies from time to time. News in the field and and a column on teaching techniques utilizing audio-visual media appear in the front.

A spring issue has a roundup of the best filmstrips and slides of the year, while reviews of award-winning films appear in the fall. Also, twice a year, in September and April, *Previews* lists new and forthcoming material with more than a thousand titles in each issue. There is no attempt at evaluation, as in the reviews, merely a few words describing the content. Included are 16mm. and 8mm. sound films, 8mm. silent loops, filmstrips (sound and silent), transparencies, slides, discs, tapes, prints, maps, charts, games, and kits, arranged by subject and ranging from preschool to college and adult level. A directory of distributors accompanies this feature. Each issue has an index by title in the back.

Previews is a major audio-visual reviewing tool. Although it covers much young adult and adult as well as children's material, it should be of importance to children's media specialist/librarians, particularly in a situation where much audio-visual material is being purchased. Most of the other reviewing tools have some reviews of nonbook material, but most concentrate heavily on books, with a few exceptions, such as *Media Review,* which also reviews only audio-visual media. *School Library Journal,* discussed below, is published by the same company as *Previews,* but now reviews only books, leaving audio-visual material to *Previews.*

> *School Library Journal,* edited by Lillian N. Gerhardt. R. R. Bowker Company. Subscription Department, P.O. Box 67, Whitinsville, Massachusetts 01588. Monthly, September through May. $13.

School Library Journal is specifically directed toward the children's or young adult school librarian but is also useful for public librarians. Regular features include an often lively exchange of letters, editorials, news, and articles on such topics as censorship, using books with children, programs tried in various children's libraries, awards, people (authors, illustrators, library leaders, and so forth), occasional special bibliographies, and a page of Professional Reading which reviews two or three books of interest to the children's librarian. The Book Review section itself has an editor, associate editor, and two assistant editors, but most of the reviews are written by a nationwide group of two hundred fifty to three hundred school and public librarians and ten subject specialists, whose names appear at the ends of the reviews, although these reviews may be edited by the staff. There are two sections of children's books, PreSchool and Primary Grades, and Grades 3-6. The arrangement in each group is alphabetical by author's last name with no division of fiction and nonfiction. Reviews are one paragraph long and are not necessarily favorable; some reviews are quite critical. Sometimes there are collective reviews for a group of related books. A book of particular quality for its type receives an asterisk and suggested grade levels are given for all books. (There are also several sections of reviews for young adults.) Altogether more than 150 children's books are usually reviewed each month.

In May, the Special Best Books for Spring are listed with annotations: these consist of about twenty children's books (and the same number of young adult books) from among the one thousand published since the preceding January. A yearly award is also given for the worst picture book and worst book for older readers! Twice a year there is a list of books to come. Indexes appear in each issue and annually. There are occasional special columns on beginning-to-read, mystery, and sports books.

School Library Journal is read by many librarians and reviews most of the children's books published each year, approximately two hundred per issue and nearly two thousand each year, so it is comprehensive enough to be a major selection guide, but this should be weighed against the policies of some of the other publications, which select only certain books for review or publish only reviews of recommended books. Certainly *School Library Journal* is a widely known and much-used tool, and some people prefer reviews written by "practicing librarians" rather than by professional reviewers. *School Library Journal* also sells sets of catalog cards for children's books, and the reviews themselves are available on three by five-inch cards for ready reference. Once a year all the reviews from *School Library Journal* are published in one volume titled *School Library Journal Book Reviews, 19—*. The cutoff date each year is May 31.

ADDITIONAL SOURCES OF REVIEWS AND NEWS

Supplementing the major reviewing tools above are several sources of occasional reviews which may also prove helpful. None of these aids is primarily concerned with the reviewing of children's books. Some deal mostly with methods of teaching, others mainly with reviewing adult books; children's books are reviewed only occasionally. One or two are included because, although they review few, if any, children's books,

PreSchool & Primary Grades

ADAMS, Pam, color illus. *Old Macdonald Had a Farm.* unpaged. Grosset. Nov. 1976. PSm $3.95. ISBN 0-448-12579-X; PLB $5.99. ISBN 0-448-13375-X. LC 76-6817.

PreS-Gr 2—In this new version of the cumulative song each new animal appears through a cut-out while the sound the animal makes is shown on the facing page. Throughout the book the farmer's wife stands placidly feeding her chickens, serenaded by an ever increasing chorus of grunts, quacks, and squeals, until on the last page she is surprised by an animal invasion. The familiar verses are presented but not the tune, and despite the novelty of the cut-outs, the cartoon-style illustrations in flat full colors are only midly amusing.—*Margaret Maxwell, Graduate Library School, University of Arizona, Tucson*

ALLEN, Marjorie N. & Carl Allen. *Farley, Are You For Real?* illus, some color, by Joel Schick. 63p. CIP. (Break-of-Day Bks.) Coward. Dec. 1976. PLB $4.99. ISBN 0-698-30633-3. LC 76-15628.

Gr 2-3—As genies go, Farley is strictly small time. Rusty from years of retirement, he cuts Archie, the young Doubting Thomas who finds him, down to his own size (about two inches tall); then has trouble returning the boy to his normal height. The miniaturized Archie has predictable run-ins with a suddenly menacing owl and cat, but from his change in perspective he comes away with a new sense of nature's wonder. As usual Schick's cross-hatched pen drawings are droll with an eye for offbeat detail, but he's no genie and can't transform the story into anything more than what it is—a prosaic easy reader.—*Jane Abramson, "School Library Journal"*

BAUM, Thomas. *Hugo the Hippo.* 64p. color illus. CIP. HBJ. Oct. 1976. PLB $5.95. ISBN 0-15-237300-4; pap. $2.50. ISBN 0-515-04188-2. LC 76-14354.

K-Gr 6—Adapted from an animated film, this is the cartoon story of Hugo, a baby hippo whose family is moved from their jungle home to Zanzibar to counteract a shark problem. When the hippos are no longer useful they are shot in cold blood. Only Hugo escapes, fleeing to Dar es Salaam where the children, especially a boy named Jorma, take care of him. Eventually, the Sultan of Zanzibar comes to Hugo's rescue. Illustrations are bold and eye-catching—Hugo is a shocking pink; the sharks look like Hell's Angels in funny hats. The story, sad and funny by turns, will be enjoyed by children although the inhumanity of grown-ups to animals is laid on a bit thick.—*Helen Gregory, Albion Public Library, Mich.*

BAYLOR, Byrd, sel. *And It Is Still That Way: Legends Told by Arizona Indian Children.* 85p. illus. CIP. Scribners. Dec. 1976. PLB $6.95. ISBN 0-684-14676-2. LC 76-42242.

Gr 1-6—Forty-one favorite traditional legends retold by Arizona Indian children with each story credited to contributor(s) and tribe. Baylor also includes an informative and perceptive introduction about storytelling in Indian life and comments on the sources of the selected legends. Some readers may object to the way stories jump from one subject to another, but the simple children's style is consistently clear throughout, and children's own drawings, which accompany most of the legends, are another plus. Although the subject material is presented in other collections, this is unusual because of the large part children have had in the selection and retelling of the stories. A good group effort.—*Marily Richards, Reading Specialist, Philadelphia*

School Library Journal, January 1977. Reprinted with permission of School Library Journal. R. R. Bowker. A Xerox Corporation.

they do an excellent job of reporting the important happenings in the far-reaching world of children's literature. None should be purchased solely for its reviews except in the case of special issues, because the reviews are not extensive enough. If purchased for their articles, teaching ideas, or news value, the reviews are certainly worth consulting.

>*Audio-Visual Instructor.* Official publication of the Association of Educational Communication and Technology, 1126 16th Street, N.W., Washington, D.C. 20036. Ten times a year. $18 to nonmembers.

Audio-Visual Instructor consists of articles on the theory and usage of audio-visual materials in libraries and schools. It is not restricted to the use of nonprint media with children but often includes it as well as young adult and adult audio-visual usage.

>*Childhood Education.* Association for Childhood Education International (ACEI), 3615 Wisconsin Avenue, N.W., Washington, D.C. 20016. Six times a year. $12 includes membership in ACEI.

Each issue of this children's education journal contains about twenty-five reviews of children's books, written by librarians, administrators, subject specialists, and the ACEI children's book editor. The signed reviews, generally well written, are one paragraph long, and give age levels. There is no statement as to whether or not inclusion of a review is a recommendation, and no symbols are used to indicate the reviewer's opinion, but most reviews are commendatory. Every three years, the reviews from *Childhood Education* are compiled into *Bibliography of Books for Children* (see entry for *Bibliography: Books for Children*). The ACEI also publishes many excellent and inexpensive pamphlets and books about children and their development and education, and a series of books of story collections for children called *Umbrella* books. Almost any librarian, teacher, parent, or other adult concerned about children would be likely to find something of interest. These are listed in a publication catalog available free from ACEI.

>*Film Library Quarterly.* Film Library Information Council, P.O. Box 348, Radio City Station, New York, New York 10019. Quarterly. $10 to nonmembers.

Although not devoted particularly to children's materials, occasionally the entire issue of *Film Library Quarterly* is about children's films. The fall 1976 issue, for example, included articles about the state of the art of children's films in this country, children as filmmakers, and a bibliography of films about minority groups and about girls and women.

Drexel Library Quarterly. Graduate School of Library Science, Drexel University, Philadelphia, Pennsylvania 19104. Quarterly. $12 to individuals, $16 to institutions.

Although most issues of *Drexel Library Quarterly* do not have articles about children's literature, an occasional issue will consist solely of articles about children's books and other materials, librarianship for children, and related topics.

Instructor. The Instructor Publications, Inc., P.O. Box 6099, Duluth, Minnesota 55806. Monthly, September through May. $12.

Consisting mostly of "how-to" articles for the elementary school teacher, *Instructor* usually has some reviews of children's books in a section near the back, divided by subject area and sometimes including professional books. Trade and textbooks are often mixed together, as are book and nonprint media. This is certainly not a major reviewing journal of children's books but is well known and popular. Sometimes an entire issue is devoted to the children's library field.

K-Eight: Learning through Media. North American Publishing Company, 134 North 13th Street, Philadelphia, Pennsylvania 19107. Seven times a year: bimonthly, September through December; monthly, January through May. $7.

K-Eight concerns itself with media, *including books,* for use with children in kindergarten through the eighth grade. It is the result of a merger of *Modern Media Teacher* and *Educate* and is considered a "sibling" of *Media and Methods* (see below). The articles generally deal with ways of using media for teaching in the classroom or media center; often there are bibliographies at the end of the articles about the materials discussed.

Language Arts (formerly, *Elementary English*). Official journal of the Elementary Section of the National Council of Teachers of English. Eight times a year, October through May. $15 includes membership in NCTE.

Language Arts contains timely articles on the theory and practice of teaching elementary school language arts and reviews of children's books and audio-visual media. The articles are frequently long and scholarly and often deal directly with children's literature; occasionally almost an entire issue will be devoted to children's literature. Between twenty-five and forty children's books are usually reviewed in each issue, but the titles of the columns in which they are found vary from issue to issue. The reviews differ greatly in length and may include text as well as trade books. *Language Arts* is a useful supplement for its articles alone, especially the issues solely about children's literature.

> *Media and Methods.* North American Publishing Company, North American Building, 401 North Broad Street, Philadelphia, Pennsylvania 19108. Monthly, September through May/June., $9.

Media and Methods is mainly devoted to articles about issues in education and the theory and practice of using both book and nonprint materials in schools, often in conjunction with each other. Reviews of children's and young adult books, both text and trade, or of teacher's materials are sometimes included, as well as articles about hardware (that is, audio-visual equipment). *Media and Methods* might be useful in a situation where much audio-visual material is being purchased and/or used or even made.

> *New York Times Book Review.* New York Times Book Review Subscription Department, 299 West 43rd Street, New York, New York 10036. Weekly. $13 yearly or $.25 per copy.

Twice each year, once in the fall and once in the spring, the *New York Times Book Review* (published as a supplement to the Sunday *New York Times*) devotes a special section to about fifty children's books. Reviews are often longer than those in tools that regularly review children's books and many have a black-and-white illustration from the book. The reviewers are authors (although not necessarily of children's books) or members of the *New York Times* staff. Since no recommendations are made for purchase, the user must read and judge each review individually. Another section, Outstanding Books, gives a sentence or two of review for Teen-Age Fiction, Ages 9 to 12 Fiction and Non-Fiction, Ages 6 to 9, and Picture Books — about fifty in addition to the fifty with lengthy reviews. Some of these were previously reviewed in the Book Review section, and all are apparently well thought of. The fall issue also includes the results of a yearly competition for the best illustrated children's books. Three judges each select three books (in their opinions) and these nine are reviewed with representative illustrations. In addition to these two special issues, a very few children's books are reviewed each week.

The New York Times Book Review does not review children's books often enough to be a major selection tool, but because of its low price per issue and ready availability it may be known to librarians, teachers, parents, or older children unfamiliar with other tools. It may also be ordered separately from the rest of the newspaper (see above) and is now being sold weekly in bookstores and on newsstands.

Publishers Weekly. R.R. Bowker Company, 1180 Avenue of the Americas, New York, New York 10036. Weekly. $25. Single issue $1.50 (special issues $3.75).

Although *Publishers Weekly* mainly consists of adult book reviews, between five and fifteen children's books, most of them fiction, are reviewed in each issue. The paragraph-length reviews may be either favorable or unfavorable and are written by the children's book editor. There are also articles about books and publishing nationally and internationally, and news items, only occasionally about children's books. Two special issues of *Publishers Weekly* list the forthcoming children's books for fall in July, and for spring, usually in January. These have articles about children's book publishing and short annotations (not reviews) for about 650 forthcoming books; a few have sample illustrations. A special Prepare for Christmas issue in August lists popular children's gift books (not about Christmas) arranged by publisher. Each issue is indexed and every six months a cumulative index is published. Overall, *Publishers Weekly* is aimed more toward the bookstore than the library, but large libraries often subscribe to it, using it more as an acquisitions tool than as a selection aid.

School Media Quarterly. Official publication of the American Association of School Librarians, a division of the American Library Association, 50 East Huron Street, Chicago, Illinois 60611. Quarterly. ASSL members $7.50 (included in dues); nonmembers $15.

School Media Quarterly consists of articles and news about school media centers (libraries), their role, functions, operations, and so forth. Reviews are of books for adults working with children and/or libraries, not of children's books.

Teacher. Macmillan Professional Magazines, *Teacher* subscription service, 262 Madison Street, Greenwich, Connecticut 06830. Monthly, September through May/June. $12.

Teacher is comprised of articles on education and teaching in the elementary school. A column called Book Bonanza discusses a varying number of both older and new children's books and ways to use them.

Top of the News. Children's Services Division and Young Adult Services Division of the American Library Association, 50 East Huron Street, Chicago, Illinois 60611. $7.50 to members included in membership dues; $15 to nonmembers.

Primarily a journal of articles about children's literature, with some news of happenings in the field, *Top of the News* occasionally has a list of recommended children's or young adult books. Articles are rather long and well written. While children's books are not reviewed, books for the adult working with children are. One other feature, the *Notable Children's Film List,* is selected by the Children's Services Division of the American Library Association and appears each year in the June issue of *Top of the News.* The list is annotated.

> *Wilson Library Bulletin.* H.W. Wilson Company, 950 University Avenue, Bronx, New York 10452. Monthly, September through June. $11. $1 per copy.

Wilson Library Bulletin contains news and information, letters, and articles about libraries in general. Five picture books are reviewed by the children's book editor in each issue in a section called Picturely Books for Children. Usually these are favorable reviews. *Wilson Library Bulletin* devotes an entire issue to children's literature or school media centers from time to time. These single issues are well worth having and may be purchased individually.

In addition, some newspapers and magazines occasionally carry reviews of children's books. Some of the well-known ones which do this, especially in early November (National Book Week) or around Christmastime, for holiday giving, are the *Boston Herald, Chicago Tribune, Christian Science Monitor, San Francisco Chronicle, Saturday Review,* and *Washington Post,* to name only a few.

YEARLY LISTS

In addition to those yearly lists already mentioned in connection with a particular reviewing tool, several others are prepared each year. These can be very useful, are often quite inexpensive, and all books are recommended. Because of the length of time that may have elapsed since a particular book came out, many may already have been ordered from periodical reviewing sources.

> *Children's Books of the Year, 19--,* by the Children's Book Committee of the Child Study Association of America, Inc. Child Study Press, 50 Madison Avenue, New York, New York 10010. $2.50.

Every year the Child Study Association's Book Committee, a group of professionals and nonprofessionals interested in children and their development, selects about six hundred books primarily published during the past year. The books are chosen for their benefits (developmental values) to children as well as for their literary qualities, and new editions of old favorites are also included as is a section on paperback books. Each entry has a one or two-sentence annotation, and books of special merit are starred. There are four large groups of books: Ages Three, Four, and Five; Ages Five, Six, and Seven; Ages Seven, Eight, and Nine; and For Older Boys and Girls Ages Nine Up. (Note the overlap of ages.) The upper cutoff age is about fourteen. Within most of these categories are broad subject groupings. Also, some books are arranged by type or topic rather than placed in an age group. The index is arranged by title. *Children's Books of the Year* is a good tool for those interested in helping children deal with their feelings (a topic of much current interest), or who are concerned with behavioral objectives in books. (The Child Study Association has also published *Children's Bookshelf: A Guide to Books for and about Children* [Bantam, 1974], which annotates some recommended books for children as well as books and articles for the adult about children's reading and books.)

> *Classroom Choices: Children's Trade Books, 19--,* by the Children's Book Council, 67 Irving Place, New York, New York 10003. Free.

This new yearly listing of books, begun in 1974, is an attempt by the International Reading Association/Children's Book Council Joint Committee to encourage the use of trade books in the classroom as important components of the curriculum. From a list of books, preselected by instructors of children's literature and classroom teachers, *children* select the final books to be included. There are almost one hundred of those published in the preceding year on the annotated list. The books are grouped in four age ranges: Seven Years and Under; Seven to Ten Years; Over Ten Years, and All Ages. The list is published in the *The Reading Teacher,* or a copy may be obtained by writing to the Children's Book Council and enclosing a stamped, self-addressed envelope.

> *Fanfare 19--, The Horn Book's Honor List, Selected from the Books of 19--* (preceding year), The Horn Book, Inc., 585 Boylston Street, Boston, Massachusetts 02116. Free.

Once a year, *Horn Book* publishes a list of about thirty of the outstanding children's books of the past year. It is a very select list, considering the number of children's books published each year. The list may include such categories as Picture Books, Stories, Folk Tales and Legends, Poetry, History, Nature, Architecture, Of Interest to Adults, and so on, but these vary somewhat from year to year. There are no annotations or reviews. A free copy can be obtained by sending a self-addressed, stamped envelope to the above address. *Fanfare* also appears in *Horn Book.*

Library of Congress Children's Books, 19--, A List of Books for Preschool through Junior High School Age. Library of Congress. (Order from Superintendent of Documents, U.S. Government Printing Office, Washington, D.C. 20402.) $.15.

Each year the Library of Congress Children's Books Section and the Office of Education compile a list of about two hundred of the best books for children from those published during the preceding year. They are divided into Picture and Picture-Story Books; Stories for the Middle Group; Fiction for Older Readers; Folklore; Poetry and Rhymes; Arts and Hobbies; Biography; History, People, and Places; and Science and Nature. Each review is about two sentences long and suggested grade levels and LC order card numbers are given. This is a good list that will provide the "top 10 percent" of the children's books of the past year.

Notable Children's Books for 19--, Children's Services Division, American Library Association, 50 East Huron Street, Chicago, Illinois 60611. $.10.

The American Library Association's Children's Services Division Book Evaluation Committee, assisted by school and public children's librarians throughout the country, each year selects a list of about sixty or seventy children's books from those published the previous year. The list with annotations appears in a spring issue of *Booklist.* Most books, but not all, were reviewed by *Booklist,* and a citation to the original review appears after the brief annotation. Copies are available in quantity from the Order Department, at the above address: single copies, $.10; 3 to 50 copies, 10 percent discount; 51 to 250 copies, 20 percent discount; 251 to 1,000 copies, 30 percent discount; 1,001 to 5,000 copies, 40 percent discount; 5,000 copies, 50 percent discount. It is also possible to get one free copy of the list from Children's Services Division by sending a self-addressed, stamped envelope. Copies of the Newbery and Caldecott Medal books are also available from CSD for $.10 a copy or at a discount for quantities. Any of these lists makes good give away material. (In 1966, three hundred of the Notable Books from 1940 to 1959 were selected and published in a volume titled *Notable Children's Books, 1940-1959.* Each book was reevaluated for inclusion on the basis of at least five years use. *Notable Children's Books, 1940-1970* replaced this in the spring of 1977.)

Notable Children's Film List for 19--, American Library Association, 50 East Huron Street, Chicago, Illinois 60611. Free.

Every year the Children's Services Division Film Evaluation Committee of the American Library Association chooses the best children's films (16mm.) from those released in the past two years. These are mainly designed for library use, but classroom-designed films may be included if they are of good enough quality. Each film has been used with children in public and school libraries. The list is not long—less than twenty films in some years, for example. It is published with annotations in *Top of the News* each year in June; a single copy may be obtained free from Children's Services Division at the above address.

> *Notable Children's Trade Books in the Field of Social Studies,* by the National Council for the Social Studies/Children's Book Council Joint Liaison Committee. Children's Book Council, 67 Irving Place, New York, New York 10003. Single copies free; send a $.26 stamped, self-addressed envelope.

This is a yearly publication which lists with short descriptive annotations the best children's social studies books (library books, not texts) for the past year. The members of the selection committee are all administrators, teachers, or librarians at various schools, and each annotation has the initials of the person who wrote it. Such topics as American Heritage, Ancient and Medieval History, Arts and Crafts, Communications, Contemporary Concerns, Pluralistic Cultures in Our Society, Native Americans, Understanding Oneself and Others, Women, World Areas, and World of Work, from a recent list, give an idea of the types of books included. The categories vary from year to year but usually include topics deemed to be of interest to today's child and likely to be used in curriculum units. Human relations and new ways of looking at topics are emphasized. Books are suitable for children from kindergarten to eighth grade and are coded P for primary, I for intermediate, and A for advanced; some have combination codes. The bibilographic information is complete enough to use in ordering. About 130 books are included, and the list is published in *Social Education.*

Considering that it represents the best children's social studies books, in the opinion of the compilers, and that it is free, many libraries will want to consider writing for a copy of *Notable Children's Trade Books in the Field of Social Studies.* Also, previous years' lists are also useful if they are not too out-of-date.

> *U.S.A. Children's Books of International Interest* (formerly known as *Bookshelf: Children's Books of International Interest),* by the International Relations Commission of the American Library Association's Children's Services Division, 50 East Huron Street, Chicago, Illinois 60611.

The Children's Services Division of the American Library Association prepares a yearly annotated mimeographed list of around one hundred books published in the United States "which, because of their literary value, universality, or indication of new publishing trends, will interest those persons in foreign countries who are concerned with children's literature." There is bibliographic information with suggested age levels and a short descriptive annotation for each. For 1975 the categories were Picture Books, Picture Book Folklore, Folklore, Fiction, and Non-Fiction. The list appears in *Today's Education.*

SCIENCE BOOKS

Basic Collection

The *AAAS Science Book List for Children* is the one major source devoted exclusively to building a basic collection of science books for children; for mathematics books (with some science books for the upper grades) *Mathematics Library* provides a comprehensive listing. In addition both *Children's Catalog* and *Elementary School Library Collection* are good sources of recommended science and math books and may provide sufficient numbers of books for some children's libraries. The decision to purchase special aids for science and math books must be made on an individual basis, taking into account the needs of that particular library, such as the emphasis on science and math in the school or community.

> *AAAS Science Book List for Children, A Selected and Annotated List of Science and Mathematics Books for Children in Elementary Schools, and for Children's Collections in Public Libraries,* 3rd edition, compiled by Hilary J. Deason. American Association for the Advancement of Science, 1515 Massachusetts Avenue, N.W., Washington, D.C. 20005. 1972. 253pp. $8.95.

The American Association for the Advancement of Science, a well-known and prestigious organization of scientists, sponsors the *AAAS Science Book List for Children* to encourage scientific reading and an interest in reading in general among children. This list, consisting of entries for about fifteen hundred science books with a short descriptive paragraph of each, contains enough titles to provide a complete basic library collection and to facilitate lesson planning. All books, which are in the fields of pure (physical and biological) and applied science, including mathematics, were carefully examined and are recommended for purchase. Arrangement in the list is by DDC except for biographies, which are grouped according to the subject area to which a person's work relates rather than separately. Neither age nor precise grade levels are given, but a system of symbols is used, as follows: K for preschool or kindergarten, E-P for primary, E-I for intermediate, and E-A for advanced. (Range is from preschool to eighth grade.) A few young adult or adult books for the advanced upper elementary school student are in the last has avoided the usual historical geology approach to the subject, probably with the intention of capturing the reader's interest rather than educating the already interested reader.

May, Julian. *They Turned to Stone*. Holiday House, 1965. Unpaged (40 pp.). Illus. LB $3.50. 65-8130. (EP-EI)
This beautifully illustrated introduction to paleontology explains various representative fossil remains. The discovery, excavation and preservation of fossils are mentioned, and the reader is told where and how he can look for fossils.

Petersen, Kai. *Prehistoric Life on Earth*. Dutton, 1961. 1963 pp. illus. $4.95. 59-11505. (EA)
Adapted from the Danish original, this refreshing investigation of the development of life on earth is valuable both as advanced reading and as a reference. In addition to precise and extensive coverage of animal evolution, it contains information on the plant environment, on classification, heredity and selection, and on the contributions of the men who have greatly influenced our understanding of evolution. Print is small and set in double columns; the illustrations are beautiful.

Rhodes, Frank H. T., Herbert S. Zim, and Paul R. Shaffer. *Fossils: A Guide to Prehistoric Life*. Golden Press, 1962. 160 pp. illus. LB $2.89; paper $1.25. 62-21640. (EI-EA)
Extensively illustrated with excellent, accurate, color pictures, this handbook is full of useful information for the fossil collector. Introductory material on fossil hunting is followed by a survey of life of the past; then invertebrate and vertebrate animal fossils are described and a brief account of fossil plants is given.

561 PALEOBOTANY

Cosgrove, Margaret. *Plants in Time*. Dodd, Mead, 1967. 63 pp. illus. LB $2.99. AC 67-10441. (EI-EA)
The author presents the story of the evolution of plants beginning with the primordial cell and progressing through the development of the first true stems, first roots, first leaves, Gymnosperms, and finally the Angiosperms which branch into the dicotyledons and monocotyledons.

AAAS Science Book List for Children, 3rd Edition, Hilary J. Deason, p. 81, 1972. Copyright 1972 by the American Association for the Advancement of Science.

category. (For a list of books for young adults, see the *AAAS Science Book List.*)

The preface explains that each book was carefully evaluated on its merits, whether or not it appeared on any other list of recommended books or received favorable reviews in reviewing tools. A panel of undergraduate college students excelling in science, elementary school science teachers, children's librarians, and instructors of children's literature were all involved in the selection and evaluation process. Every title from the second edition was reevaluated before being included in the third; new inclusions were largely based on books in the AAAS reviewing journal, *Science Books and Films,* discussed below. The criteria for selection is summarized in this manner: "No science fiction, per se, has been included but we have not found the use of a fictionalized story line objectionable in certain books about individual animals as long as the basic scientific facts are correct. We have excluded whenever possible those books that are overly sentimental, that contain objectionable and unwarranted anthropomorphisms, and that cover so much subject matter superficially that the reader actually learns nothing by reading the book. Such books may convey erroneous ideas and will be repugnant to many bright children. The best science books for children are those that deal with a single basic idea, concept or subject which is developed accurately and completely, using whenever possible the appropriate technical terms" (preface, p. xi). Books with controlled vocabularies were omitted, and a strong plea is made for numbering the pages and including an index and/or tables of contents in all books except those for the very youngest children (preface, p. xii). The work has one index by author and one by subject and title; the arrangement itself and the table of contents serve also as a subject approach to the books.

The *AAAS Science Book List for Children* is undoubtedly a good source of a basic collection, selected by those who work directly with children and science books and produced under the auspices of a prominent scientific body. Moreover, the purchase of fifteen hundred science books should not be beyond the capabilities and needs of most children's libraries. The best course where budgets are limited might be to start with the *AAAS Science Book List for Children* together with *Children's Catalog* or *Elementary Library Collection* and purchase only those books that are listed in both the former and one or both of the latter, adding more as funds permit. The important thing is to consider specific needs of the library, the budget, the shelf space, and the curriculum if applicable, and to try to build the best scientific collection possible under the circumstances. Also, the *AAAS Science Film Catalog,* compiled by Ann Seltz-Petrash (Bowker, 1975) lists, with annotations, six thousand science

Primary Grades

Abbott, Janet S. *Learn to Fold—Fold to Learn.* Franklin Mathematics Series. Franklin, 1968, 120 pp., $1.80, paper. Grades 3-4.

> An excellent workbook, do-it-yourself type. Supplementary material that helps the reader investigate, by use of paper folding, these geometric ideas, among others: point, line segment, line, horizontal and vertical lines, parallel lines, circle, triangle, rectangle, square, and congruent figures.

_____. *Mirror Magic.* The Franklin Mathematics Series. Franklin, 1968, 120 pp., $2.10, paper. Grades 3-5.

> An excellent workbook, do-it-yourself type. Supplementary material that helps the reader investigate the concept of reflexive symmetry.

Abisch, Roz. *Do You Know What Time It Is?* Illustrated by Boche Kaplan. Prentice, 1968, 32 pp., $4.50. Grades K-3.

> Simple instructions for telling time from clock faces and for making a paper-plate clock face.

Adams, Pamela. *The First Book of Number Rhymes,* Watts, 1970, unpaged, $1.49. Grades K-1.

> A collection of illustrated rhymes which use number words.

Adler, Irving, and Ruth Adler. *The Calendar.* Day, 1967, 48 pp., $2.68. Grades 3-6.

> A discussion of what a calendar is, why we need calendars, and the history of important changes in calendar organization.

_____. *Sets.* Day, 1967, 48 pp., $2.68. Grades 3-6.

> An excellent introduction, with exercises, to the ideas of naming sets, forming subsets, finding solution sets for simple equations, forming unions and intersections of sets, and finding the number of a set.

1

films that can be bought, borrowed, or rented. There is a section of films for children, arranged by DDC.

> *Mathematics Library, Elementary and Junior High School,* 2d edition, by Clarence Ethel Hardgrove and Herbert F. Miller. National Council of Mathematics, 1906 Association Drive, Reston, Virginia 22091. 1973. 70pp. $2pb.

Mathematics Library is an annotated bibliography of about six hundred books, mainly about mathematics, for children from kindergarten to ninth grade. It is divided into books for Primary Grades, Intermediate Grades, and Junior High School, but a book may be listed in more than one section if it is suitable for a wide age range. Each entry has bibliographic information and a short annotation. In addition, broad grade levels are given for each book after the bibliographic information. Science books on subjects other than mathematics are covered to some extent for the intermediate and junior high groups. All books were chosen to supplement the curriculum and the annotations sometimes give curricula-related suggestions. (For books for young adults, see *High School Mathematics Library,* 5th edition, 1973.)

This work has neither an index nor a subject arrangement, which is a serious drawback to its use. Nonetheless, it is the only tool devoted primarily to mathematics books for children. It could be used in the same manner as the *AAAS Science Book List,* in conjunction with a general basic collection tool, bearing in mind the needs of the specific library.

Keeping Up-to-Date

The following are reviewing journals which serve the same purpose for science books as the general reviewing journals in the earlier section do for the entire collection, that is, keeping the collection current in regard to the many children's science books constantly being published.

Of course, a number of general reviewing journals have good science book coverage. Such sources as *Booklist, School Library Journal,* and *Horn Book* regularly review nonfiction, hence science books, and the latter has a special short column for science books.

> *AAAS Science Books and Films.* American Association for the Advancement of Science, 1515 Massachusetts Avenue, N.W., Washington, D.C. 20005. Quarterly. $16. Single Copy $4.25.

A portion of each issue of *AAAS Science Books and Films* is devoted to reviews of children's science trade books and a few textbooks. The remainder deal with reviews of young adult, college, and adult materials. Seventy or more children's science books are reviewed in each issue. As

Children's Books

The Social Sciences

301.3   Ecology and Community

VENTURA, PIERO   Piero Ventura's Book of Cities. (Illus. by the author.) NY: Random House, 1975. Unpaged (52 pp.). $4.95. 74-4927. ISBN 0-394-82744-9; 0-394-92744-3. C.I.P.

EP-EI ★   This is an excellent introduction to the wonders of cities. By selecting cities like London, New York, Kyoto and Venice, the author shows how cities can vary widely in form. By employing artistic license in the delightful drawings on each page, the author captures the flavor of each city more accurately than would be possible with a photograph or a more faithful illustration. The action detailed in the illustrations will delight and hold the attention of children of all ages. The author highlights the differing lifestyles found in the cities of the world while introducing subjects such as city living, transportation, employment economics, and leisure and recreation activities. Unfortunately, the subject matter makes it impossible to avoid using some difficult words, and there is some variation in type size which may confuse young readers.—*Arthur B. Hatton*

338   Production

PERL, LILA   The Global Food Shortage: Food Scarcity on Our Planet and What We Can Do About It. (Illus. with photos; Morrow Junior Books.) NY: Morrow, 1976. 128 pp. $5.95. 75-35860. ISBN 0-688-22068-1; 0-688-32068-6. Index; C.I.P.

EA-JH-SH Ac   "Is the world really running short of food?" Perl believes it is, as a result of rapid population growth, wasteful resource management, environmental deprivation and economic or political decisions that promote disasterous world consumption patterns. These malfunctioning elements are discussed individually and relative to each other. To ameliorate the global food shortage, the author stresses recognition of the symbiotic relationships existing between people, rich and poor, and between the human species and nature. Essentially the book is an essay in text and pictures, written from a personal view, with no attempt to be comprehensive. Its limitations are less from omitting significant factors than from oversimplifying the problems and solutions.—*G. Terry Sharrer* in the *AAAS Science Book List* above, reviews are written by scientists, teachers, or librarians, edited by the *Science Books and Films* staff, and are signed. (A directory of reviewers and their affiliations is in each issue.)

Following very complete bibilographic information are rather long paragraph-length reviews. The books are rated with two asterisks for highly recommended, one asterisk for recommended, AC for acceptable, or NR for not recommended. Reviews may cite specific examples of a book's strengths or weaknesses, compare it to others, and point out possible uses for that book. As in any nonfiction book, accuracy is a primary concern; the AAAS policy also requires the reviewer to consider scope, clarity, and quality of illustrations, and books with controlled vocabularies are usually omitted. Children's books are graded K for preschool and kindergarten, EP for grades one and two, EI for grades three and four, and EA for grades five and six. (Junior and senior high school book reviews are placed with the children's books.) In actual practice, most books have a combination of symbols encompassing a wide grade range. Arrangement is by DDC, alphabetically within each category. Between nine hundred and one thousand science books are reviewed yearly; between three hundred and five hundred of these are children's books.

Films for all ages are lumped together, so it is necessary to look through the reviews to find children's films. The format is the same, with the designation of quality and grade levels as outlined above. The bibliographic information gives distributor, length, cost, and rental fee, if any, as is standard for media reviews. No media other than films are reviewed.

AAAS Science Books and Films is a good, technical, detailed source of reviews of current science books that is used by many children's libraries. A library that plans to expand in the science area will find it particularly useful.

> *Appraisal, Children's Science Books*, edited by Diane Holzheimer. Children's Science Book Review Committee, Longfellow Hall, 13 Appian Way, Cambridge, Massachusetts 02138. Three times a year. $4 a year or $7.50 for two years.

The Children's Science Book Review Committee, which publishes *Appraisal*, is jointly sponsored by the Harvard Graduate School of Education and the New England Round Table of Children's Literature. The unique feature of *Appraisal* is that it has two reviews for each book: one by a librarian and one by a scientific specialist in whatever field the book deals with. Fifty to seventy books are reviewed in each issue (150-200 for the year), including some for young adults as well as for children. Age levels, given after the bibliographic information, are followed by the two

Kaufman, John. *Flying Reptiles in the Age of Dinosaurs;* illus. by the author. William Morrow & Company, 1976. 40 p. $4.59, $4.95.Age 6-10.

G LIBRARIAN: An interesting book about a creature which inhabited the world over one hundred million years ago is simply but adequately described for younger children. Although the author says that scientists learned about the prehistoric reptiles from fossil bones, he goes on to describe other parts of ancient reptilian anatomy and how the creatures lived without explaining how scientists know these facts. Throughout the text the reader wonders what is scientifically proven fact and what is surmised. Black-and-white drawings illustrate the simple text and make the creatures very lifelike.   S.H.E.

VG SPECIALIST: The subject matter is well organized and well illustrated, but it seems highly specialized for the six-to-ten year old "target audience." It might be best utilized as an informational supplement for the young reader with a strong interest and a more general background in the nature and evolution of Mesozoic reptiles.   R.J.K.

Kellner, Esther. *Animals Come to my House;* illus. by Heidi Palmer. G.P. Putnam's Sons, 1976. 160 p. $7.95.   Age 8-12.

VG LIBRARIAN: Even for the most cold-hearted non-lover of possums, groundhogs, chickaree squirrels, raccoons, cottontail rabbits, fox squirrels and other small animals of the wilderness, this warm-hearted account of care and love for them would be irresistable. The Kellners are obviously very special in their humaneness and their special quality shines through this account. Never sentimental or maudlin, this also contains specific directions for feeding, handling and ultimately releasing the animals back to their native habitat. Inviting illustrations in black and white are truly humorous and whimsical in content and style. A charming book! An adequate index is included.   V.A.T.

reviews, first the librarian's and then the specialist's. Generally these are a long paragraph in length. Each review has a symbol, as follows: EX for excellent, VG for very good, G for good, F for fair, and UN for unsatisfactory. Often the librarian and the specialist agree closely on the quality of a particular book (although possibly for different reasons), but sometimes they differ widely. *Appraisal* explains that the librarian's review often evaluates the book's literary style and appeal to children, while the scientist may judge the book's subject matter and accuracy. This division does not always exist, however. There is an author-title index in each issue and a cumulative one once a year in the fall issue, but no subject index. Arrangement is by author's last name rather than by subject or by DDN.

The parallel reviews in *Appraisal* are interesting to read because they are very outspoken. The criticism could be made that all the librarians who write the reviews are from Massachusetts except for two from Maine; some might feel that this would result in reviews that are not as reliable in other parts of the country which have different community or school standards. However, against this must be weighed the fact that many of the scientific specialists are from all over the country, although a number are from the New England area.

> *Growing Up with Science Books,* compiled by Eleanor J. Widdoes. R.R. Bowker Company, 1180 Avenue of the Americas, New York, New York 10036. (Order from Frieda M. Johnson, Bookseller Services.) 1975. 32pp. $12.25 per 100 copies. (One copy free; send a self-addressed, stamped envelope.)

This small pamphlet, another in the same series as *Growing Up with Books* and *Growing Up with Paperbacks,* lists and briefly annotates about 160 science books for children from ages two to eleven and up. The books were selected from those reviewed and recommended by *School Library Journal* and other reviewing tools. The format is the same as *Growing Up with Books*—division by age and then by broad subject areas. See the discussion of *Growing Up with Books* in the chapter on Selecting Books for Children, Other General Bibliographies, for the special uses of this series.

> *Outstanding Science Trade Books for Children, 19--,* National Science Teachers Association/Children's Book Council, 67 Irving Place, New York, New York 10003. Free.

This committee annually selects around a hundred of the best children's science books published during the past calendar year. These books' brief annotations are initialed by committee members—scientists, teachers, and librarians. Names and credentials are given. The com-

In general, books selected for this bibliography meet the following criteria: (1) accurate, (2) readable, and (3) pleasing format. Committee members considered the following: Does the book encourage independent work? If experiments are used, do they lead to some understanding of basic principles? Are they feasible and safe? Are facts and theories clearly distinguished? Are significant facts omitted? Are generalizations supported with facts? Are differing views presented on controversial subjects? Is the book a good value? Are animals and plants anthropomorphized? and, Does the book violate our basic principles against racism, sexism, and violence?

mittee uses rather strict criteria for book selection and the list in their opinion represents about a fourth of the best children's science books. It is available as a pull-out in *Science and Children* each spring or may be ordered from the Children's Book Council. For a free copy, send a self-addressed, stamped envelope.

Other Sources of Reviews

> *Science and Children.* National Science Teachers Association, an affiliate of the American Association for the Advancement of Science, 1742 Connecticut Avenue, N.W., Washington, D.C. 20009. September through May. $14. Single copy $2.

Mainly consisting of articles about teaching science to elementary and secondary school children, *Science and Children* also has a monthly column, Resources Reviews, of between half a dozen and two dozen children's science books. The materials to be reviewed are screened beforehand and the reviewers, who sign their annotations, are instructed to choose books for review that are "up-to-date, accurate, and worthy of use in the elementary and secondary school science programs." Reviews are then edited by the column chairman. This would seem to indicate that books reviewed in *Science and Children* are recommended for purchase, although no statement is made to this effect; the reviews are often favorable and suggested grade levels are given. There are usually a few shorter reviews by the chairman as well. From time to time reviews of texts and of books for adults about science and children appear, but overall the scope is mainly children's science trade books. Sometimes a few audio-visual aids are reviewed.

Science Teacher and *Science World,* two other periodicals devoted to articles about children, science, and education, also regularly review a few children's science books in each issue.

For those interested in the philosophy of writing, selecting, and reviewing science books for children and young adults, the April 1974 issue of *Library Trends* was on "Science Materials for Children and Young People." Although *Library Trends* does not normally focus on children's literature, this special issue is well worth having. It can be ordered from the Subscription Department, University of Illinois Press, Urbana, Illinois 61801, for $2.50. One article, "AAAS Science Books: A Selection Tool" by Kathryn Wolff, fully explains the procedure and philosophy of this reviewing journal. "Science as Literature," by Zena Sutherland, has a bibliography of science books for children, and "Science Media for Elementary School Libraries," by Robert E. Muller, is a bibliography of nonprint science media for children. There are twelve articles in all.

INDEXES AND ABSTRACTS OF REVIEWS

Because of the number of journals that review children's books and the many articles about children's literature written, there are now several guides to finding specific reviews or articles. (Most of the journals have their own indexes, of course, often in each issue and also cumulatively once or twice a year, but these only provide access to that journal.) Some of the following tools are indexes only; others provide extracts from reviews or abstracts of articles as well. Many may be too expensive for a children's library but could be consulted when necessary at a nearby large public, university, or state library.

> *Book Review Digest.* H.W. Wilson Company, 950 University Avenue, Bronx, New York 10452. Ten times a year. Monthly, except February and July. Sold on service basis.

Every month *Book Review Digest* compiles reviews of fiction and nonfiction books for adults, young adults, and children, published in the United States and reviewed in the past year and a half. Each entry is alphabetical by author, followed by title and the usual bibliographic information, including paperback and/or library bindings, if available, in addition to the regular binding. A suggested Dewey Decimal Number is given, as are suggested subject headings, ISBNs, and LC card numbers. Next is a description of the book, quoted from a review or from the publisher's note (such as would be found in an advertisement or on the dust jacket of the book). This first quotation of two or three sentences is descriptive rather than critical. Excerpts from a number of critical reviews are then given. In each case, a fiction book must have been reviewed in at least four of the seventy-two journals used; for nonfiction, in at least two. Citations are given for those reviews not quoted. At the end of each are the reviewer's name (or initials), the abbreviated name of journal, the page, month, day (if any), and year, and the number of words in the original review. Young adult, but not children's books, are so indicated. In adddition to the author arrangement, there is a subject and title index. Look in the index under Juvenile Literature (Individual Titles) for a listing of children's books alphabetically by author, or under Juvenile Literature (Collections). About six thousands books are indexed every year.

Book Review Digest is actually a reviewing tool of sorts and could have been included with that section. However, as its preface states, it is really intended to be an *index* to the reviews. Since several reviews of a book have been brought together, it is not necessary to look up the original reviews, although *Book Review Digest* intends the user to do so.

Note that only those books that have received the minimum number of reviews are included. Although the scope of this tool is so wide (adult, young adult, and children's) that a children's library may not wish to subscribe to it, if a children's librarian has access to it, such as at a subscribing public library, it should not be overlooked. *Children's Literature Review,* discussed below, is a somewhat similar tool that deals only with children's books.

> *Book Review Index,* edited by Robert C. Thomas. Gale Research Company, Book Tower, Detroit, Michigan 48226. Bimonthly and yearly cumulation. $68 per year.

Book Review Index is an index to all books that have received reviews, from one to any number. It contains only a citation as to where the review(s) appeared. All books are covered — children's, young adult, and adult. Arrangement is by author only. There are no quotations from reviews, and a book need not have received a minimum number of reviews. For a similar tool, see *Current Book Review Citations.*

> *Children's Book Review Index,* edited by Gary C. Tarbert. Gale Research Company, Book Tower, Detroit, Michigan 48226. Annual. $18.

Formerly published three times a year, *Children's Book Review Index,* now an annual publication, provides citations to children's books only. These are drawn from *Book Review Index* (discussed previously) and furnish indexing to reviews from more than two hundred children's book reviewing journals. Each entry consists of author, title, and the abbreviated citation to the journal. The new annual format will also include a title index. This publication therefore provides bibliographic access to virtually all children's book reviews in the United States and should be very useful to most children's librarians.

> *Children's Literature Abstracts,* edited by Colin H. Ray. International Federation of Library Associations and Institutions, 45 Stephenson Tower, Station Street, Birmingham B5, 4DR, England. Quarterly. £2.50 per year.

Published by the Sub-Section on Library Work with Children of the International Federation of Library Associations and Institutions, this quarterly consists of abstracts of articles about children's literature which have appeared in various periodicals. They are written by a staff of abstractors (not by the authors of the articles) and vary in length from one sentence to a full page. All abstracts are initialed; the names can be found in a list in the front. There are about one hundred abstracts per issue, in a subject arrangement; occasionally, reference is made to

A

AARDEMA. **Verna** - Why Mosquitoes Buzz In People's Ears / CLW - v48 - F '77 p307

ABELL. **Kathleen** - King Orville And The Bullfrogs / GP - v15 - Ap '77 - p3083

ABELL. **Kathleen** - King Orville And The Bullfrogs / JB - v41 - F '77 - p12

ABERCROMBIE. **Barbara** - The Other Side Of A Poem / BL - v73 - Mr 15 '77 - p1086

ABERCROMBIE. **Barbara** - The Other Side Of A Poem / CSM - v69 - My 4 '77 - pB4

ABERCROMBIE. **Barbara** - The Other Side Of A Poem / KR - v45 - Ap 1 '77 - p353

ABERCROMBIE. **Barbara** - The Other Side Of A Poem / NYTBR - My 1 '77 - p33

ABERCROMBIE. **Barbara** - The Other Side Of A Poem / SLJ - v23 - My '77 - p58

ABRAHAM Lincoln: **The Moving True-Life Story Of The Leader During The Darkest Days In The History Of The United States** / SLJ - v23 - Ap '77 - p59

ADAMS. **A** - Talent, Wonder And Delight / JB - v41 - F '77 - p28

ADAMS. **Richard** - The Tyger Voyage / HB - v53 - Ap '77 - p181

ADAMS. **Richard** - Watership Down (Lawrence) / JB - v41 - Ap '77 - p104

ADKINS. **Jan** - Inside / Cur R - v16 - F '77 - p61

ADLER. **David A** - The House On The Roof / BL - v73 - Ap 1 '77 - p1174

ADLER. **David A** - A Little At A Time / CCB-B - v30 - Ap '77 - p117

ADLER. **David A** - A Little At A Time / CE - v53 - Mr '77 - p257

ADLER. **David A** - A Little At A Time / CLW - v48 - Ap '77 - p404

ADLER. **David A** - A Little At A Time / LA - v54 - Ap '77 - p440

ADLER. **David A** - Roman Numerals / KR - v45 - My 15 '77 - p540

ADLER. **Irving** - The Environment / ACSB - v10 - Spring 77 - p5

ADLER. **Irving** - The Environment / HB - v53 - Ap '77 - p196

ADLER. **Irving** - The Environment / SB - v13 - My '77 - p41

ADLER. **Irving** - The Environment / SE - v41 - Ap '77 - p349

ADLER. **Irving** - How Life Began / BL - v73 - Je 15 '77 - p1567

ADLER. **Irving** - How Life Began / BL - v73 - Je 15 '77 - p1572

ADOFF. **Arnold** - Big Sister Tells Me That I'm Black / RT - v30 - My '77 - p946

ADOFF. **Arnold** - Make A Circle Keep Us In / Cur R - v16 - F '77 - p17

AESOPUS - The Fables Of Aesop (Baber) / BB - v5 - Mr '77 - p1

AFANAS'EV. **Aleksandr** - Russian Fairy Tales / TLS - Mr 25 '77 - p357

AHLBERG. **Janet** - Burglar Bill / KR - v45 - Mr 15 '77 - p279

AHLBERG. **Janet** - Burglar Bill / NYTBR - Ap 10 '77 - p19

AHLBERG. **Janet** - Burglar Bill / SLJ - v23 - My '77 - p47

AHLBERG. **Janet** - Burglar Bill / SR - v4 - My 28 '77 - p33 another article or abstract. The range is international, although the preponderance of abstracts has generally been from jounrals published in the United States and England, with a number also from West Germany. Other countries are also represented to a lesser extent. All abstracts are in English, although the article itself may not have been. There is an author and subject indexes, plus a list of journals abstracted.

Although *Children's Literature Abstracts* may seem to be mainly useful to the academic library where children's literature is taught, the fact that many of the articles are from well-known American journals may actually increase its usefulness to the ordinary children's library, especially if it has a good many adult patrons interested in keeping up with the international children's literature field. (An effort is being made to expand the geographical coverage.) Remember that the abstracts are from *articles about* children's literature only; abstracts of children's books or of books about children's books are not included. A library that did not take most of the journals abstracted would obviously find this tool of somewhat lessened value; although a certain amount of information can be obtained just from the abstracts, any one wanting the complete article would have to refer to the journal in which it appeared.

> *Children's Literature Review, Excerpts from Reviews, Criticism, and Commentary on Books for Children and Young People,* edited by Ann Block and Carolyn Riley. Gale Research Company, Book Tower, Detroit, Michigan 48226. Twice a year. $25 per volume.

A rather new publication, *Children's Literature Review* combines several elements: contemporary and "older" writers, biographical and critical data, and quotations from reviews and citations to other reviews. Each volume contains information about forty or fifty generally well-known children's and/or young adult authors. For each author there is very brief biographical information such as date of birth and death, nationality, and awards received, and usually some general remarks about the person's work from various sources. Following this introductory material are the titles for each author arranged in alphabetical order with the review(s) or quotations from them. (Many of the reviews come from journals discussed in Keeping Up to Date.) There may be from one to as many as six or more reviews for each title. Citations are also given for other reviews not quoted and cross-references are made to entries in *Contemporary Authors* and *Something about the Author,* published by the same company. (See the chapter on Authors, Illustrators, and Awards for information on the latter.)

Children's Literature Review presents an excellent overview of critical comments about each author's work conveniently arranged in one place. Since the titles are alphabetical rather than chronological, the develop-

Children's Literature Abstracts

United States

74/385 MCELDERRY, Margaret K.

The best of times, the worst of times: children's book publishing 1924-1974. Horn Book Magazine 50 October 1974, pp. 85-94

Recollections and insights--from a well-known editor whose children's book work began at the New York Public Library in the Depression thirties. She points to early editors, important for developing pioneering precepts and principles, the encouraging librarians with whom strong friendships were formed, creative authors and artists of the thirties and forties, the effects of World War II followed by a period of expansion and the resuming of international trends in publishing relations, new trends in the fifties, the incredible sixties, and the seventies with their new challenges. "The new generation of children's book editors, authors, and illustrators will require the same--or greater--resilience, toughmindedness, and strong-fibered beliefs that have carried the publishing of children's books through these fifty years of varied challenge."

V.H.

U.S.S.R

74/386

Literatura infantil na Russia (Children's literature in Russia) Folha de Sao Paulo 26 October 1974

The development of publishing for children in the U.S.S.R. Describes "houses of children's books". In these establishments children's reactions are passed on to authors, teachers, librarians and parents.

M.N.C.P.

74/387 SULAJMANOV, Murza

Kirgizskaya detskaya literatura (Kirgizian children's literature) Detskaya Literatura 12 (108) 1974, pp. 6-10

A short introduction to the literature for young people in the Kirgizian Soviet Republic; main names, main themes.

P.S.

ment of a writer's work is not particularly evident, however. The biographical information, while slight, is useful. It is necessary to purchase all volumes (at the rate of two per year with around fifty authors per volume) if a library intends to build up a set of this kind of information about various authors. It can be used to decide whether to purchase a considerable number of books by one author, not just recent publications by that author, and brings together virtually all of the reviews of a title from the major reviewing journals. Also, the inclusion of "older" authors extends its usefulness. An academic library would find it useful as would a children's library. There are three indexes—by author, critic's name, and title.

> Current Book Review Citations, H.W. Wilson Company, 950 University Avenue, Bronx, New York 10452. Monthly, except August. Annual cumulation: $75.

Somewhat similar to Book Review Index, Current Book Review Citations is an index to reviews of children's, young adult, and adult books from more than over one thousand journals. The arrangement is by author with an index by title. Each entry consists only of information on where to find a review. Many of the reviewing journals cited are ones that are in the section on Keeping Up to Date. Counting reviews of adult, young adult, and children's books, more than fifty thousand reviews are referenced every year!

> Media Review Digest (formerly Multi-Media Reviews Index), Pierian Press, P.O. Box 1808, Ann Arbor, Michigan 48106. Every year with supplement. $65.

Media Review Digest is a combination of an index to reviews of educational media and annotations and excerpts from reviews. Each entry is rated + for good to excellent, − for fair to poor, or + − for both positive and negative attributes; movie ratings are also given. It should be useful for a children's library which is buying enough nonbook media to need an index to audio-visual reviews and also provides some additional information in its annotations, brief quotes from reviews, and ratings. Children's, young adult, and adult materials are covered; subject headings are given, as are Dewey Decimal Numbers. Entries are divided by type of media with an alphabetical by title arrangement within each category. Entries by subject refer the user to specific titles.

3

Special Help for Special Fields

MAGAZINES AND ARTICLES IN MAGAZINES

The use of children's magazines for leisure reading has long been established, but their use for curricula-related reasons seems to have been growing in recent years. For children's magazines and magazine articles there are basically four tools. Two of these, *ACEI Guide to Children's Magazines, Newspapers, Reference Books* and *Periodicals for School Libraries,* deal with selection. Another, *Dobler World Directory of Youth Periodicals,* is primarily for acquisitions, and the last is an index to articles that have appeared in children's magazines, *Subject Index to Children's Magazines.*

> *ACEI Guide to Children's Magazines, Newspapers, Reference Books,* 1974 edition, by Judy Mathews and Lillian Drag. Association for Childhood Education International, 3615 Wisconsin Avenue, N.W., Washington, D.C. 20016. 12pp. $.50.

This pamphlet lists and briefly describes about one hundred magazines for use with children, as well as a number of reference books, which will be discussed later. (There seem to be few, if any, newspapers.) Magazine entries, arranged alphabetically, have title, frequency of publication, name and address of publisher, price per year, and a sentence or two of description. Grade/age recommendations are given for broad ranges such as "all ages," "upper elementary," and so on. Some magazines suitable for adults as well as for children, such as *American Heritage,* are included; these are marked with an asterisk. There are curricula suggestions for a good many of these magazines, some of which are recommended for boys or for girls. Although there is no statement to that effect, inclusion of a title in the *Guide* seems to constitute a recommendation, and a wide variety of topics, not all curricula-related, is covered.

ACEI Guide to Children's Magazines, Newspapers, Reference Books is an inexpensive aid; however, it is not by any means as extensive in the amount of information it gives as *Periodicals for School Libraries.*

> *Dobler World Directory of Youth Periodicals,* 3rd enlarged edition, compiled and edited by Lavinia Dobler and Muriel Fuller. Citation Press, 50 West 44th Street, New York, New York 10036. 1970. 108pp. OP.

This is primarily a listing of about one thousand children's and young adult magazines. The entries are alphabetical by title within broad subject areas such as general periodicals, religious periodicals, and school and classroom periodicals, and further divided by school subjects. Each entry contains this information: name of magazine; date it began publication; yearly circulation; frequency of issue; price for a yearly subscription and for a single copy; age level for usage; name of editor; name and address of publisher; type of fiction, nonfiction, and artwork used; rates paid, and a sentence or two (sometimes less) of description of content, usually supplied by the publisher. A set of symbols at the end indicates where the periodical is recommended (such as *Elementary School Library Collection* or *Periodicals for School Libraries,* for example) and where it is indexed (such as in *Subject Index to Children's Magazines* or *Reader's Guide.)* Also indicated is whether the periodical accepts free-lance work and whether it publishes book reviews. Some entries recommend the periodical for boys or for girls. There are sections on periodicals published in English in other countries and on non-English-language periodicals, arranged by countries. Many of the latter have title and publisher information only.

Inclusion in *Dobler World Directory of Youth Periodicals* is comprehensive, that is, the directory attempts to include a listing of *all* periodicals for children and young adults. For this reason, it should not be used as a selection aid. It also does not give enough information about the content of a particular periodical to make it useful for selection. (It is most unlikely that a public or school children's library would want to purchase all the American and foreign children's magazines that are published.) It *is* a good place to verify ordering information after making a selection from some other source such as *Periodicals for School Libraries.* Also, a children's library which does have need of foreign-language materials or those in English but published in another country, will find it helpful. This could include academic libraries where courses in international children's literature are taught or children's libraries which serve a large number of children with close ties to another country.

Other features of interest are: a currency and exchange rates table for converting foreign currency to American currency (however, these fluctuate rapidly, so the table may be out of date); two short articles on children's and young adult periodicals in the United States and around

ACEI Guide to Children's Magazines, Newspapers, Reference Books

CURIOUS NATURALIST, THE.* *Monthly (Sept.-May). Massachusetts Audubon Society, Lincoln, MA 01773. $3 per year.* Facts and projects to help beginning nature lovers discover more about the exciting world of nature. Amply illustrated.

CURRENT SCIENCE. *Weekly. American Education Publications, Inc., 1250 Fairview Ave., Columbus, OH 43216. $2.20 per year.* Newspaper format with articles on current scientific news, puzzles and quizzes. Braille and teacher editions. Useful for *upper elementary-junior* high children.

DANCE MAGAZINE.* *Monthly. Danad Publishing Co., 268 W. 47th St., New York, NY 10036. $12 per year. Ages 10 up.* Complete world coverage on dance news. Short, well-written articles of appeal to youthful and more mature dancers.

DOGS.* *Bimonthly. Country Wide Publications, Inc., 222 Park Ave. S., New York, NY 10003. $6 per year. Elementary & up.* Emphasis is on the dog as a pet—with illustrations and information. Relevant too for the professional and his showdog.

DOWN BEAT.* *Biweekly. Maher Publishers, 222 W. Adams St., Chicago, IL 60606. $9 per year.* For the pop-music fans of all ages. News on jazz events and artists plus excellent critical reviews of records. Reading level, *mature 6th-graders & up.*

EBONY.* *Monthly. Ebony Publishers, 1820 S. Michigan Ave., Chicago, IL 60616. $8 per year.* Pictorial magazine directed toward the black community. Excellent for articles about blacks in history, literature, sports, politics, entertainment. Readable for *upper elementary grades & mature readers.*

EBONY, JR! *Monthly (except June-July & Aug.-Sept.). Johnson Publishing Co.. 820 Michigan Ave., Chicago, IL 60605. $6 per year; for Can. & Pan Am. add $1; other foreign add $2. Elementary grades.* Stories, games, puzzles, history, biography based on the idea learning is fun. For the young black of today.

ELECTRONICS ILLUSTRATED.* *Bimonthly. Fawcett Publishing, Inc., 1515 Broadway, New York, NY 10036. $3 per year.* Appeal for radio and stereo buffs. Articles informally written but with sound technical information. Readable for *mature 5th- & 6th-graders & older* enthusiasts.

FARM JOURNAL.* *Monthly. Farm Journal, Inc., 230 W. Washington Sq., Philadelphia, PA 19105. Five editions for specific areas of the country: Central, Southeastern, Western, Southwestern, Eastern. $2 per year.* Attractive, colorful pictures. Not only supplies important information for people living on farms, but will help the city dweller better understand American farm life. Excellent for social studies in *elementary grades* and practical information for 4Hers.

FIELD AND STREAM.* *Monthly. Holt, Rinehart & Winston, Inc., 383 Madison Ave., New York, NY 10017. $5 per year; single copy 50¢; other countries $7.* Major American sports magazine; emphasis on "where-to-go" and "how-to-do-it." Strong statements on conservation. Appeal to all who love the out-of-doors. Reading level, *upper elementary.*

FLOWER AND GARDEN MAGAZINE.* *Monthly. Mid-America Publishing Corp., 4251 Pennsylvania Ave., Kansas City, MO 64111. $3 per year. Northern, Southern, Western editions. Upper elementary & up.* Written in popular style, with ideas and practical suggestions for indoor and outdoor gardening.

FLYING.* *Monthly. Ziff-Davis Publishing Co., Cir-Dept., Portland Pl., Boulder, CO 80302. $7 per year for U.S. and Possessions and Can; all other countries $8. Ages 12-adult.* Of special appeal to the aviation-minded. Up-to-date information; great photography in color and black-and-white.

FOOTBALL DIGEST. *Monthly. Century Publishing Co., 1020 Church St., Evanston, IL 60201. $6 per year.* Contains news stories, personal interviews and photographs. For the youthful sports fan.

FUN JOURNAL. *3 issues per year. Fun Publishing Co., P.O. Box 40283, Indianapolis, IN. $6.* Contains original poems, stories and articles by children nationwide. *Teacher's edition, $3;* also workbook for children.

GALAXY. *Bimonthly. Universal Publishing Co., 235 E. 45th St., New York, NY 10017. $9 per year.* Very popular science-fiction magazine. Contains both short stories and serials; also a nonfiction section with useful, factual scientific information. Braille edition. Can be read by *mature, upper elementary* as well as *older* readers.

GEMS AND MINERALS.* *Monthly. California Federation of Mineralogical Societies. Gremac Corp., Box 687, Mentone, CA 92359. $4.50 per year in U.S.* Wide range of articles with helpful hints for collecting, cutting, polishing. Reading level *12th grade & older.*

HIGHLIGHTS FOR CHILDREN. *Monthly (except July &Aug.); semimonthly in Feb. Highlights for Children, P.O. Box 269, Columbus, OH 43216. $7.95 per year, incl. Resources/Index Issue; $19.95 for 3 years in U.S.; Can. $21.45; foreign countries $22.95. Ages 3-12.* Stories, puzzles, riddles, fun with words, problems to solve, writings and drawings of children, craft activities. School and teacher subscriptions include quarterly professional bulletin, *Highlights for Teachers.* Much useful material for teachers of retarded children.

HOT ROD MAGAZINE.* *Monthly. Peterson Publishing Co., 8490 Sunset Blvd., Los Angeles, CA* the world; a list of agents (with their addresses) for ordering foreign periodicals; a list of periodicals that have ceased publication or changed title, and an index by title only. Since the arrangement is by topic, the lack of a subject index is not as serious as it might otherwise have been.

> *Periodicals for School Libraries, A Guide to Magazines, Newspapers, and Periodical Indexes,* revised edition, compiled and edited by Marion H. Scott. American Library Association, 50 East Huron Street, Chicago, Illinois 60611. 1973. $4.95 pb.

This is a general guide to about five hundred recommended magazines and newspapers for elementary, junior high, and high school students, subject to possible reservations in the specific review. Arranged alphabetically by title, each magazine or newspaper has an entry giving its name, publisher's name and address, suggested usage range (E for elementary; J for junior high, grades seven through nine; and S for senior high, grades ten through twelve), frequency of publication (such as W for weekly and M for monthly — see the chart in the front), yearly price, and a paragraph of description. These are critical reviews which may compare a periodical to other similar publications and possibly give a suggested curricula usage, either in the classroom or library. If articles from the periodical are indexed in a magazine index, this is noted at the end of the review. If back issues are available on microfilm, this is also indicated. The selection of periodicals for inclusion has been tied somewhat to school curcicula and to students' interests, and highly specialized materials are not included. Occasionally, there will be a combination review of several similar periodicals.

A list in the back of the book of sixteen indexes which index children's magazines may be useful (see *Subject Index to Children's Magazines* below). Many of these are definitely more for the young adult than the child, however, and do not tell which magazines are found in which indexes. This aid itself has an index by subjects, and suggestions on the use of periodicals. Users are referred in the introductory material to the reviews of periodicals that appear from time to time in *Booklist*. *Periodicals for School Libraries* is a very helpful source for selection and ordering children's magazines. A new edition is expected soon, edited by Selma K. Richardson.

> *Subject Index to Children's Magazines,* edited by Gladys Cavanagh. 2223 Chamberlain Avenue, Madison, Wisconsin 53705. Monthly, except June and July; bi-monthly, April/May. $12 yearly.

Devoted entirely to the indexing of sixty-five to seventy magazines for elementary and junior high school children, *Subject Index to Children's*

Animal Kingdom   E J S
    New York Zoological Society,   BiM
    Zoological Park, 185th St. and Southern Blvd.,
    New York, N.Y. 10460 $4.50 yr.

The habits and behavior of wild animals around the globe comprise the coverage of *Animal Kingdom*, with approximately five articles in each issue, written clearly and authoritatively by zoo curators, zoologists, and conservationists. Although these articles are more specialized than those in *Natural History*, they have the same tone and quality of writing. "Animal Kingdom Report" carries New York Zoological Society notes and news of animals in the zoos. There is a column with brief identification of contributing authors, and usually three to four short book reviews. This is a small publication with good paper, format designed for readability, articles illustrated with black-and-white photographs, and color photographs featured on the front and back covers. On the elementary level, children can enjoy the fine illustrations and teachers will find useful material for the classroom; on the secondary level, there is good browsing material, and some of the information will be relevant to science classes and projects.
Biol.Abstr.

Animals   E J S
    Nigel Sitwell Ltd.,   M
    21 22 Great Castle St., London, W. 1, England $9 yr.

The editor and publisher of *Animals* (Nigel Sitwell) is vitally concerned with the protection of animals threatened with extinction anywhere in the world, and the magazine reflects this concern in articles as well as in editorials. Interest in unusual animals is developed through articles describing little-known species in strange habitats. A "Zoo News" feature reports on the latest additions to zoos; "Zooguide" lists zoo addresses, opening times, admission charges, etc. A new "Books by Post" section reviews natural history books which may be ordered from publishers through the magazine. This is an excellent magazine for conservation study, comparing favorably with *Audubon*, but with emphasis on Britain. The content is of interest to pupils from 6th grade

Magazines fills a need for bibliographic control over the numerous magazines now found in so many children's libraries. It is somewhat similar in format and purpose to *Reader's Guide to Periodical Literature;* the *Guide,* however, includes few, if any, children's magazines. The subject arrangement makes it possible to find what children's magazine articles have been written each month via a topic approach. The arrangement is simple: each entry gives the title, author, name of the magazine (abbreviated), volume number, page(s), month, and year for the article. (Naturally, it is necessary for a library to subscribe to many of the magazines indexed in order to have any use for the *Subject Index.*) A few magazines indexed, such as *Horn Book,* are actually more for the adult working with children than for the child to use directly. The subject heading Book Reviews may be of interest to the librarian or teacher, as many of these citations are to *Horn Book.* "Easy reading" material is marked with a #, but there appears to be little of this. "See" and "See also" references are used for subjects, but there are no author or title entries. The backs of most issues have questions for class discussion or practice, a guide to usage, publisher's address, and so on. This is a very valuable tool for any library that subscribes to many children's magazines, especially if they are used for curricula-related purposes. Back issues are available.

REMEDIAL (HIGH INTEREST/LOW VOCABULARY)

Growing concern about the child who reads far below his or her grade level has led to the publication of several tools that are mainly bibliographies of books with interest levels well above their vocabulary (reading difficulty) levels. These are not exactly the same as the beginning-to-read and easy-to-read books that are intended for the child who is just starting to read but is not in any sense a retarded reader. The two types are often lumped together under the term "easy reading," however, as in *Booklist's* monthly reviewing column of that name which reviews both books for the beginning reader and for the so-called retarded reader. ("Retarded" here means behind in reading, not mentally retarded.)

Good Reading for Poor Readers, now in its ninth edition, is well known to reading specialists; it is the source of a device widely used for determining the "readability" of a book, the Spache Readability Formula, devised by its author. (There is a difference of opinion about the reliability and desirability of such formulas, however.) One tool, *Gateways to Readable Books,* has been included even though it is really intended for the retarded adolescent reader, since it is potentially useful for some elementary school-age children. The last title in this section, *Books for Mentally Retarded Children,* is for the truly mentally retarded child.

The Chicago Public Library also publishes *What's New in Children's*

Subject Index to Children's Magazines

ANDERSON, JOHN
John Anderson: a renegade.
L.Lettieri.   Texas Hist
36:23-5 Ja '76
ANECDOTES
Was my face red!   Young Miss
22:82-3 Mr '76
ANGOLA
And now...Angola.   Jr Schol
78:2-4 F 24 '76
Nation building.   Explorer
38:7 Mr 2 '76
Why fight over Angola?   Jr Schol
78:5 F 24 '76
ANIMAL SOUNDS
What to say when you meet a duck
in Thailand. W.Christophersen.
Jack & Jill 38:40 Mr '76
ANIMALS: see also Night Creatures;
Pets; Zoos; also groups of
animals, as Birds; also names
of animals, as Antelopes;
Cats; Chimpanzees; Dogs; Pigs
Animal prospectors sniff for
minerals. L.Grele.   Current
Sci 61:8 Mr 3 '76
Animal senses: touch.   Pict Ed
50:14+ Ja '76
Animal water tanks. H.Hathaway.
Boys' Life 66:70-1 Mr '76
Bigfoot. M.Walsh.   Child D
25:50-8 Mr '76
Okapi watch.   Zoonooz 49:9-11
F '76
ANIMALS - HOUSES
Animal homes. E.Myers.
Playmate 47:31-3 Mr '76
Home sweet home.   J.Bartenbach.
Ranger Rick 10:37-9 Mr '76
ANIMALS - PROTECTION
Death Match: should this show go
on? J.Ball.   Read 25:4-7
Mr 3 '76
Happy Bee.   Ranger Rick 10:26-31
Mr '76
Six more animals endangered.
Sr Wkly R 30:12-3 Mr 17 '76

ANTELOPES
Birth of a bontebok.   D.Sweeney
& B.Joseph.   Zoonooz 49:8-9+
F. '76
A slender-horned gazelle with
twins. M.M.Lieras.   Zoonooz
49:6-7 F '76
South African greater kudu.
(Picture only)   Zoonooz
49:1 F '76
ANTS
Beware the fire ant.   EYE 54:6
Mr 17 '76
AQUARIUMS
A visit to Sea World.   B.A.Tay-
lor.   EYE 54:7-10 Mr 17 '76
ARCHEOLOGY
Chinese anchors?   Sci World
32:24-5 Mr 9 '76
Did the Asians beat Columbus?
Current Sci 61:10 F 25 '76
Scientists make new find.
Parade 57:7 Mr 17 '76
ARCTIC REGIONS
Chilling thought.   NewsTime
48:6 Mr 9 '76
ARGENTINA
Argentina protects its wildlife
treasures. W.G.Conway.
Nat Geog M 149:290-7 Mr '76
ARIZONA
Creation of an Arizona landscape.
Ariz Highw 52:16-33 Mr '76
Texas Canyon: rocks, rocks every-
where. R.Jones.   Ariz Highw
52:42-5 Mr '76
ARMADILLOS
Research corner: "identical"
quadruplets and the nine-banded
armadillo. K.Benirschke.
Zoonooz 49:17 F '76
ART: see also Artists; Arts and
Crafts; Design; also branches
of art, as Music
Thracian treasures.   Pict Ed
50:24 F '76
ART, RESTORATION

Books, a monthly roundup of some new titles purchased by the library; some issues are solely annotations of new children's books, in which case the For Reluctant Readers page will have high interest/low vocabulary books. A yearly subscription is $2 from the Publications Department, Chicago Public Library, 78 East Washington Street, Chicago, Illinois 60602. Also, the National Council of Teachers of English has a bibliography called *High Interest-Easy Reading* (Citation Press, 1972) intended for junior and senior high reluctant readers but which could possibly be used for upper elementary school children. For the adult or young adult with reading problems, the Free Library of Philadelphia has the *Reading Development Bibliography* (New Readers Press, P.O. Box 131, Syracuse, New York 13210. 1974. 75p).

> *Gateways to Readable Books, An Annotated Graded List of Books in Many Fields for Adolescents Who Are Reluctant to Read or Find Reading Difficult,* 5th edition, by Dorothy E. Withrow, Helen B. Carey, and Bertha M. Hirzel. H.W. Wilson Company, 950 University Avenue, Bronx, New York 10452. 1975. 299pp. $12.

This annotated bibliography of one thousand books is included even though it is not actually within the scope of this book since it was written for the young adult, rather than the child, who is a reluctant or retarded reader. But even though its interest level is for the adolescent reader, most of the books included have a fifth or sixth grade reading *difficulty,* so it may well be used with older elementary school-age students. Each chapter covers a topic, such as sports or adventure stories, which is then further subdivided by type. Many books on contemporary issues likely to be of interest to young adults have been added to this fifth edition, but the fiction is divided into boys' fiction and girls' fiction with an additional separate section for girls' stories, but none for boys. The division of books into those for boys or for girls is not entirely acceptable to everyone today, although the intent is merely to appeal to the interests of retarded readers, who are believed to have strong sexually determined reading interests.

Vocabulary, a plot with action, conversation, length of sentences, physical format, and literary quality were all considered in selecting books for inclusion. A Reading Difficulty (rd) level is given by one grade level for each book. There are no interest levels specifically stated, as this is intended to be junior/senior high level in general. There are about two sentences of description as well as author, title, publisher, date of publication, number of pages, and price. Most of the books are trade books, but there is a separate chapter on texts and one on books in series that are graded in a few cases as low as preprimer or first grade. Both trade and text books are included in the series book chapter. The chapters on

86   GATEWAYS TO READABLE BOOKS

LESTER, JULIUS. To Be a Slave. (rd6) Dial, 1968. 156p. (paper, Dell)
The history of the African slave in America is related through records of narratives by slaves. Vivid pictures describe all aspects of slavery to the post—Civil War period.

MEADOWCROFT, ENID LaMONTE. When Nantucket Men Went Whaling. (rd4) Garrard, 1966. 96p.
Here is the true and dramatic story of the men who "went down to the sea in ships," facing great dangers of killer whales and unknown seas. Their lives at sea, on the wharves, and at home come alive in this vivid portrayal of Nantucket people in the early 1800s. (How They Lived Books)

NICKEL, HELMUT. Warriors and Worthies: Arms and Armor Through the Ages. (rd6) Atheneum, 1969. 122p.
Beautiful illustrations add greatly to the information given by an expert on arms and armor, from earliest civilizations to nineteenth century America. While it makes an excellent reference book, it is also a delightful source of material for hobbyists.

PHELAN, MARY KAY. Four Days in Philadelphia—1776. (rd6) Crowell, 1967. 189p.
The crucial four days of July 1 through July 4, 1776, when the Second Continental Congress debated and finally adopted the Declaration of Independence, are dramatically presented. It is especially appropriate for the Bicentennial year.

REIT, SEYMOUR. Growing Up in the White House: The Story of the Presidents' Children. (rd5) Macmillan, 1968. 118p.
One way to be a part of the life of famous or important people is to share their experiences. The story of the young people who have lived in the White House gives insights into presidential lives and times.

RICHARDS, NORMAN. The Story of Old Ironsides. (rd4) Childrens, 1967. 31p.
The story is told of the exciting role played by the famous frigate Constitution in developing U.S. naval power. The many illustrations are quite helpful. (Cornerstone of Freedom Series)

SCHELL, ORVILLE and ESHERICK, JOSEPH. Modern China: The Story of a Revolution. (rd6) Knopf, 1972. 149p. (paper, Random)
This is a very readable book on China's modern history, from the Opium War through the Communist Revolution, showing how war, famine, and social change have affected peasant life.

magazines and newspapers and those on simplified newspapers are especially likely to be useful. The introduction gives some suggestions on how to use the list in programs for the reluctant reader; students can use it directly as the annotations were written for their reading level. Libraries can also use it, of course, as a buying guide, and teachers can use it in planning lessons. There are indexes by author, by title, and by reading difficulty, but not by subject. The table of contents can be used as a subject approach, however.

> *Good Reading for Poor Readers,* 9th edition, by George D. Spache. Garrard Publishing Company, 1607 North Market Street, Champaign, Illinois 61820. 1974. 303pp. $5.75pb.

The first part of *Good Reading for Poor Readers* consists of chapters titled The Right Book for the Right Child, Choosing the Right Type of Book, Using Books to Help Solve Children's Problems, and Estimating Readability, which discuss the various factors involved in reading difficulties and suggestions for working with the retarded reader. There are extensive bibliographies at the end of each chapter for the adult working with children with reading difficulties. After the introductory material, much of the book consists of annotated bibliographies of titles for use with retarded readers or by the reading specialist. These are divided into chapters titled Trade Books Useful with Poor Readers (about eight hundred listings); Adapted and Simplified Material; Textbooks, Workbooks, and Games; Magazines and Newspapers; Series Books; Book Clubs; Indexes and Reading Lists; Programmed Materials; Auditory and Visual Perception; and Resources for Teachers of the Disadvantaged. There are subdivisions by topic within each chapter. Each entry has a Reading Level (R.D.), usually by one or two grades and an Interest Level (I.L.), usually by a fairly wide grade range, as well as author, title, publisher, date of publication, and a short one-sentence description of the book. Some texts as well as trade books are included. Generally speaking, most of the books were selected for inclusion because they were found useful by classroom teachers or clinicians.

While *Good Reading for Poor Readers* undoubtedly fills a need for books useful with the retarded or reluctant reader, it should be used with some caution. Some of the books included are of questionable quality and are not likely to be found recommended elsewhere. There would seem to be little advantage in giving children who are having difficulties material of rather pedestrian quality, no matter how easy it is to read. Furthermore, *Good Reading* recommends adapted or simplified versions of books, which are usually better avoided altogether, in the opinion of many librarians. Bibliotherapy, the use of books to resolve personal problems, which Spache seems to favor strongly, is also strongly opposed by

Aviation and Space Adventure

Caidin, Martin, *The Winged Armada*. New York: Dutton, 1964. The subtitle, the story of the Strategic Air Command, is apt. The daily tensions and activities are presented with accuracy and enthusiasm. R.L. 5–6 I.L. 6 up.

Corson, Hazel W., *Peter and the Rocket Ship*. Chicago: Benefic, 1955. A very simple science fiction tale. One of the Air Age series. R.L. 2 (Spache) I.L. 3 up.

Furman, A. L., ed., *Teen-Age Outer Space Stories*. New York: Lantern, 1962. Teenage adventures in tomorrow's world of outer space. One of the Teenage series. R.L. 7–8 I.L. up.

George, J. C., *Hold Zero!* New York: Crowell, 1936. Four boys upset their neighbors by building a rocket. R.L. 6–7 I.L. 7 up.

Hamre, Leif, *Perilous Wings*. New York: Harcourt, 1961. Adventure in the new supersonic planes in the Norwegian Air Force. R.L. 7–8 I.L. 7–10.

Hill, Robert, *What Colonel Glenn Did All Day*. New York: John Day, 1962. The story of Glenn's day in outer space. R.L. 4–5 I.L. 4 up.

Norton, Andre, *Moon of Three Rings*. New York: Viking, 1966. Simple space-age adventure. R.L. 5–6 I.L. 5 up.

Sarnoff, Paul, *Ice Pilot—Bob Bartlett*. New York: Messner, 1966. Story of a bush pilot who lived with danger. R.L. 5–6 (D-C) I.L. 5–8.

Stapp, Arthur D., *Ordeal by Mountains*. New York: Viking Press, 1970. R.L. 5–6 I.L. 5 up. A mountain boy aids three victims of an airplane crash.

Zimmerman, Naoma and Schuyler, Ruby, *Corky in Orbit*. Chicago: Reilly, 1962. Two boys' adventures in space flight. R.L. 3.1 (Spache) I.L. 3–5.

Reprinted from *Good Reading for Poor Readers*, 9th edition, by George D. Spache, published by Garrard Publishing Company.

some; this is particularly important in that the retarded reader is often believed to have adjustment problems. The Spache Readability Formula and the information on its use at the end of the book will be of considerable interest to many people; this is a well-known and highly regarded way of calculating the readability (that is, reading difficulty) of a book, but here again some are opposed to the idea of setting exact reading levels for books. (For the reluctant or retarded reader the practice may be much more defensible than for the ordinary reader, however.) *Good Reading for Poor Readers* has an index by author and one by title, but not by subject; it would be enriched by one, as the table of contents is not sufficiently detailed to be used as a subject index.

> *Books for Mentally Retarded Children,* by the Public Library of Cincinnati and Hamilton County. 800 Vine, Cincinnati, Ohio 45234. 1969. 32pp. OP.

A small pamphlet of one-sentence annotations for about three hundred books for educable and trainable mentally retarded children, *Books for Mentally Retarded Children* has four sections. The first three list books for educable mentally retarded children, divided by ages (six to nine, ten to twelve, and twelve to fifteen); the fourth lists books for trainable mentally retarded children ages eleven to thirteen. (Books for other ages of trainable mentally retarded children are not included.) For the first three groups, an asterisk is used to indicate books with which the child will need adult help. This is not done for entries for the trainable children as they are not generally able to read and must be read to. All the books were selected from ordinary library books, not from materials especially prepared for the mentally retarded child. There are many well-known and well-regarded titles here, although a few seem questionable and are not usually found on lists of recommended children's books. All books were used with mentally retarded children and inclusion was based to some extent on their responses. The introduction states that most of the books are realistic rather than fantasy, but examination of the list reveals that for the younger children especially there are quite a number of animal fantasies. The sections for educable children ages ten to twelve and twelve to fifteen have informational books, but those for educable children ages six to nine and trainable children do not. Bibliographic information is confined to title, author, and name of publisher, and there are no indexes. Arrangement is alphabetical by title in each of the four sections.

Although it is slightly out of date, *Books for Mentally Retarded Children* is still likely to be of considerably usefulness to those who work with the mentally retarded, particularly as there are few, if any, similar tools. It could be used as a starting point and expanded by individual librarians or teachers who find that their libraries have other books that are suitable.

Those concerned with texts for the retarded reader may wish to consult *Books for the Retarded Reader*, 5th edition, by J. A. Hart. Lawrence Verry, Inc., 16 Holmes Street, Mystic, Connecticut 06355. 1973. $5.50.

REFERENCE BOOKS

Reference books can be broadly defined as those intended to answer specific questions rather than to be read in their entirety. As educational methods change, reference books are used more and more by children, even quite small children. This is due to several developments: less reliance on only one textbook by the teacher, more nonfiction being published for children, and more individualized instruction in many schools. Children may also use a reference book for information about a personal interest such as a hobby. Since reference books are among the more expensive of the books in a children's library, ranging from two or three dollars for a paperback copy of an almanac to $600 to $1,000 or more for a set of encyclopedias, for example, it is necessary for the librarian to choose carefully. No less important is the fact that children's lifetime opinions may well be formed while they are still in elementary school, and it behooves librarians and teachers to see that the information they receive is as accurate and well written as possible.

The aids in this section are primarily selection guides; they may be consulted when considering the purchase of a particular reference book or to check against a collection to determine its strengths and weaknesses. In addition to being used for selection, these books could be used, as several of their authors point out, to answer reference questions by giving the librarian an idea of where to look to find the answer to a specific question. (*Children's Catalog* and *Elementary School Library Collection* can also be used in the same way.) Naturally, the success of this method depends on having access to a good many of the books described in the aids; as interlibrary loan is not well established for children's books, this would probably mean owning most of the books. Having a good collection of children's reference books and being thoroughly familiar with them is, of course, the best way, but these books could be used as described above as a starting point, especially for the inexperienced librarian. Also, in reference books, as in other categories, one tool may be used to reinforce another. On occasion older children might use the books in this section directly.

The Department of Public Instruction in North Carolina has an ongoing evaluation process for reference books for children and young adults; a number of reference books are evaluated and an annotated list is published from time to time. This is not a complete listing of reference books for libraries, but rather an evaluation of each group of books since the last list was compiled. There is a list of all titles evaluated since September 1969 but this is not annotated. (No comprehensive listing of all titles evaluated is available.) State libraries can request copies of the lists from the Materials Review and Evaluation Department, Department of Public Instruction, State of North Carolina, Raleigh, North Carolina 27611, but cost prohibits the Department of Public Instruction from supplying a list to individual libraries.

In addition, *Booklist* regularly reviews reference books for both children and adults in its section at the back of each issue, Reference and Subscription Books Reviews. Libraries already subscribing to *Booklist* for its children's book reviews would thus already have a good source of reference book reviews, although not every issue would necessarily cover any children's reference books. Every two years all these reference book reviews are brought together and published in one volume, the latest of which is *Reference and Subscription Books Reviews, 1972-1974, Reprinted from the Booklist,* volumes 69-70, September 1, 1972 to August 1974, prepared by the ALA Reference and Subscription Books Review Committee. These are the reviews exactly as they appeared in *Booklist.* They are long and end with the indication Recommended or Not Recommended. Note that reference books are an exception to the usual *Booklist* policy of publishing only reviews of recommended books. *(Reference and Subscription Books Reviews, 1974-1975, Reprinted from the Booklist,* volume 71, September 1, 1974, to July 15, 1975, and *Reference and Subscription Books Reviews 1975-1976, Reprinted from the Booklist,* volume 72, September 1, 1975, to July 15, 1976, both were published in 1977. Hereafter, this will be an annual publication.)

> *ACEI Guide to Children's Magazines, Newspapers, Reference Books, 1974,* by Judy Mathews and Lillian K. Drag. Association for Childhood Education International, 3615 Wisconsin Avenue, N.W., Washington, D.C. 20016. 12pp. $.50.

The magazine and newspaper section of this pamphlet has already been discussed. The reference books section which comprises four pages of the *Guide,* although necessarily limited, is a good source of a beginning reference collection for children. As well as bibliographic information, the annotations have several sentences of description for atlases, biographies, dictionaries, encyclopedias, handbooks, almanacs, and reference books on fine arts, music, literature, recreation, science, and social science (about thirty in all). Some entries are somewhat critical but

Guide to Reference Books for School Media Centers

1013.   Langdon, William C. **Everyday Things in American Life, 1607-1776.** New York, Scribner's, 1965. 353p. $7.95.

1014.   Langdon, William C. **Everyday Things in American Life, 1776-1876.** New York, Scribner's, 1941. 393p. $7.95.
These are histories of social life and customs and are not in reference book format or design. However, the range of subjects covered and detail provided in text and illustrative matter recommend the volumes for reference use in schools. They describe modes of travel, furniture, clothing, buildings, eating habits, agriculture, and many other topics. A similar compendium abridged from Alice Morse Earle's *Home Life in Colonial Days* and *Child Life in Colonial Days* is Shirley Glubok's *Home and Child Life in Colonial Days* (Macmillan, 1969. 357p. $6.95). (ESLC, WJ, WS)

1015.   Lord, Clifford L., ed. Localized History Series. New York, Teachers College Press.
The Localized History Series presents an approach to history teaching based on study of primary sources and first-hand observation, making the local community "a laboratory for learning history." While this has much to recommend it, a glance at some of the introductory notes to students indicates how much instruction on basic reference materials, use of libraries and archives, planning of field trips, interview techniques and notetaking is required. Fortunately, Lord has prepared a teacher's guide, *Teaching History with Community Resources* (1967. 85p. $2.50pa.) to accompany the booklets. To date there are 30 local history titles covering individual states, five for cities, eight on watersheds, and six for minorities. (See Teachers College Press catalog for list of titles.) The booklets range in size from 32 to 64 pages and in price from $1.50 to $2.50. While they vary somewhat in detail, the general format is similar providing brief surveys of significant periods of development followed by a short list of selected readings. Suggestions for field trips are also provided. The survey articles provide concise background information on each topic which in itself is of some reference value in secondary schools.

1016.   Morison, Samuel Eliot. **The Oxford History of the American People.** New York, Oxford University Press, 1965. 1150p. $15.00. New American Library, 1972. 3v. $1.95 ea. vol. LC 65-12468.
A one-volume general history of America from the earliest civilizations through the assassination of John F. Kennedy. The New American Library reprint (1972) is issued in three volumes: vol. 1, prehistory to 1789. vol. 2, 1789 through the Reconstruction; vol. 3, 1869 to 1963. Morison has included political, military, social, and cultural history, with special emphasis on the American Indian and the growth of Canada. No bibliographies are included. (ARBA 73, Winchell)

1017.   Tunis, Edwin. **Colonial Living.** New York, World, 1957. 155p. $6.95; $7.70PLB.
A detailed illustrated description of the common everyday aspects of colonial life—food, clothing, tools, methods of building, making candles, weaving, and other topics. Tunis is author and illustrator of this work, a standard title for children and young people. His drawings, numbering over 200, are an excellent source of information. A companion volume is his *Frontier Living* (World, 1961. $7.70PLB), which provides similar meticulous illustrations. (ESLC, WC, WJ, WS)

Guide to Reference Books for School Media Centers, by Christine L. Wynar. Reprinted with permission. Published by Libraries Unlimited, Littleton, Colorado, 1973.

all are considered to be recommended. Fifty cents is certainly a modest price and would be an especially appropriate expense for a library that could not afford more costly bibliographies of children's reference books. There are not enough entries to provide more than a beginning collection, however. The entire *Guide* is also found in the *ACEI Bibliography of Books for Children.*

> *Guide to Reference Books for School Media Centers,* by Christine L. Wynar. Libraries Unlimited, P.O. Box 263, Littleton, Colorado 80120, 1973. 473pp. $17.50.

This lengthy work consists of entries for reference books and other media for elementary and secondary schools, and some material suitable for vocational and two-year colleges. In this respect it is similar to Peterson (see below) but its scope is much wider. Its coverage of selection aids in the first several chapters is another similarity to Peterson but here, too, its range is wider. There are more than 2500 entries in all, arranged by type, such as history, crafts, and so on. These are then subdivided, with general works first for each category, and then an alphabetical arrangement within each smaller category. The usual bibliographic information is given, including LC card number. The annotations, some of which compare a book to another title of similar content, vary from a few sentences to rather long paragraphs, and availability of a title in paperback is noted. At the end of each description is a notation of where reviews of the title appeared. The index is by author, title, and subject together.

Guide to Reference Books for School Media Centers is a monumental work that should be of value to a library wanting a wider range of material than is found in Peterson or wishing to supplement or reinforce her book; the ordinary children's library will probably find Peterson of primary importance. Many entries in the Wynar book are not, of course, intended for children and it is sometimes rather difficult to tell which are, in fact, suitable for use with children if one is not already familiar with the titles. The *Guide to Reference Books for School Media Centers: 1974-1975 Supplement,* $8, by the same author adds about three hundred new titles and brings the work up-to-date.

Readers interested in purchasing reference books in paperback may wish to consult *Reference Books in Paperback: An Annotated Guide,* by Bohdan L. Wynar (Libraries Unlimited, Littleton, Colorado 80120, 1972. 199pp). It is similar to the previous entry in that it covers a range of books for children from elementary school through high school or early college. The savings for purchasing expensive reference books in paperback may be considerable, but against this must be weighed the heavy use these books may receive and the fact that paperback books never, of course, last as long as hardbacks.

GEOGRAPHY

Geography as a subject in the curriculum begins very early in elementary school and pervades the social studies program thereafter. Unfortunately, this is a rather neglected area as far as beginning reference tools are concerned. While geographical reference works for students in the middle grades are practically nonexistent, trade books in this field are not adequate to meet the needs. Many of them are sadly out of date; a 1970 book describing the countries of Africa will hardly be applicable today. Revision policies for series books on countries usually leave the old edition with wrong information to remain in print too long before the new edition is published. Since providing wrong information is worse than providing no information at all, geography is an area in which the library's collection should be carefully monitored and weeded frequently by the librarian. It is imperative that the school library acquire reference sources that are revised annually or at least frequently to include the latest world developments.

The titles included in this chapter are sources either recently published or subject to frequent revision. While many of them are in fact designed for adult use, most are easily used by children. The specific titles chosen for the library's reference shelf will depend upon the curriculum demands of a particular school. The books listed here include a number of general works covering the entire world, and a variety of sources dealing with specific geographical locales. Related material can be found in the chapter on atlases.

Webster's New Geographical Dictionary; A Dictionary of Names of Places with Geographical and Historical Information and Pronunciations. Springfield, Mass.: Merriam, 1972. 1370p. $14.95.

First published in 1949 and revised periodically to bring it up to date, Webster's New Geographical Dictionary includes over 47,000 entries. Listing both ancient and modern place names, it gives a brief statement of geographical and historical information and the pronunciation for each entry. It contains special sections on signs and symbols, geographical terms, and maps and map projection. It includes 217 small maps prepared by Hammond. Concisely written and easy to understand, it is an indispensable tool for elementary and junior high libraries.

137

Reference Books for Elementary and Junior High School Libraries by Carolyn Sue Peterson. Published by Scarecrow Press, 1975. Reprinted with permission.

Reference Books for Elementary and Junior High School Libraries, 2d edition, by Carolyn Sue Peterson. Scarecrow Press, 52 Liberty Street, P.O. Box 656, Metuchen, New Jersey 08840, 1975. 314pp. $10.

As its title suggests, this book recommends reference books for use by elementary and junior high school students, from kindgergarten to ninth grade. About nine hundred books are discussed, and inclusion was selective. (Some adult sources are also included when necessary for the advanced student.) The first chapter gives some remarks on the use of reference material for children, excellent general guidelines for evaluating a children's reference book, and sample reference collections for primary grades, intermediate grades, and junior high school. The other chapters are devoted to different types of reference books as follows: general encyclopedias, English language dictionaries, factbooks and yearbooks, indexes, atlases, biographical reference books, foreign language dictionaries, English and language arts, music and art, philosophy and religion, history, the social sciences, ethnic groups in America, natural science and mathematics, applied science, recreation and hobbies, and bibliographies. In most of the categories there are then further subdivisions by type. Each chapter opens with some remarks, usually brief, about the type of material and how to evaluate it; it then lists recommended titles with annotations, arranged by level of difficulty whenever possible, otherwise alphabetically. There is complete bibliographic information and a paragraph of description for each title. There are subject and author-title indexes. This is a good basic guide to reference books that any children's library should find of considerable value.

INTERNATIONAL

Due to the large amount of material available and the somewhat small part that books in a language other than English and/or books published in a country other than the United States play in most children's libraries in this country, this section has been purposely limited. Also, several excellent sources are rather out of date, considering the changes in our world in the past few years and the arbitrary cutoff date of pre-1970 for this book. Nonetheless, one or two earlier books have been included since they are, in my opinion, too good to be omitted. These are bibliographies of children's books from an international viewpoint, a journal of articles about children's literature, and sources for further reading.

Many of the large publishing houses have displays of international children's books at conventions; this can be an interesting and good way to actually see some of the books. State departments of education and state libraries often publish lists and there are *many* articles in journals,

FOLKLORE

467 Brown, Marcia. The Flying Carpet. Ill. by the author.
     Scribner's, 1956. A good readaloud and story-telling
     version of the story from "Arabian Nights," taken
     from Richard Burton's translation. E, I
468 Bryson, Bernarda. Gilgamesh, Man's First Story. Ill.
     by the author. Holt, 1967. A splendidly designed
     and illustrated book of the Sumerian legend of Gil-
     gamesh and his companion, Enkidu, from which we
     may find possible sources of the great mythological
     heroes, Hercules, Jason and Theseus. YA
469 Davis, Russell and Ashabranner, Brent. Ten Thousand
     Desert Swords; The Epic Story of a Great Bedouin
     Tribe. Ill. by Leonard Everett Fisher. Little
     Brown, 1960. An Arabian epic of the "Bani Hilal,"
     Sons of Hilah, a great tribe of desert warriors of
     ancient Arabia, Iraq and Syria. YA
470 Ensor, Dorothy. The Adventures of Hatim Tai. Ill.
     by Pauline Baynes. Henry Z. Walck, 1962. An
     adaptation of Duncan Forbes' translation of the orig-
     inal legends of Hatim Tai, the great Persian hero
     of the 6th century. The author's note will interest
     students of Persian legends and folklore. I
471 Hampden, John. Endless Treasure, Unfamiliar Tales
     from Arabian Nights. Ill. by Kurt Werth. World,
     1968. Fifteen stories which Mr. Hampden considered
     the best of (what he calls) "Shahrazad's" tales, with
     an interesting introduction. I
472 Hauff, Wilhelm. The Caravan. Ill. by Burt Silverman.
     Tr. by Alma Overholt. Thomas Y. Crowell, 1964.
     Original fairy tales, strung along night after night by
     the various members of a caravan crossing the
     Arabian desert, with a new story at each camping
     place. I
473 Hodges, Elizabeth Jamison. A Song for Gilgamesh.
     Ill. by David Omar White. Atheneum, 1971. Fic-
     tion based on the Gilgamesh legend, about a potter
     who discovers the mysteries of writing and nearly
     loses his life because of his ability to communicate
     by means of written symbols. Appended is a basic
     glossary of "Historical, Mythological, Geographical
     and Literary Words. " YA up
474 Ish-Kishor, Sulamith. The Carpet of Solomon, A He-
     brew Legend. Ill. by Uri Shulevitz. Pantheon,
     1966. When the great King Solomon of the Old
     Testament is flown high above the earth on a magic

often with very good bibliographies. For reviews of recent African children's books, see *African Library Journal.*

> *African-Asian Reading Guide for Children and Young Adults,* by Jeanette Hotchkiss. Scarecrow Press, Inc., 52 Liberty Street, P.O. Box 656, Metuchen, New Jersey 08840, 1976. 269pp. $9.

As the title indicates, this is an annotated bibliography of more than twelve hundred books on Africa and Asia for children, young adults, and adults. It is divided by regions and countries; for each section there are nonfiction books, biographies, folklore, and fiction, except for picture books, which are in a separate section divided by country. Each section also has a short introduction to that region, mentioning its countries and when they came into being. Books are classified as follows: PB for picture books; E for elementary from kindergarten to second grade; I for intermediate up to junior high; I Up for intermediate up to senior high; YA for young adult (mainly junior high); YA Up for junior and senior high; and A for adult. Each entry has bibliographic information and a descriptive annotation from one sentence to a paragraph in length. (Most are two or three sentences.) The entire list is selective, with books included on the basis of their merit. It is easy to locate entries in this guide; it was in fact intended for use by children and young adults. It has an author index, a title index, an illustrator index, and a biographical index. There is no subject index, but the arrangement of the book itself is a subject approach.

African-Asian Reading Guide is clearly organized and provides access to a considerable number of books. It should be most valuable for any library wishing a descriptive listing of books on this area of the world.

> *Africana for Children and Young People, A Current Guide for Teachers and Librarians,* compiled by James P. Johnson. (African Bibliographic Center, Special Bibliographic Series, volume 8, number 1). Negro Universities Press, an affiliate of Greenwood Press, 51 Riverside Drive, Westport, Connecticut 06880. 172pp. $9pb.

Africana is a generally *unannotated, nonselective* bibliography of about six hundred books and audio-visual items for use with children and young adults from preschool to twelfth grade, plus more than two hundred bibliographies and background readings of Africa. The entries, almost all of which are for books which were published in the United States in 1969 and 1970, are divided into Africa — General, Central Africa, East Africa, North Africa, South Africa, and West Africa, with nonfiction and fiction categories which are further divided into book and audio-visual items. Some entries have a few words of annotation when

Africana for Children and Young People

Larson, Charles R., ed. AFRICAN SHORT STORIES. New York: Macmillan, 1970. 185p. pap. $1.50.   (488)

Lester, Julius. BLACK FOLKTALES. illus. by Tom Feelings. New York: Baron, 1969. 159p. $4.50; New York: Grove, 1970. pap. 95¢.   (489)

Lomax, Alan and Raoul Abdul. eds, 3000 YEARS OF BLACK POETRY. New York: Dodd, 1970. 261p. $6.95, pap. $3.50. Gr 7-up.   (490)

Lurie, Morris. THE TWENTY-SEVENTH ANNUAL AFRICAN HIPPOPOTAMUS RACE. illus. by Richard Sawers. New York: Simon and Shuster, 1969. 56p. $3.95. Gr 1-5.   (491)

Martin, Minnie. TALES OF THE AFRICAN WILDS. illus. by Ivan Mitford-Barberton. 2d ed. Cape Town: Maskew Miller, 1969. 96p. illus. 75¢   (492)

Mitchison, Naomi. SUN AND MOON. London: Bodley Head, 1970. 11 sh.
                                                                     (493)

Nunn, Jessio A, comp. AFRICAN FOLK TALES. illus. by Ernest Crichlow. New York: Funk and Wagnalls, 1969. 141p. $4.95. Gr 4-6.   (494)

Power, Rhoda. THE BIG BOOK OF STORIES FROM MANY LANDS. illus. by Bernadette Watts. New York: Watts, 1970, c 1931. 240p. $5.95.   (495)

Radford, William, ed. AFRICAN POETRY FOR SCHOOLS. Nairobi, Kenya: East African Pub. House, 1970.   (496)

the title is not descriptive, but the majority include just full bibliographic information, and only some have suggested grade levels. Standard reviewing journals as well as publishers' catalogs were used for selection. The index is by author, illustrator, country, and title, and in some cases by place and subject.

Africana was not intended to be used for selection but rather to provide a comprehensive listing. (The author plans a more selective bibliography with annotations based on this work.) It provides a very complete listing of books and audio-visual materials about Africa for children and should be used by the researcher or the library amassing an examination collection of books on Africa; otherwise, it should be used for selection only with another aid.

> *The Best of the Best, Catalogs of the International Youth Library, Picture, Children's and Youth Books from 57 Countries or Languages,* edited by Walter Scherf as a publication of the International Youth Library. Published in the United States by R.R. Bowker Company, 1180 Avenue of the Americas, New York, New York 10036, 1969. 189pp. $9.50.

This compilation is a bibliography (1) in the original language of publication, (2) in German, and, (3) in English of the best children's books from more than fifty of the countries or languages in the world. Entries are arranged alphabetically by country, divided by ages within each country, and consist of bibliographic information only. The idea for this work came from Margaret Nilson at a UNESCO conference in Denmark several years ago; she felt that children of minority groups within a country need books in their languages and about their cultures. Accordingly, the books to be included were suggested by adults knowledgeable about children's books in each country represented. An attempt was made to avoid stereotyping any group, so this is therefore a selective listing. There is a list of exporters and importers which will be helpful for anyone who wishes to order any of these books. (It is also possible to obtain a list of titles suitable for translation from the International Youth Library in Munich.) Altogether, there are about fifteen hundred entries, and as the title says, these are "the best of the best." Naturally, many of them are not in English. The librarian looking for titles in languages other than English will find this useful. A new edition was published in 1976.

> *Bookbird, Literature for Children and Young People, News from All Over the World, Recommendations for Translation.* International Board on Books for Young People and of the International Institute for Children's Literature and Reading Research, Fuhrmannsgasse 18a, A-1080, Vienna, Austria. Quarterly. A.S. 250 per year.

Bookbird is a journal of articles from various countries about children's literature, children's libraries and librarians, and children's book programs. There are short reports of happenings in the children's literature field, biographies of authors or illustrators, and announcements of award winners in many different countries. There are no reviews of children's books, but a section called Professional Literature has short reviews for adults of books about children's books and library work. Frequently, there is a list of books which the editors feel would be good for translation. Overall, the emphasis is more international than most other journals in the field, which tend to concentrate on one country, although individual articles in *Bookbird* may be related to one country. It should be of value to children's librarians who wish to widen their scope from American children's literature and programs.

> *Books from Other Countries, 1968-1971, A Bibliography of Translated Books for Young People Available in the United States,* compiled by Elana Rabban. American Association of School Librarians, American Library Association, 50 East Huron Street, Chicago, Illinois 60611, 1972. 48pp. $1pb.

Compiled for International Book Year with the assistance of a grant from the Professional Division Program of the Scarsdale (New York) school system, *Books from Other Countries* lists translated books from twenty-two countries. There are from one to about fifty entries per country, about 180 titles in all; the bibliographic information includes name of author, title, translator, illustrator, company, date of publication, price, LC card number, and a short descriptive annotation. The stated purpose of the work was to make books from other countries available to American children, and most of the books were used in the Scarsdale schools, but publishers actually supplied the short annotations, so it should be used with this information in mind. No bilingual texts, adaptations, or folk literature were included. For each entry a Reading Range (RR) is given as follows: PB for preschool; L for kindergarten to grade three; U for grades four to seven; and JR for junior high. (Combination ranges are sometimes used.) In addition, each entry has been assigned one or more numbers from one to five. These refer to units of study in social studies, a key to which may be found at the front of the book. (These categories were also supplied by the publishers.) There are indexes by author and by title; no country index is needed since the arrangement is alphabetical by country. There is no subject index.

While this is a good source for children's books that are available in English translation, it should be used with the reservation that much of the descriptive material was supplied by the publishers, although many of the books, as has been noted, were used in the Scarsdale schools. A revision is underway.

Israel

Livne, Zvi. The Children of the Cave, translated by Zipora Raphael. Henry Z. Walck, 1970, $4.50. LC No. 76-100707. RR: JR. Category: 3, 5.
A group of children who survive the massacre of their village organize a commune in first-century Palestine in this absorbing story by an Israeli writer.

Italy

Boldrini, Giuliana. The Etruscan Leopards, translated by Isabel Quigly, illustrated by J. C. Kocsis. Pantheon, 1968, $4.95. LC No. 68-12650. RR: U, JR. Category: 1, 2.
Vel, the son of a wealthy Etruscan merchant, sets out on his first sea voyage and meets with numerous adventures. This is a vibrant story of a most advanced civilization brought to life by the fine writing and scholarship of the author.

Bufalari, Giuseppe. The Devil's Boat, translated by Douglass Paige, illustrated by Wayne Gallup. Knopf, 1971, $4.50. LC No. 78-113051. RR: U. Category: 4.
The story of a young coral diver who goes to sea with his father in search of a legendary coral bank in the Mediterranean. Through Gino's eyes we see his village of Porto San Stefano and meet the people he knows there as well as share his secret fears about the boat of the evil eye.

Bufalari, Giuseppe. The Yellow Boat, translated by Alfeo Marzi, illustrated with photographs by Peter Neide. Knopf, 1969, $3.95. LC No. 68-22244. RR: U. Category: 2.
A naturalistic story told from the point of view of a thirteen-year-old boy named Enrico who lives in a fishing village in Italy. As a fledgling coral diver, Enrico explores the underwater world of fish and sunken galleons.

> *Bookshelf, 19--, Children's Books of International Interest,* by the Children's Services Division of the American Library Association. 50 East Huron Street, Chicago, Illinois 60611. Free.

Bookshelf is a yearly mimeographed list of children's books which are of international interest. Accordingly, some of the titles reflect American children and their way of life, while others have settings in other countries; some have no particular geographical setting but might be of interest to children in any country because of their universality. All were published in the United States or occasionally in England since the last compilation and are in English. There is simplified bibliographic information for each of the eighty to one hundred books, with a sentence or two of annotation, divided into categories of picture books, fiction, folklore, and nonfiction. The list may be ordered from the American Library Association by sending a stamped, self-addressed envelope, with $.26 postage. This is an inexpensive way to obtain a list of books about other countries, written in English.

> *Children's Books of International Interest, A Selection from Four Decades of American Publishing,* edited by Virginia Haviland. American Library Association, 50 East Huron Street, Chicago, Illinois 60611, 1972. 69pp. $2.50.

This title is something of a turnabout from the others in this section: it presents an annotated bibliography of about four hundred children's books published in the United States that may be of interest abroad, whether in their original forms or in translations. Part of the purpose of the work, which was prepared for International Book Year (1972) and concerns itself with children's books published in the United States during the preceding forty years, was to encourage the publication of American children's books abroad. The previous lists of *Children's Books of International Interest (Bookshelf)* were used as a basis, although about half of the books from that source were not used, and some other titles were added. Some classics were omitted unless there was a new edition, but librarians and teachers will recognize many old favorites. It is divided into Books for Younger Children, with two categories, Picture Books and First Reading; and Books for Older Children, which consists of Fiction; Folklore; Poetry; Biography; History, Peoples, and Places; the Arts; and Science and Nature. The editor mentions that the preponderance of fiction is due to its generally longer-lasting appeal. Each of the entries has bibliographic information and one or two sentences of description. There are no indexes; arrangement is alphabetical within each category.

While the majority of children's librarians in the United States may never be concerned with purchasing children's books to be used abroad, this is a good list to keep in mind for general purchasing, and could, in

ℬooks for Older Children

Fiction

Alexander, Lloyd. **The Book of Three.** Holt. 1964. 217p. $3.95.

Inspired by legends of ancient Wales, the author has created Prydain, mythical land of kings and villains, in which Taran, an Assistant Pig-Keeper, becomes a hero. Four sequels include **The Castle of Llyr, The Black Cauldron, Taran Wanderer,** and **The High King,** the last winning the Newbery Medal award and the National Book Award. Each part of the chronicle sees confrontations between the forces of good and evil as Taran pursues his quest to find the truth about himself. Ages 9–12.

Alexander, Lloyd. **The Marvelous Misadventures of Sebastian.** Dutton. 1970. 208p. $5.95.

The swift-paced comic adventures of an eighteenth-century court fiddler who comes to own a magical violin, his encounters with a cat accused of witchcraft and his meeting with a runaway princess. Ages 9–13.

Andersen, Hans Christian. **Seven Tales.** Tr. from the Danish by Eva Le Gallienne. Illus. by Maurice Sendak. Harper. 1959. 127p. $3.95.

21

Reprinted by permission of the American Library Association from *Children's Books of International Interest* by Virginia Haviland, copyright © 1972 by the American Library Association.

fact, have been included in the first chapter, Building the Basic Collection. Most of the titles included, however, will be found elsewhere in the tools in that section. Note its inexpensive price.

> *Children's Books on Africa and Their Authors, An Annotated Bibliography,* by Nancy J. Schmidt. Africana Publishing Company, 101 Fifth Avenue, New York, New York 10003, 1975. 291 pp. $15.

Schmidt has prepared a very extensive annotated bibliography of more than eight hundred books for children and young adults set in Africa or about Africa. Each entry is by author and has a sentence of biographical information about the author to show how he or she is qualified to write children's books about Africa. This is followed by the title, publisher, date, number of pages, illustration statement, and the symbol YA if the book is for young adults or E if it is for younger elementary school children. (If the book is for upper elementary or junior high school children, there is no designation.) The annotations are a paragraph long, are generally descriptive rather than critical, and are based more on the content of the African information than on the book's literary or artistic quality. Annotations end with a one-sentence statement about the illustrations, mainly telling whether they have an African setting or whether they complement the text. Books are not designated as recommended or not recommended as the compiler feels that almost any book on the subject could be usable for some purposes. (The exceptions are a few books which are totally without merit, and these are so indicated.) The inclusion was not selective and almost all books that the compiler was able to examine are included. Both old (1880s) and new (1973) books are included, whether published in the United States or abroad, but most are from the 1960s and early 1970s. Fiction, nonfiction, and folklore are all included, plus some texts, but no attempt was made to include all texts about Africa. There are no foreign-language books. There are entries for many books in series, because many books on Africa have often been published in series. There are indexes by country; name of coauthor, consultant, editor, illustrator, or pseudonym; series name, divided into those for African readers and non-African readers; subject; title; and tribe.

Librarians could use this aid for selection by reading the annotations carefully and selecting only those books whose annotations say that they give an accurate portrayal of African people and countries (since the list is not selective and no indication of recommended books is given) unless, of course, a comprehensive, retrospective collection is purposely being acquired. One drawback, especially in selecting for younger children, is the limited information about the illustrations. The student of African children's literature would undoubtedly find it of great value—the information in the introduction alone should be read by anyone interested in this topic. Schmidt is also the editor of *Children's Literature and Audio-Visual Materials in Africa* (Conch Magazines, Ltd., 1977, $10), which was not available in time for inclusion here.

> *The Chinese in Children's Books*, by the New York Public Library, Fifth Avenue and 42 Street, Room 58, New York, New York 10018. 1973. 30pp. $2pb.

The Chinese in Children's Books is primarily an annotated bibliography of children's books written in Chinese or set in China. The books, selected by children's librarians, avoid stereotypes of the Chinese or their way of life. The first section, Books in Chinese, has entries for thirty-seven books. The title, author, and illustrator for each of these books are given in Chinese characters and in Arabic transliteration but not in English. The annotations, a short sentence or so long, are in English, however. There are no suggested age or grade levels, but a few books are recommended for older or for younger children. Fiction and nonfiction books, including picture books, are listed. The second section, In China, has six parts: Picture Books; Stories for Younger Children; Stories for Older Children; Folk Tales; People and Places; and Arts and Culture. It contains entries for seventy-eight books in English set in China, some published in the United States, some abroad. The annotations are slightly longer than those in the previous section, and the books were mostly published in the 1960s and 1970s. Entries do not have grade or age levels. The final section, The Chinese in the United States, has twelve books about Chinese-Americans (Nisei). There are no indexes for the work, and it is sometimes hard to tell whether a book is fiction or nonfiction.

As ethnic awareness seems to be growing in the United States, librarians can probably expect to see an increase of interest in books about China and Chinese-Americans. *The Chinese in Children's Books* should prove useful, especially as these sources are hard to find elsewhere. Some old favorites (such as *Story about Ping, Little Pear,* and *Moy Moy*) can be found here, but the majority are probably unfamiliar to many children's librarians.

> *The Wide World of Children's Books, An Exhibition for International Book Year, An Annotated Catalog*, compiled by Virginia Haviland. Library of Congress, 1972. (Order from Superintendent of Documents, U.S. Government Printing Office, Washington, D.C. 20402.) 84pp. $.50.

Intended as a catalog to accompany a display of children's books for International Book Year (1972), *Wide World of Children's Books* is an annotated bibliography of 130 books from thirty-eight countries, primarily picture books, with sample black and white illustrations. Each country

BOOKS
IN
CHINESE

愛漂亮的蝴蝶. 潘遂文. 陳壽美 圖.

Ai p'iao liang ti hu tieh. By P'an Sui. Illustrated by Chen Shou-mei. (13014)

A picture book about a frivolous butterfly who does not think ahead to winter.

鷄兒喔喔啼. 朱介凡文 黃昌惠. 圖.

Chi êrh wo wo t'i. Compiled by Chu Chieh-fan. Illustrated by Huang Ch'ang-hui. (21023)

Nursery rhymes from different provinces of China. Illustrated with collages.

奇妙的機器. 呂廷和 文. 陳正枝圖.

Ch'i miao ti chi ch'i. By Lü T'ing-ho. Illustrated by Ch'en Cheng-chih. (63011)

The structure and functions of the human body.

中國歷史人物故事.

Chung Kuo li shih jen wu. Hong Kong, Chung Hwa Shu Chu.

A collection of booklets, each dealing with outstanding historical figures and events from Chinese history. For older children.

中國名著圖畫故事集

Chung Kuo ming chu t'u hwa ku shih chi. 4v. Hong Kong, Hsing Ya Erh Tung Chia Yu Ch'u Pan She.

In this set of illustrated classic tales, volumes 1 and 2 tell of the adventures of Monkey. Volumes 3 and 4 contain the biography of Yüeh Fei, the national hero.

FRANCE

1

Aymé, Marcel. Les Contes du chat perché. [Stories told by the perching cat] [Paris] Gallimard [1968] 309 p. (Collection Soleil, 239)

PZ26.3.A9 1968

The full collection of this novelist's tales about two little girls who live on a farm where the animals talk. Single chapters and groups of the tales have also been published separately. American editions have appeared as *The Wonderful Farm* and *The Magic Pictures*, both illustrated by Maurice Sendak.

2

Boland, Josette, *and* Suzanne Boland. Séraphine et le marcassin. [Séraphine and the wild boar] Raconté par Claude Voilier. [Paris] Hachette, 1969. [30] p. col. illus. (Grands albums Hachette) PZ23.B564S4

Of Belgian origin, this story describes the delight of small farm children playing with a foundling wild baby boar until, in the springtime, it hears a call of the wild.

Haviland, Virginia, compiler. *The Wide World of Children's Books; an Exhibition for International Book Year.*

has from one to seven entries. Books themselves are in the original language of publication; however, the bibliographic information for each one also has an English translation of the title, and the annotations are in English. Most of the books are rather recent publications and were selected for their literary and artistic merit and for their importance to the country's whole body of literature, not just its children's literature. Some have won awards or have appeared on recommended lists in their countries of origin. There is no index, but the arrangement by country provides an approach via the table of contents.

A wide variety of regions of the world is represented here—Europe, Asia, North and South America, Australia, and Africa, although the preponderance of entries are for Europe. Note that with three exceptions of translated books only a few of the books are in English, such as those from the United States, Australia, or Canada, which originally appeared in English.

> *The World of Children's Literature*, by Anne Pellowski. R. R. Bowker Company, 1180 Avenue of the Americans, New York, New York 10036. 1968. 538pp. $18.75.

Although strictly speaking this book is too old (1968) to be included, it is too imposing a work to be omitted. Pellowski explains in the preface that her intent was "to give an overview of the development of children's literature in every country where it presently exists." *World of Children's Literature* contains annotated bibliographies of books and articles about children's books, children's libraries, children's programs, and so forth, divided into eight geographical areas and subdivided by countries. Each section begins with a discussion of the state of the art of children's literature in that country followed by the annotated bibliography for the country. Reviews of children's books themselves are not included. The bibliography on pages 14-20, following the introduction, is a good source for anyone interested in a general approach to internationalism in children's literature, not in any one particular country.

The World of Children's Literature is a still massive work that should provide the definitive source of references for anyone interested in reading in depth about children's literature of almost any region or country. The articles and books themselves would have to be obtained, of course, since this is a bibliography. In eight years there have been a number of articles and books which are more current, but there are no plans for updating.

Several organizations also publish inexpensive lists, often in mimeographed or pamphlet form, of children's books from their respective countries or areas or of books that promote friendship and understanding among people in general. While not all of this material was

2050.   Chmielowski, Piotr. "Czasopisma polskie dla młodego wieku," *Encyklopedia wychowawcza*, 1885, Tom 6, pp. 134–141.

2051.   Čukovskij, Kornej. *Od dwóch do pieciu.* Warszawa, Nasza Księgarnia, 1962. 310p.
A translation of 1877, made by Wiktor Woroszylski and illustrated by children from Warsaw Public School No. 50.

2052.   Dąbrowska, Wanda. *Wybor ksiązek dla dzieci i młodziezy; powiesci, opowiadania, poezje.* Warszawa, Skłod Głowny: Poradnia Bibljoteczna, 1936. 63p. DLC.

2053.   Dmochowska, Maria. "Moja praca w bibliotece dziecięcej," *Bibliotekarz*, Warszawa, Rok 28, No. 7–8, 1961, pp. 229–232. DLC, NNY.
"My work in a children's library." A fragment of a study which won the 1960 contest for a descriptive essay on library experience. This librarian wrote of work in the Warsaw central children's library.

2054.   Douglas, Mary Peacock. *Biblioteka w szkole podstawowej i jej dzielalność.* Warszawa, Pánstwowe Zaklady Wydawnictw Szkolnych, 1964. 130p.
A translation of *The Primary School Library and Its Services* made by Wanda Koszutska.

2055.   Durajowa, Barbara. "Młodociani czytelnicy korespondują z autorem," *Bibliotekarz*, Warszawa, Rocznik 18, Nos. 3–4, Mar.–Apr., 1951, pp. 56–58. DLC, NNY.
"Young readers correspond with authors." The librarian in Łódż describes a special reading club and program for young adults.

available for examination, readers needing more information on this topic may find it worthwhile to write directly to the addresses below; much of this material is inexpensive or free. Titles are indicated when known, but it will probably be best to simply ask for any children's book lists that the organization publishes. (Some of them also have lists for adults.) Many of the lists are revised on an occasional basis, and may be annotated or unannotated:

American Friends Service Committee, Children's Program Publications, 160 North 15th Street, Philadelphia, Pennsylvania 19106.
  Books for Friendship, 4th edition, edited by Mary Esther McWhirter, 1968. $1.25.
American Jewish Committee, 165 East 56th Street, New York, New York 10002. (See entry for *About 100 Books.*)
Asia Society, 112 East 64th Street, New York, New York 10021.
  Asia: A Guide to Books for Children, 1966. $.50.
Educational Resource Center, New Delhi, India.
  A Guide to Indian Books Recommended for Use in American Schools. Free.
Information Center on Children's Cultures, United States Commission for UNICEF, 331 East 38th Street, New York, New York 10016.
  Latin America: An Annotated List of Materials for Children, edited by Elena de Gonzales and Anne Pellowski. $1.
  The New East and North Africa: An Annotated List of Materials for Children, 1970.
  Africa: An Annotated List of Printed Materials Suitable for Children, 76pp. $1.
National Conference of Christians and Jews, 43 West 57th Street, New York, New York 10019. (Attention: Edith Selig.)
  Books for Brotherhood. $.20.
Also see the Multiethnic section of this book for some related materials.

PARTIALLY SIGHTED AND DEAF

While books for the physically handicapped child are generally outside the scope of this book, a few suggestions for partially sighted and deaf children, who may be using the same library facilities as nonhandicapped children, are included. These are unfortunately rather out of date. Addresses are provided for those who wish to write for more information.

> *Books for the Partially Sighted Child,* edited by Thomas D. Horn and Dorothy W. Ebert. National Council of Teachers of English,

1111 Kenyon Road, Champaign, Illinois 61820. 1965. 79pp. OP.

Reprinted from *Elementary English* (now *Language Arts*), *Books for the Partially Sighted Child* is an annotated bibliography of more than six hundred books for children with partial vision who can read type that is sufficiently large and dark enough, and has enough space between the lines. The books were selected on the basis of these three criteria, which are explained in considerable detail in the front of the book, and for the type of illustrations and the literary quality of the book. Books considered for inclusion were ordinary books from libraries in the Austin, Texas area, not books especially prepared for partially sighted children. Each annotation has bibliographic information and two or three short sentences of description. The size of type is given for each book (no books with less than 14-point type were included), and suggested grade levels are included. These were intended to indicate interest levels only, not reading difficulty. The annotations include remarks about the leading (space between lines) and the illustrations. An asterisk by the author's name means the book is Especially Recommended; two asterisks means it is Doubly Recommended. All the nonfiction books are arranged by simplified DDS in Part I; fiction, in Part II, is divided into fifteen interest categories (an unusual arrangement for fiction), and Part III has seventeen categories of easy books, most of which are fiction. Other than separating the easy books into one category, there is no age or grade level division. There are no indexes and no table of contents, although the subject arrangement can be used instead to some extent.

Obviously, *Books for the Partially Sighted Child* is badly out of date, but it is included here because of the difficulty in finding a more recent similar tool. Some of the books or titles are often well regarded, but others are not those usually found on lists of children's recommended books, including some with controlled vocabularies. However, teachers and librarians could pick and choose among those listed and perhaps use the explanation in the front as a guide to making their own selections of books for partially sighted children from their libraries' collections.

> *Books for Deaf Children, A Graded Annotated Bibliography,* by Mary Griffin Newton. Alexander Graham Bell Association for the Deaf, Inc., The Volta Bureau, 3417 Volta Place, Washington, D.C. 20007. 1962. 173 pp. OP.

This annotated bibliography of more than eight hundred books for children who are totally deaf or hard of hearing is fifteen years old, but unfortunately it is one of the few tools of its kind and has never been updated. Each entry has bibliographic information and a short paragraph of descriptive annotation. Books included were intended to supplement school curricula as well as to be used for leisure reading and were

selected on the basis of whether deaf children could understand them
and for their literary and artistic merit. Some adaptations were included,
a practice which is not usually followed for lists of recommended books
for children. A number of easy-to-read books, which were rather a new
idea at the time the bibliography was published, were included, as the
compiler felt they were especially suited to the needs of deaf children.
The introduction explains that deaf children often prefer nonfiction, including biography, because it is easier to grasp, so fiction titles were
selected to tempt the reluctant fiction reader and include mysteries,
sports stories, and "romances." There are also hobby books.

The books are divided into chapters for the totally deaf child by
grades: Nursery and Kindergarten; Reading Readiness; and Grades I, II,
. . . IX. They are further graded in each annotation as follows: N for nursery; K for kindergarten; P for picture use (presumably meaning children
can enjoy and learn from the illustrations without necessarily being able
to read the text); S for storytelling; an asterisk for the grade at which the
child can read the book alone (such as *2); and R for reference use. These
symbols are usually combined for each book to give an indication of
when it can be used for storytelling, if applicable, when the child can
read it with help, and when it can be used by the child alone. Text and
trade books are both included, but the later predominate. Some material
produced by religious institutions is also included. Often the annotation
indicates that a book should be used at school, at home, for pleasure, or
with adult help. There are subject and author/title indexes.

Books for Deaf Children could be used by librarians or teachers of deaf
children as a starting point but needs, of course, to be brought up to date,
and some titles are questionable. It might be well to check entries against
another list such as *Children's Catalog* or *Elementary School Library Collection.*

The Bell Association also publishes, for teachers, parents, clinicians,
and the like, a great many titles which are related to library books. A list
of materials is available from the address above. One of their publications, *The Raindrop,* is a collection of folk tales and classic stories to use
with deaf children.

The Center on Deafness, 600 Waukegan Road, Glenview, Illinois
60025, has a set of readers for the deaf child which combine sign language and the printed word. While libraries do not usually purchase
texts, there might be occasion to do so for the deaf child who often has
trouble with reading.

For the blind child, there are two services by the American Foundation
for the Blind: *Talking Books,* which lists children's talking books available
free to the blind or physically handicapped and is revised yearly, and

Sources of Reading Material for the Visually Handicapped, a collection of pamphlets on how to obtain services and materials for visually handicapped and blind people.

There is also a publication similar to *Books in Print* (discussed in a later chapter) called *Large Type Books in Print* (R.R. Bowker Company, 2d edition, 1976) which lists all titles available in large type for people of all ages with visual impairments. It is not a list of recommended books but rather includes all that is available.

The Reference Section of the Library of Congress, Division for the Blind and Physically Handicapped, Washington, D.C. 20542, has a number of publications and services for partially sighted or blind children. Two of special interest are *Magazines in Special Media, Braille, Cassette, Disc, Large Type, Moon Type, Open-Reel Tape* and *Sources of Children's Book/Record, Book/Cassette, and Print/Braille Combinations, 1974,* both free by writing to the above address. The former has a list in the back of organizations concerned with helping people with various handicaps. *Extensive* interlibrary loan is available for materials for the handicapped; information on this may also be obtained from the Library of Congress Reference Section.

Finally, a very new book titled *The Special Child and the Library,* edited by Barbara Baskin and Karen Harris (American Library Association, 50 East Huron Street, Chicago, Illinois 60611. 1976. 208pp. $9) is specifically concerned with library services for children with various disabilities. Although published too late in 1976 for inclusion in this book, it may be of interest to any librarian faced with providing for the special needs of the special child.

MULTIETHNIC AND NONSEXIST

The tremendous burgeoning of interest in children's books that reflect a wide diversity of ethnic backgrounds in recent years has led to a rather large number of publications in this area, beginning with materials about blacks. In the even more recent past, many criticisms have been made of the way that Indians (native Americans), Chicanos (Mexican-Americans), and women are portrayed in children's books. Unfortunately, there is still not a great deal of material giving recommendations of books on these last three topics, except for pamphlets and newspaper and magazine articles. While many of these are excellent, titles considered here are limited to books and pamphlets that are fairly easy to obtain and were published separately.

In regard to blacks as portrayed in children's books, there is a great deal of material, much of it published between the mid-1960s and the present. These take the form of bibliographies, usually of recommended books, articles about the need for more positive images of blacks, and discussions of specific titles with black characters or with themes relating to blacks. Many of the journals in the chapter on Keeping Up-to-Date contain excellent articles on these topics. Because there is so much available, only a few of the possible aids, excluding articles, can be covered here. For further information see Masha Kabakow Rudman's *Children's Literature, An Issues Approach* (D. C. Heath and Company, 125 Spring Street, Lexington, Massachusetts 02173. 1976. $6.95pb), pp. 208-215, which contains a good listing of nearly sixty references.

Because of the amount of material, this section is long, and it probably represents more than many children's librarians will need. Examination of the description of the titles should reveal several that meet a library's needs in various areas. Most are bibliographies of recommended books, but there are also tools that review current books, readings about the ways minorities and women are written about in children's books, and books that give ideas on how to encourage acceptance of diversity among children. The latter, of course, usually cover a wide scope of different ethnic groups rather than just one. Although multiethnic books are not *ipso facto* for the disadvantaged child, these resources have been included in this section because past library service to children has demonstrated that children of a minority background are fairly often disadvantaged in the sense of having little about their culture or about people of their color to read about. Perhaps the future will be different, but for now the examination of bibliographies for disadvantaged children usually reveals that they are, in fact, multiethnic in nature.

For further reading on ethnic diversity in children's literature, the reader may wish to consult *Reading, Children's Books, and our Pluralistic Society,* edited by Harold Tanyzer and Jean Karl (Perspectives in Reading, no. 16, International Reading Association, P.O. Box 695, Newark, Delaware 19711. 1972. 89pp. $3.50), which consists of papers on the topic.

Due to the changes in the way ethnic minorities and women view themselves, the 1970 cut off date has, with few exceptions, been carefully adhered to, even though this means exclusion of some well-known sources. Even so, since this is an area of as much controversy as any other in children's literature, some books in almost any list of recommended titles may be criticized by some people or groups as being unrealistic, derogatory, or inappropriate.

Blacks

For readers who may be unfamiliar with the criticisms that have been made of the way a number of children's books, some of them well known, portray black people, the first two titles in this subsection, *The Black American in Books for Children* and *Image of the Black in Children's Fiction,* will be of help as general orientation to the issue. The next three, *The Black Experience in Children's Books, The Black Experience in Children's Audio-Visual Materials,* and *Black World,* are lists of recommended books and audio-visual materials, while *Starting Out Right* combines remarks on the portrayal of blacks with recommended and nonrecommended books.

> *The Black American in Books for Children: Readings in Racism,* compiled by Donnarae MacCann and Gloria Woodard. Scarecrow Press, Inc., 52 Liberty Street, P.O. Box 656, Metuchen, New Jersey 08840. 1972. 223pp. $7.50.

This title is a collection of articles, most of them post-1965, from various sources such as *Interracial Bulletin for Children, School Library Journal,* and *Publishers Weekly,* on aspects of the portrayal of blacks in children's books. The sections are: Black Perspective, the Basic Criterion; Racism in Newbery Prize Books, More Modern Examples; Some Early Examples; and Racism and Publishing. A number of well-known titles like *Amos Fortune, Free Man, The Cay,* and *Charlie and the Chocolate Factory,* are sharply criticized. There are also discussions of some lesser-known books of historical significance. Several chapters contain a plea for better books about blacks for children. A few recommended books are included in some of the articles, but overall the chapters are critical of the treatment of blacks in children's books.

This is good background reading for anyone interested in how blacks are shown in children's books; it covers a number of young adult as well as children's books, and is indexed by title and author.

> *Image of the Black in Children's Fiction,* by Dorothy M. Broderick. R.R. Bowker Company, 1180 Avenue of the Americas, New York, New York 10036. 1973. 219p. $14.

Image of the Black is somewhat similar to *The Black American in Books for Children* in that it is a book about the portrayal of blacks in children's books rather than a bibliography of recommended titles. It was written entirely by Broderick, however, rather than being a collection of articles by different people. The various chapters deal with different aspects of this topic as seen in books published from 1927 to 1967, but the author concludes that the picture has changed little since then (that is, between her cutoff date of 1967 and the copyright date of 1973). Overall, Broderick concludes that the image of blacks in children's books has been a generally negative or unrealistic one. There are a few illustrations from children's books and many passages are quoted to make her points.

SCIENCE

The Color of Man. By Robert Cohen. With an afterword by Dr. Juan Camas. Illustrated by Ken Heyman. Random House, 1968. $3.95. A book on human coloring including facts of anthropology and heredity and a discussion of prejudice. Illustrated with photographs of people all over the world.

Red Man, White Man, African Chief. By Marguerite Rush Lerner. Medical Books for Children/Lerner, 1960. $2.95. The scientific explanation of color in all living things, presented as a picture book.

Straight Hair, Curly Hair. By Augusta Goldin. Illustrated by Ed Emberley. Crowell, 1966. $3.75. A simply written science picture book about hair.

What Color Are You? By Darwin Walton. Photographs: Hal Franklin. An Ebony Jr! Book/Johnson, 1973. $4.95. A study of skin color which emphasizes that color has little to do with the basic worth of the individual.

What Happens When You Go to the Hospital. By Arthur Shay. Reilly and Lee, 1969. $4.50. A factual account of Karen's trip to the hospital to have her tonsils out, told through a simple text and black and white photographs.

Why People Are Different Colors. By Julian May. Illustrated by Symeon Shimin. Holiday House, 1971. $4.95. Sensitive illustrations accompany a simple introduction to the variety of races in the world.

Your Skin and Mine. By Paul Showers. Illustrated by Paul Galdone. Crowell, 1965. $3.75. Simple clear information about the skin with attractive illustrations showing people of different races. Another in the well-known "Let's Read and Find Out" series is **Look at Your Eyes,** 1962.

In selecting titles to consider, she restricted herself to certain subject headings in one of her two sources, *Children's Catalog*; therefore, some well-known titles dealing with blacks are not found in this work since they were not listed in *Children's Catalog* under the subject headings selected. This book would probably be most useful for children's librarians in the same way as *Black American in Books for Children* — as background reading.

> *The Black Experience in Children's Books*, selected by Barbara Rollock. Office of Branch Libraries, New York Public Library, 8 East 40th Street, New York, New York 10016. 1974. 122p. $2.50pb.

This latest edition of what was probably the first list of recommended books for black children is an annotated bibliography of nearly one thousand books. They are arranged in three main categories: The United States, South and Central America and the Caribbean, and Africa. Each category has divisions by topic and also to some extent by age range (picture books, for example). The first section, The United States, is much longer than the other two. Both fiction and nonfiction are included, and each book has bibliographic information and a brief annotation of one or two sentences. No age or grade levels are given; some books would be suitable for children, others for young adults. The work is actually a catalog of a collection of books in one of the New York Public Library's branches and includes some books that are very sharply criticized in some of the other books in this section — *Sounder* and *Bright April*, for example; the latter is the subject of considerable criticism in *Starting Out Right*. However, the intent was to include a wide range of books, and there are many new titles that help black children see themselves in positive ways and/or use black English (introduction, p.i.). There is an author-title index; for a subject approach the table of contents is sufficiently detailed.

The Black Experience in Children's Books (originally titled *Books About Negro Life for Children*, and first compiled in 1949 by Augusta Baker) is probably the oldest and one of the best-known lists of recommended books for black children. The criticism that might be leveled against it in some quarters is that it includes books that some blacks evidently find very unacceptable. As noted above, however, this was done intentionally to reflect a diversity of feeling; for that reason it may be more satisfactory to those who do not take a militant stand. Because of the considerable difference of opinion in this area, libraries should make every effort not to rely solely on one selection aid.

> *The Black Experience in Children's Audio-Visual Materials*, compiled by Diane DeVeaux, Marilyn Berg Iarusso, and Viola Jones

The Black Experience in Audio-Visual Materials

RECORDS AND CASSETTES

Africa; an Evening with Belafonte and Makeba. RCA Victor LSP 3420. The majority of these South African songs are in the Zulu tongue. Many are protest songs.

African and Afro American Drums. Folkways/Scholastic 4502. A two record anthology of drumming from Africa, South America, the West Indies and United States street bands which illustrates the influence of the musical traditions brought to the western world by African slaves. Collected by Harold Courlander. Also available as separate records African Drums (Folk. 4502AB) and Afro-American Drums (Folk. 4502CD).

African Folk Tales. Vols. 1-2. CMS 547/550. Cassettes: x4547/ x4550. Told by Bertha Parker.

African Folk Tales and Legends. Vol. 3. Tales and Legends of the Congo. CMS 591. Cassette: x4591. Brock Peters retells short, appealing stories. Includes explanation of words from Tshiluba dialect.

African Musical Instruments. Folkways 8460. A good introduction to African music by Bilal Abdurahman.

African Village Folktales. Caedmon TC 1309/1310/1312. Cassettes: CDL 51309/51310/51312. Brock Peters and Diana Sands tell a wide range of tribal tales.

Afro-American Music. Folkways/Asch AA 702. (2 Vol. set) Dr. Willis James, an authority on Afro-American ethnic music, gives a detailed explanation of African roots of Afro-American music with musical illustrations. For teachers and serious students.

Clark. Office of Branch Libraries, New York Public Library, 8 East 40th Street, New York, New York 10016. 1973. 32p. $1pb.

The Black Experience in Children's Audio-Visual Materials is a list of brief descriptive annotations for more than two hundred audio-visual items for children. Entries are divided into Records and Cassettes; Films; Filmstrips; and Multi-Media Sets, with the arrangement alphabetical by title in each of the four categories. Each entry has a notation of whether the item is in black and white or color, the length in minutes, and the distributor, followed by a description of the item. No prices are given since they change so quickly. The Countee Cullen Branch of the New York Public Library, which was named for the famous black poet and where this list was compiled, has long been known for its work with black people. This listing is actually a catalog of Countee Cullen Branch's holdings, and the introduction explains that most of the items relate to the black experience; some however are by famous blacks but not necessarily about being black. All were evaluated for both quality and their appeal to children. Future issues will have other kinds of media in addition to the four types listed. No age levels are given but some of the entries are probably more suitable for young adults or adults than for children.

Although prepared for the New York Public Library and somewhat geared to usage there, this bibliography will be helpful elsewhere and is certainly inexpensive. There is a list of hard-to-find distributors' addresses.

Black World in Literature for Children, A Bibliography of Print and Non-Print Materials, edited by Joyce White Mills. Atlanta University School of Library Science, Atlanta, Georgia 30314. 1975. 42pp. $2.50.

Black World is an annotated bibliography of more than two hundred children's books and audio-visual materials about black people, the black experience, or with black characters. All the items included were published in 1974 or the first half of 1975 and were read by a committee of librarians, teachers, and so on. Each entry has bibliographic information and a critical/descriptive annotation which varies in length from a sentence to a short paragraph; illustrations as well as text are discussed in the annotations. The book is divided into For Younger Children: Ages 3-8, and For Older Children: Ages 9-13; each is further subdivided by type. Both fiction and nonfiction books are included, and a rating scale of highly recommended, recommended, or not recommended was used. There are also a few adult references for further reading. Grade levels are given for the audio-visual items and for junior fiction (fiction for upper elementary school children and young adults). The audio-visual items are sometimes based on children's books and sometimes not—the original book may or may not be recommended itself. There is an index by publisher, which could be useful in ordering, and one by author-title, but none by subject. A page in the front has some suggestions for parents of black children of ways to introduce their children to books in general and to books about blacks in particular.

Black World should probably be used with certain reservations; it was intended to include books that are not recommended, as well as those that are, but a good many of the entries, perhaps as many as half, do not in fact have any indication of recommended/not recommended at all. Two sources were used for selection of audio-visual material, one of which is a catalog published by a jobber (that is, a seller of children's books and audio-visual items). However, the other audio-visual source was a well-known reviewing journal. This aid might be used in conjunction with another; it is very up to date, and there are plans for it to become an annual publication.

For reviews of new children's books and audio-visual media, see the usual reviewing sources in the first chapter and the *Bulletin of Interracial Books for Children* in the following chapter.

> *Starting Out Right, Choosing Books about Black People for Young Children, Pre-School through Third Grade,* compiled by the Children's Literature Review Board, Bettye I. Latimer, editor. Wisconsin Department of Public Instruction, 126 Langdon Street, Madison, Wisconsin 53702. 1972. 96pp. Free.

Compiled using funds from the Office of Equal Educational Opportunity, *Starting Out Right* presents a searching look at the way blacks are often portrayed in children's books, stern critiques of several classic books about blacks, and reviews of books about blacks for children, some of which are recommended and some of which *are not*. The names of the chapters indicate very well what is covered: Chapter 1, The Child's Book World: From Segregation to Token Integration; Chapter 2, Criteria for Judging Books Involving Black People; Chapter 3, Syndrome Patterns in Books Involving Black People. All discuss the racial situation as it has been and still often is. Chapter 4, Bright April—A Critique of a Classic, points out serious stereotypes and degrading aspects, in the opinion of the compilers, of this well-known and often well-thought-of classic (see *Black Experience in Children's Books* for the opposite point of view). Chapter 5, Reviews of Books for Pre-School through Third Grade, and Chapter 6, Moving Beyond Token Integration, present often lengthy reviews of more than 250 books, arranged alphabetically by title, and some suggestions for improving children's reading experiences about black people. Chapter 5 is by far the longest; the reviews are usually

Starting Out Right

The Big Pile of Dirt, by Eleanor Clymer, Holt, 1968.

This vibrant story shows how some city children took the iniative to secure a playground for themselves. The story also reflects some of the real hardships of the urban poor, but most of all we get an idea of the inventive and creative minds of poor children. Two qualities seem to make this story exceptionally appealing to children; it is narrated by a child in unpretentious, yet colorful language and the bold illustrations are expressionistic and warm without blurring the blackness and whiteess of the people involved. For advanced primary readers.

Binky Brothers, Detectives, by James Lawrence, Harper & Row, 1968.

Chub's baseball mitt disappears and with the help of his friend Pinky and Pinky's younger brother, Dinky, the mystery is solved. Children will enjoy the unravelling of this story as the members of one baseball team eventually outsmart and outplay the other team. Two of the characters in the story, Chub and Joe Parker, are Black youngsters. Appropriate for K-3.

Birthday Presents, by Eugene Fern, Farrar, 1967.

A small and colorful picture book showing a variety of birthday presents received by individual children in Joseph's city neighborhood. Joe receives a song which is printed in the book and which he later gives to the whole world. Good representation of Black faces throughout the story. For pre-schoolers through 2nd grade.

Black and White, by David Arkin, Ward Ritchie Press, 1966.

Using the 1954 Supreme Court decision as its focus, this picture book attempts to simplify that event. Its faults are numerous.

By reducing the decision to a catechism, the book undercuts a child's potential understanding of a historic case. Moreover, the author conveys a sense of paternalism. The emphasis is on nine justices who assume the image of the "great white father" dispensing some measure of freedom and equality to black people. This amounts to a distortion of history. By disregarding the political initiative historically exerted by Blacks, one can conclude that they have played a passive role in their own fight for freedom.

Its poetic style is extremely monotonous. The drawings are dreary and humdrum as they attempt to portray a black and a white child as exactly alike. The emphasis on black and white goes to the extreme. Samples:

The board is black; the chalk is white.

Their robes are black; their hair is white.

Black and White was written for pre-school through second grade level, but it is *not recommended* for use.

Starting Out Right, edited by Bettye I. Latimer. Published by the Office of Equal Education Opportunity of the Wisconsin Department of Public Instruction, 1972.

detailed and include quotes to illustrate either specific objections or good qualities. They may have the words Recommended or Not Recommended, but some have neither. The author index has, however, an asterisk by books that are not recommended. Some texts or series of texts are included in the reviews, which cover only books for preschool to grade three.

Starting Out Right should be useful to children's libraries that wish to upgrade the images of blacks that their children encounter in their reading.

Multiethnic and Disadvantaged

> *About 100 Books, A Gateway to Better Intergroup Understanding,* 8th edition, by Ann G. Wolfe. The American Jewish Committee, Institute of Human Relations, 165 East 56th Street, New York, New York 10022. 1977. 40 pp. $1.00.

About 100 Books is an annotated list of more than one hundred books for children and young adults which have as their theme better intergroup relations or better understanding and acceptance of differences among people. Many of the books deal with the heritage and/or problems of being Jewish, Black, Chicano, Oriental, American Indian, or female. Some deal with living in poverty, rural or urban, especially during the Depression. Others merely portray the way of life of a particular group of people, the struggle for freedom of people over the years, and have minority children as main characters. There are three groups of stories: Just Beginning, for children five to nine; The World Is Big, for children eight to thirteen; and Those Teen Years, for young adults eleven to sixteen. Arrangement is alphabetical by author within each group, and the fiction and nonfiction are not separated or otherwise designated. There are also annotations for a number of books about Jewish folklore and customs, as well as some about Nazi Germany, modern-day Israel, the Vietnam War, and nonstereotyped girls and women. The paragraph-long entries were selected from over six hundred books published since 1972, so earlier editions may still be useful. Both content and quality of illustrations were considered for the inclusion of a book. A few reference books and some books on the history of the women's rights movement are also included. There are no indexes.

The purpose of *About 100 Books,* to help children learn to be more tolerant of others, is laudable. Jewish material especially is sometimes hard to find, and a number of books with Jewish themes can be found here. For all minority groups, books are included that show past heritage

COHEN, BARBARA
The Carp in the Bathtub
New York. Lothrop, Lee & Shepard Co., 1972. 48 pp. $3.95.

A grandmother reminisces about the time she and her brother tried to save a live carp being kept in the family bathtub from being turned into gefilte fish for Passover. Parents will enjoy reading this blend of humor, nostalgia, and history aloud to their children, and remembering their own backgrounds together. Age 6-10

COHEN, BARBARA
Where's Florrie?
New York. Lothrop, Lee & Shepard Co., 1976. 48 pp. $4.95.

Florrie runs away because she is afraid her father will be angry if he finds out she disobeyed him. Jewishness is not the point of the story, but its setting in East New York during World War I offers insights into the Jewish life of the period. Age 6-10

DOBRIN, ARNOLD
Josephine's Imagination: A Tale of Haiti
New York. Four Winds Press, 1973. 48 pp. $5.95.

The lives of most American children are very different from that of Josephine, who comes from a poor rural area in Haiti. Imagination and effort bring her the doll she has always longed for and some other good fortune as well. A well-written story with an authentic setting. Age 5-8 and the present way of life. A subject index would have been an important addition.

> *Building Bridges of Understanding Between Cultures,* by Charlotte Matthews Keating. Palo Verde Publishing Company, 609 North 4th Avenue, Tucson, Arizona 87505. 1971. 233pp. OP.

This is an easy-to-use, informally written, annotated list of more than eight hundred recommended books for children, divided into twelve chapters whose headings give a good indication of their contents: Black Americans; Indians and Eskimos; Spanish-Speaking Americans (Mexican-Americans, Puerto Ricans, and Hispanos); Asian Americans; Nationality Groups and Religious Minorities; Selections with Multi-Ethnic Representation; Books for Bilingual/Bicultural Children; Books that Belong but Don't Fit; Africa; Asia; Caribbean; and Mexico. Each section has three divisions: Pre-School and Primary Levels, Upper-Elementary Levels, and Junior-High and High-School Levels; fiction and nonfiction are not separated or designated. Each book also has suggested age levels usually by three or four ages, and many of the annotations include comments made by Keating's sons. (Quite a number of books are recommended for one sex only.) Selection was apparently based on Keating's extensive tutoring experience and travels throughout the United States as well as her obviously deep concern about the acceptance of diversity in our culture, and not on any other lists of recommended books or reviewing journals; some titles which she includes have been criticized elsewhere. Also, some series books are included that librarians might hesitate to buy, either because of their content or questionable physical durability. The list was actually intended for parents and teachers rather than librarians, and often has suggestions for home, classroom, or church use.

In spite of these possible limitations, *Building Bridges* is still a useful source which covers quite a wide range of ethnic groups and recommends books that are readily available (and which may already be familiar to many librarians or teachers). It might be best to use it with another aid for selection purposes. It could be used directly by children as its casual style has much appeal. There is an index by author and one by title.

> *Bulletin of the Council on Interracial Books for Children,* 1841 Broadway, New York, New York 10023. Eight times a year. $10 to individuals; $15 to institutions.

The CIBC *Bulletin* is devoted almost exclusively to articles about children's literature and reviews of children's books from the standpoint of whether or not they violate the council's canons against sexism, racism, and antihumanistic values. It comes out eight times a year in a

Part 2
UPPER-ELEMENTARY LEVELS

Margaret Crary.   *Mexican Whirlwind.*   ages 11–15

New York: Ives Washburn, 1969.

Highly entertaining fiction that features an affluent Mexican for a change. Charming, wealthy Maria Estrada captivates her host family and her peers when she comes to an Iowa town as a high-school exchange student. The Websters, especially teenaged Taffy, learn much from their vivacious guest. Maria, in turn, learns to play basketball and help with housework.

The concern of American youth for social problems helps Maria become involved in a community-action project for her own people. Constructive social commentaries are expressed with humor and tact. True-to-life characterization and plot make this a junior novel girls should relish.

Maurine H. Gee.   *Timothy and The Snakes.*   ages 8–12

Illustrated by Charles Geer.
New York: Morrow, 1960.

The Coachella Valley·of California is new territory for Tim Adams. Beto, a Mexican-American boy, helps Tim learn about snakes, chickens, cats, and tree houses. Boys will appreciate Tim's struggle to earn money for a new bike. My boys found this entertaining.

Arlene Harris Kurtis.
Puerto Ricans from Island to Mainland.   ages 8–12

New York: Messner, 1969.

Reading this book develops interest in this exotic commonwealth and an appreciation of its culture. It intrigued me from page one and should liven up social-studies classes where educators make the book available. Spanish-speaking students will find it appealing. Teachers will appreciate the pronunciation guide and glossary. An absorbing, comprehensive text that should swell the tourist travel to Puerto Rico and make readers want to learn Spanish pronto.

Building Bridges of Understanding Between Cultures by Charlotte Matthews Keating. Published by Palo Verde Publishing Company, 1971. Reprinted with permission.

Bulletin of the Council on Interracial Books for Children

SPECIAL ISSUE ON CHICANO MATERIALS

Interracial Books
FOR CHILDREN

Vol. 5 Numbers 7 & 8, 1975

Bulletin

BILINGUAL EDUCATION

COUNTERING THE
CULTURAL DEPRIVATION MYTH

By Gloria Gomez

Ideally, bilingual education should promote and nurture diverse life styles. By embracing and sanctioning the behavioral norms of both white Americans and those of a given ethnic minority, it can help produce well-rounded and self-respecting individuals. This means, really, that bilingual education is meant for everyone in our multicultural and multilingual nation, not for ethnic minorities alone.

Appreciation of the above concept requires abandoning the myth of "cultural deprivation," a euphemism for asserting that all non-Anglo cultures are inferior, and that when their members enter the public school system remedial programs must be conducted to uplift them. Bilingual education programs, if they are to fulfill their potential, must rest on the premise that

equality is to be found in diversity; it must be a tool for sharing cultures, not a scalpel to excise minority ones. row focus results in the neglect of Chicanitos' intellectual, physical, emotional, social and esthetic needs that, with language, are woven into the cultural experience.

The heterogeneity of Chicano cultures requires that each bilingual project be designed individually. For example, foods that are common or popular in one geographic region may not be so in others (*sopaipillas* — blue-corn tortillas — are scarcely known in Los Angeles but are commonplace in New Mexico). There are great differences between urban and rural housing patterns, between town and city habits, between California-city and Texas-city habits. There are also a

Continued on page 15

Bulletin of the Council on Interracial Books for Children, 1841 Broadway, New York, N.Y. 10023. Institutional rate $15 for an annual subscription of eight issues, $10 for subscription by individuals.

newspaper-style format and also has reports of how the above-mentioned values are faring in schools and libraries across the country, usually via library programs and court cases. Texts as well as trade books are considered, and much of the contents of the *Bulletin* tends to be critical of traditional values and of well-known books; recommended bibliographies appear occasionally, but CIBC often finds little to recommend, and reappraisal of older titles is frequently called for. The council publishes a set of guidelines for evaluating a children's book quickly in terms of its racism and sexism. These may be obtained in pamphlet form by sending a self-addressed, stamped envelope.

Perhaps not all librarians and teachers will agree with all the viewpoints of CIBC and its *Bulletin* and guidelines (they have been the subject of much difference of opinion in several of the reviewing journals lately), but anyone working closely with ethnic minorities or in an area that requires nontraditional books about minorities and girls and women should probably consider it seriously. All librarians should at least be familiar with its point of view.

The council has also recently published a book titled *Human and Anti-Human Values in Children's Books* which evaluates two hundred and fifty children's books on the basis of CIBC's above-mentioned standards against sexism, racism, and antihumanistic values. It contains a detailed rating scale which may be used to evaluate a children's book on the basis of these criteria and is also considered very controversial.

> *Emerging Humanity: Multi-Ethnic Literature for Children and Adolescents,* by Ruth Kearney Carlson. William C. Brown Publishing Company, 2460 Kerper Boulevard, Dubuque, Iowa 52001. 1972. 246pp. OP.

Emerging Humanity was intended to develop an awareness of the cultures of the different peoples of America. The chapters contain discussions of the literary forms and traditional characters of various ethnic groups. Many titles are also discussed, as are ways to use literature with children. At the end of each chapter is a bibliography divided by age group—Primary, Intermediate, Adolescent, and Professional (Adult). There is a wealth of material here about blacks, American Indians, and Mexican-Americans, plus some about Eskimo, Polish, Japanese, Armenian, and Jewish culture and books, as well as about different religious groups. Throughout the book there are standards for evaluating literature about different ethnic or religious groups, while the conflict of many of these cultures with the mainstream of today's society is considered. At the end of each chapter are a summary, questions, and projects.

BIBLIOGRAPHY
BOOKS FOR PRIMARY CHILDREN

BUFF, MARY (Marsh). *Kemi: An Indian Boy Before the White Man Came.* Los Angeles: Ward Ritchie Press, 1966.

CLARK, ANN NOLAN. *In My Mother's House.* New York: The Viking Press, 1941.

————. *Blue Canyon Horse.* New York: The Viking Press, 1954.

CLYMER, ELEANOR. *The Spider, the Cave, and the Pottery Bowl.* New York: Atheneum Publishers, 1971.

ELTING, MARY. *The Hopi Way.* Philadelphia and New York: J. P. Lippincott Company, 1967.

EMBRY, MARGARET. *My Name is Lion.* New York: Holiday House, 1970.

JONES, WEYMAN. *The Talking Leaf.* New York: Dial Press, 1965.

SCHWEITZER, BYRD BAYLOR. *One Small Blue Bead.* New York: The Macmillan Company, 1965.

TOBIAS, TOBI. *Maria Tallchief.* New York: Thomas Y. Crowell Company, 1970.

UDRY, JANICE MAY. *The Sunflower Garden.* Irvington-on-Hudson, New York: Harvey House, 1969.

BOOKS FOR INTERMEDIATE GRADE CHILDREN

ARMER, LAURA ADAMS. *Waterless Mountain.* New York: David McKay Company, 1966.

BEATTY, PATRICIA. *The Sea Pair.* New York: William Morrow and Company, 1970.

BENNETT, KAY and ROSS. *A Navajo Saga.* San Antonio, Texas: Naylor Company, 1969.

CLARK, ANN NOLAN. *The Desert People.* New York: The Viking Press, 1962.

CROWELL, ANN. *A Hogan for Bluebird.* New York: Charles Scribner's Sons, 1969.

ERNO, RICHARD B. *Billy Lightfoot.* New York: Crown Publishers, 1969.

FALL, THOMAS. *Edge of Manhood.* New York: Dial Press, 1964.

FARNSWORTH, FRANCES J. *Winged Moccasins: The Story of Sacajawea.* New York: Julian Messner, 1954.

GOBLE, PAUL and DOROTHY. *Red Hawk's Account of Custer's Last Battle: The Battle of the Little Bighorn, June, 1876.* New York: Pantheon Books, a division of Random House, 1969.

Emerging Humanity: Multi-Ethnic Literature for Children and Adolescents by Ruth Kearney Carlson. Reprinted with the permission of the William C. Brown Company, Publishers, 2460 Kerner Boulevard, Dubuque, Iowa 52001.

This title is a combination of background reading (including criticisms of older works), an introduction to the cultures mentioned, and a bibliography of recommended books with suggestions for library or classroom use. It is an outstanding work. There is an author-title-subject index, but some subjects are not found in the index. There are a few illustrations, mostly of presentations by children based on the different cultures. If available, it should be seriously considered by anyone wanting material on the ethnic groups mentioned above, for it provides valuable information in itself even without the books it discusses.

> *Good Reading for the Disadvantaged Reader: Multi-Ethnic Resources,* revised edition, by George D. Spache. Garrard Publishing Company, 1607 North Market Street, Champaign, Illinois 61820. 1975. 311 pp. $5.75pb.

Good Reading for the Disadvantaged Reader is primarily an annotated bibliography of in-print books for children and young adults who are in one way or another disadvantaged; this has often meant children of various minority groups—hence the subtitle *Multi-Ethnic Resources.* The first three chapters discuss a child's self-concept, especially with regard to disadvantaged children and their teachers, how this concept can be helped to grow, and the disadvantaged child and learning to read. Overall, Spache's orientation is toward the teacher trying to meet the needs of the disadvantaged child as he or she is rather than trying to change the child to more middle-class values. All three chapters have bibliographies and references. The major portion of the book, the annotated bibliographies (chapters 4 through 18), cover these categories: Heritage of the Black Americans—From Africa and Other Countries; American Heritage of the Black American; The Black American Today; The American Indian, Background and History; The American Indian Today; Eskimo and Alaska; Inner City Life; Mexican-American and Migrant Workers; Orientals, Puerto-Ricans; Social Science; Reading Improvement; Materials for Instructional Units in Art, Music, Literature and Human Relations Among Minority Groups; Audio-Visual Resources; and Professional Resources (for the teacher).

With the exception of the last two categories, which are ungraded, most chapters are divided into Primary Level (up to around third or fourth grade), Intermediate Level (third or fourth grade up to fifth or sixth grade), and Junior-Senior High School Levels. A Reading Level (R.L.) is given for each book, usually by grade and month within a grade; however, some books have a whole grade or even two grades for reading level. Books in the Eskimo and Alaska and Puerto-Rican chapters are for all levels, and Social Science is divided into general and ethnic heritage units. Arrangement is alphabetical within each grouping and the annota-

Inner City Life

(Primary Level)

Appell, Clara and Morey, *Glenn Learns to Read*. Des Moines: Duell, 1964. R.L. 2-3. A reassuring story for young people struggling to learn to read.

Barr, Jene, *Miss Terry at the Library*. Chicago: Whitman, 1962. R.L. 3.1. Semi-fictional account of the work of the librarian.

Beim, Jerrold, *The Boy on Lincoln's Lap*. New York: Morrow, 1955. R.L. 2-3. Three city boys learn something about citizenship by cleaning up a statue.

Beim, Jerrold, *Shoeshine Boy*. New York: Morrow, 1954. R.L. 3-4. Simple story of a city boy.

Beim, Jerrold, *The Smallest Boy in the Class*. New York: Morrow, 1949. R.L. 3.5. Jim was the smallest, but the noisiest and busiest.

Beim, Jerrold, *Thin Ice*. New York: Morrow, 1956. R.L. 3. O.P. When his ability to read a warning sign helps prevent an accident, reading finally makes sense to Lee.

Bell, Norman, *Linda's Air Mail Letter*. Chicago: Follett, 1964. R.L. 2.8. More about community workers. Simple, factual material.

Belmont, Evelyn, *Playground Fun*. Chicago: Melmont, 1955. R.L. 1.9. Playground fun at an easy to read level.

Berg, Jean H., *The O'Learys and Friends*. Chicago: Follett, 1961. R.L. 2.0. Friends and neighbors, and their pets in the city.

Bonsall, Crosby, *The Case of the Cat's Meow*. New York: Harper, 1965. R.L. 1.5. A humorous story of the activities of city youngsters.

Bonsall, Crosby, *Mine's the Best*. New York: Harper, 1973. R.L. 1-2. A black and a white boy meet at the beach and argue which of their identical balloons is best.

Breinberg, Petronella, *Shawn Goes to School*. New York: Thomas Y. Crowell, 1973. R.L. 3-4. Shawn's first day at school is told by his sister, in non-standard English.

Brown, Virginia, et al., *Who Cares?* New York: McGraw-Hill, 1965. R.L. 3-4. Stories about underprivileged urban children.

Burchardt, Nellie, *Project Cat*. New York: Watts, 1966. R.L. 3-4. Betsy finally convinces the officials of the housing project that she should be allowed to keep a cat.

Burstein, Chaya M., *Rifka Bangs the Teakettle*. New York: Harcourt, 1970.

Reprinted from *Good Reading for the Disadvantaged Reader: Multi-Ethnic Resources*, revised edition, by George D. Spache. Garrard Publishing Company, 1975.

tions are usually one sentence long. Chapter 19 deals with adult illiteracy (below the fifth-grade level); the problem of illiteracy and some programs to combat it are summarized. Chapter 20 is a bibliography of books for use with adult illiterates. In all the chapters most of the books are trade books, but some are texts. There are two indexes, one by author and title and one by title and author, but no subject index. The directory of publishers is far more complete than is usual.

It would be well to remember in using this aid that inclusion was *not* selective; some books annotated have been criticized elsewhere on the grounds that they portray stereotypes of various minorities. (The author points out that in his opinion children need to learn to judge books on their own merits, and that they should be exposed to different books and helped to understand and distinguish between them.) Also, precise reading levels are not usually used for trade books, and there is controversy about their value and proper application. However, it is undoubtedly one of the most complete listings of material for many minorities. It could be used as a starting place and then checked for recommended entries in another aid.

> *I Read, You Read, We Read; I See, You See, We See; I Hear, You Hear, We Hear; I Learn, You Learn, We Learn,* by the Library Services to the Disadvantaged Committee of the Children's Services Division of the American Library Association, 50 East Huron Street, Chicago, Illinois 60611. 1971. 104pp. $2pb.

This briefly annotated bibliography of books for disadvantaged children is divided into four categories: For Preschool Children, which consists of Picture Books, Stories to Tell, Sound Filmstrips, Filmstrips, Recordings, Tape Cassettes, and Motion Pictures; For Boys and Girls Ages 5-8 (or kindergarten to grade three), which consists of Stories and Poems, Stories to Tell, Informational Books, and Motion Pictures and Recordings; For Boys and Girls Ages 9-11 (grades four to six), which consists of Stories, Fairy Tales and Legends for Reading and Telling, Poetry, Informational Books, History and Biography, Motion Pictures, and Recordings; and For Boys and Girls Ages 12-14 (grades seven to nine), which consists of Fiction, All-Time Greats, Poetry, Informational Books, and Motion Pictures and Recordings. There is also a section, Suggested Program Aids for Adults, which lists sources for adults working with children, plus distributors for motion pictures and records. Each entry has bibliographic information followed by a one-sentence description. If an audio-visual version of a book title is available, this is noted after the annotation with a symbol. All the entries were selected with the disadvantaged reader in mind but the criteria used for selection are not given. Some titles are ones that are criticized elsewhere; for some the reason for inclusion is not clear and the annotations are not complete enough to explain this. There is no indication of stories for or about different ethnic groups, nor are there any indexes.

This is an inexpensive source with a catchy title, but although its intentions are good, some librarians may find other titles in this section of more merit.

> *Multi-Ethnic Books for Young Children, An Annotated Bibliography for Parents and Teachers,* compiled by Louise Griffin. Publications Department, National Association for the Education of Young Children, 1834 Connecticut Avenue, N.W., Washington, D.C. 20009. 1970. 74pp. OP.

Prepared under a contract with the Office of Education of HEW, this is an annotated bibliography of about six hundred trade and text books for children in nine categories: American Indians and Eskimos; Appalachia and the Southern Mountains; Afro-American; Hawaii and the Philippines; Latin American Derivation; Asian Derivation; Jewish Derivation; European Derivation; and Diversity. A few of the books are in parallel languages, and most are library books. The arrangement is alphabetical by author in each category, the usual bibliographic information being followed by a short paragraph of description. A number of older titles are included and some of these may be unacceptable today to some people. (The 1970 publication date may reflect the differences in thinking since then.) However, the work includes some categories that are very hard to find elsewhere. Symbols are used to indicate age levels: N for nursery (up to age five), K for kindergarten (ages four to six), P for primary (ages five to nine), E for elementary, and A for adult, with no designation for young adult; combination symbols are sometimes used. A list of sources used to compile the publication, a directory of lesser-known publishers, and a list of distributors of books published abroad with an indication of their country or language of specialization may also be of interest. There are probably better sources for books about some of the better-known ethnic groups included in *Multi-Ethnic Books*, but for some of the more elusive categories it may be very helpful.

> *RIF's Guide to Book Selection,* by Reading Is Fundamental. Smithsonian Institution, Washington, D.C. 20560. 1973. 91pp. Free.

RIF's Guide is a briefly annotated bibliography of books for preschool through about the sixth grade plus some high interest/low vocabulary books that could be used with older children or young adults. There are about eighteen hundred entries with simple bibliographic information, including a very broad reading level-interest level, and a sentence of descrip-

2

Accent on Appalachia and the Southern Mountains

Budd, Lillian. *Larry.* New York: McKay, 1966. $3.25.
In this story set in the mountains of Kentucky, a small boy runs away from home and later is happily reunited with his family. KP

Carroll, Ruth R. *Tough Enough.* New York: Walck, 1954. $3.00.
The Great Smoky Mountains provide the setting for the adventures of a mischievous puppy. See also other stories about Tough Enough by this author. NKP

Caudill, Rebecca. *A Certain Small Shepherd.* New York: Holt, 1965. $3.50.
Jamie, a little boy who cannot talk, recovers his speech when he presents a gift to a baby born in the church on Christmas Eve. Only in the color illustrations is it apparent that the baby is a Negro. The excitement of Christmas in a mountain community and the drama of the storm combine with this story of mutual acceptance. KP

Caudill, Rebecca. *Did You Carry the Clay Today, Charley?* New York: Holt, 1966. $3.50.
Charley's first school experience results in trials and finally in success. Set in Appalachia, the dialogue uses the idiom of the area. A good teacher-child-family relationship is described. The book may be too long to read in one sitting to young children. Black and white illustrations. P

Caudill, Rebecca. *Happy Little Family.* New York: Holt, 1947. $2.95.
A good book to read chapter by chapter, this story describes the life of 4-year-old Bonnie in the rural mountains several generations ago. Black and white pencil illustrations. NK

Caudill, Rebecca. *A Pocketful of Cricket.* New York: Holt, 1964. $3.50.
Jay is 6 years old and lives in the hills of Appalachia. While going about his daily business, he finds Cricket and takes him home as a pet. He takes him to school, too, for the first grade Show and Tell. Interesting development of the relationships among children, and a good presentation of an understanding teacher. Fine two-color illustrations by Evaline Ness. NKP

Caudill, Rebecca. *Schoolhouse in the Woods.* New York: Holt, 1949. $2.95.
Mountain life in the Southern states is described in this story of Bonnie, as she becomes old enough to go to the one room school with her brothers and sisters. NKP

tion. The arrangement is by publisher and then by title within each publishing group, an unusual arrangement. Most titles included are library books, but a few are texts or textlike. Some of the publishers have put restrictions on ordering; for example, one must order a minimum of six titles, or there is no selection of titles from a list. The whole purpose of the RIF program is to give away books to children who would possibly otherwise never own a book of their own; therefore, all titles are paperbacks because of their inexpensive cost and appeal. It is not entirely clear whether or not this list *must* be used in implementing a RIF program; each program is organized and sponsored locally, usually with a civic or service group providing the money, but it is also possible to obtain matching government funds. Write to Ruth Graves, Executive Director, Reading Is Fundamental, Inc., L'Enfant 2500, Washington, D.C. 20560, for materials for setting up an RIF program.

One special feature of the *Guide* is the Special Booklist for Ethnic Groups, which consists of about five hundred fifty titles divided into three categories: Black Elementary, Indian Elementary, and Spanish Elementary. Almost all of these are trade books. Addresses are given for publishers of materials for Spanish-language programs.

Unfortunately, publishers' catalogs, as well as some standard selection aids, were used to some extent in selecting books to be included. Nevertheless, the RIF *Guide* can be useful whether or not one is participating in a RIF program, if care is exercised in selection. Note that it is free and that most of the books were selected with the disadvantaged child in mind — any child who does not own books is disadvantaged.

> *Reading Ladders for Human Relations*, 5th edition, by Virginia M. Reid and the Commission on Reading Ladders for Human Relations of the National Council of Teachers of English. American Council on Education, One DuPont Circle, Washington, D.C. 20036. 1972. 346pp. $10.50 ($4.50pb).

The stated purpose of *Reading Ladders for Human Relations* is "to help teachers, librarians, and other adults working with children and young people in the delicate task of extending sensitivity toward people, their values and their ways of living" (preface, p.vii). Many, although by no means all, of the eighteen hundred books included have ethnic or religious themes. The book is arranged in four "Ladders": Creating Positive Self-Image; Living with Others; Appreciating Different Cultures; and Coping with Change. Each ladder has an introduction which discusses that topic and some of the books and is then subdivided into smaller topics; for example, Ladder Three, Appreciating Different Cultures, has four sections: Appreciating Different Ethnic Cultures; Appreciating Different Religious Cultures; Appreciating Different Regional

Coping with Personal Change

Primary

ABBOTT, SARAH. *Where I Begin.* Coward, 1970, $3.75. A quiet book intended to develop the concept that parents were once children, too. As a small girl looks through a family album, she discovers the many changes time brings in its wake.

ALEXANDER, MARTHA. *Nobody Asked Me If I Wanted a Baby Sister.* il. by author. Dial, 1971, $3.50. A fine book for the older brother or sister who feels a bit neglected after the arrival of a younger sibling. In this book Oliver, disgusted at all the to-do being made over his new sister, decides to give her away. Then he discovers he is the only one who can make the baby stop crying. With this he decides she's pretty smart after all.

* BELL, GINA. *Who Wants Willy Wells?*

BELPRE, PURA. *Santiago.* il. by Symeon Shimin. Warne, 1969, $3.95. Santiago, a young Puerto Rican boy, wants to take his stereoscope to school to show pictures of his pet hen which he had to leave behind in Puerto Rico. When his classmates finally see his pictures, they view Santiago differently. Beautiful, sensitive pictures show an integrated classroom and help tell of Santiago's adjustment to a new environment.

BOUCHARD, LOIS. *The Boy Who Wouldn't Talk.* il. by Ann Grifalconi. Doubleday, 1969, $3.50. Carlos, who comes from Puerto Rico, is frustrated by the problems of adjusting to a new city and a new language. To the distress of his family, his friends, and his teacher, Carlos decides to stop using words at all until he becomes friends with Ricky, who is blind and cannot read Carlos' signs and gestures. A sensitive "boy's eye" view of the problems of a child facing a new urban environment.

BRENNER, BARBARA. *Nicky's Sister.* Knopf, 1966, $3.25. Nicky has a new baby sister over whom a great fuss is made. Nicky is disgusted; he would rather have a hamster. When the baby breaks his plastic Indian Nicky decides to run away, but he confronts McGillicuddy, the neighborhood bully, and he decides to stay to protect his sister, declaring that brothers and sisters should stick together.

Reading Ladders for Human Relations, 5th edition, by Virginia M. Reid. Published by the American Council on Education, 1972. Reprinted with permission.

Cultures; and Appreciating Different World Cultures. Within each of these sections the books are divided into five groups: Primary (up to grade three), Intermediate (grades four to six), Junior (grades seven to nine), Senior, and Mature (some of which may be "controversial"). Arrangement is alphabetical by author within each grouping. The bibliographic information is followed by an annotation that ranges from one sentence to a fairly long paragraph, written by the committee and assisted by contributors from all over the country; the quality of the annotations varies somewhat. Older classic books as well as new books are included, but all books are reevaluated for each edition. Only trade books are included, and it is pointed out that some books of rather mediocre quality are annotated and used as "place-holders" until better books are available. An asterisk by a title means that the book should be used for that category, but the actual annotation is elsewhere. Paperback editions are noted by a P, while P/several indicates several editions are available. Some short chapters at the front deal with ideas for using books with children and are followed by a list of sources for teachers and a list of review sources.

Reading Ladders is intended for use in organized programs rather than for recommending individual books to individual children, although there is no absolute reason why it could not be used for the latter purpose. It would have considerable value in an innovative school or library which could base units of study around trade rather than textbooks, or it could be used to supplement texts. In this aid it is fairly hard to find books on specific topics since there is an author-title index but no subject index. It includes many books for young adults as well as for children. However, some books, especially those for older readers, may offend some people (as the editor is careful to point out) so care should be used in selection. A few books are recommended for one sex only and some titles may be regarded as rather sexist, but it should possibly be valuable in encouraging the acceptance of ethnic, cultural, and religious differences.

The Children's Television Workshop, National Educational Television, 1865 Broadway, New York, New York 10023, has a mimeographed free list of inexpensive children's books to be used with educational television programs, such as Sesame Street. Some of these are by prominent children's authors or illustrators; others are not and may be questionable.

Indian

Recent years have seen the rise of strongly militant groups of Indians who are actively campaigning for better treatment of America's original natives as well as a reevaluation of the ways their history and culture have been portrayed. Concurrently, as has happened with blacks and is now happening with women, articles and books have been written protesting the way many authors (and illustrators) have depicted Indians and/or listing recommended books about Indians for children. Here, as in bibliographies of recommended material about other minorities or about women, there is difference of opinion as to what exactly is derogatory and what is not. Unfortunately, some selection aids about Indians are not readily available except via interlibrary loan, in which case they were placed in the bibliography rather than in this section.

> *American Indian Authors for Young Readers, A Selected Bibliography,* by Mary Gloyne Byler. Association on American Indian Affairs, 422 Park Avenue South, New York, New York 10016. 1973. 26pp. $1pb.

This is an annotated bibliography of recommended *authors* of books about American Indians and Eskimos for children. Each entry has the name of the author (usually including his or her tribe), a title or titles for the author, bibliographic information, recommended grade levels, and a descriptive annotation. About fifty authors are included, but there is more than one title for some of them. The compiler examined more than six hundred children's books about Indians and eventually decided to limit the bibliography to authors who are themselves Indian. (Not everyone, of course, agrees that an author must be of a particular ethnic group in order to write about that group.) Byler points out that some titles drawn from the oral tradition may not have been adapted for children. An introduction gives some brief condemnations, with examples, of the way Indians have usually been portrayed in children's books. At the back of the book following the regular entries is a separate miscellaneous section of seven entries; it is not clear why these were set apart. The list of publishers is good for this hard-to-find material.

This is an excellent source for anyone concerned with the way writers have treated native Americans, but the strict interpretation of who should write these books may seem unnecessary to some. The introduction alone is enough to convince almost anyone of the inaccuracy and unfairness of most books about Indians.

> *Books about Indians and Reference Material.* Idaho State Department of Education, Indian Education, Boise, Idaho 83720. 1971. 175p. OP.

Books about Indians is an annotated bibliography of about seventeen hundred books for children, young adults, and adults, intended to help further an appreciation of native American cultures and contributions. The entries are arranged by publishing company and there are usually no

American Indian Authors for Young Readers

ABEITA, LOUISE, (E-YEH-SHURE'). Isleta
Pueblo.

I am a Pueblo Indian Girl. William Morrow, 1939.
25 pp. Illus. by American Indian artists. Out of
print. Grades 2-5.

E-Yeh-Shure' describes her way of life in her pueblo. She discusses such things
as the making of bread in beehive ovens, hair washing with yucca plant roots,
the types of clothes she wears, and hunting. Two of E-Yeh-Shure's poems are
included. Beautifully illustrated.

ANAUTA, Eskimo
Children of the Blizzard, with Heluiz Chandler Wash-
burne. Dennis Dobson, 1960. 192 pp. Illus. 75s.
Grades 5 and up. Can be ordered through: British
Book Center, Inc., 996 Lexington Ave., New York,
N.Y. 10021

The author uses her own experiences as background for a series of interrelated
stories about several Baffin Island Eskimo children. Different types of work—hunting, securing food, constructing shelter, making clothes—are described, as are
friendships, relationships between adults and children, games and travel. A concluding chapter on games shows that they are not just for fun but are important
for survival. A vocabulary of Eskimo words is included.

ANAUTA, Eskimo
*Wild Like the Foxes: The True Story of an Eskimo
Girl.* John Daly, 1956. 192 pp. Grades 5 and up. Out
of print.

This story is based on the life of the author's mother, Alea, and covers her girl-
hood up until she meets Yorgke, who becomes her husband. Hunting, trapping,
playing boys' games, enduring hardships all are part of Alea's life until she is sent
to school in England by her widowed father. Her return, her love for Yorgke, and
the death of her father are described.

ANTELL, WILL, Chippewa
William Wipple Warren: Objibway Historian. Dillon
Press, 1972. Approx. 50 pp. Illus. $3.95. Grades
5 and up.

This biography of William Whipple Warren, who was born in 1825, includes
information on his family, work in the Territorial House of Representatives of
which he was the only Indian member, his articles for a newspaper in St. Paul
and his writing of a book about the Ojibways.

Reprinted from *American Indian Authors for Young Readers: A Selected Bibliography*
by Mary Gloyne Byler, with the permission of the Association on American Indian
Affairs.

age or grade levels. The books included have various copyright dates and some are rather old, which is a consideration in selecting books in an area in which attitudes have changed greatly. There is no indication of how the books were selected; the work appears to be a complete listing of all in-print titles from each publisher, and some of the books have been criticized in other sources. One strength of the work is that books by university presses have been included, thereby providing a body of material not often included in children's book lists; much of this material, however, would not be especially useful with children. There is also a list of bulletins available from the Bureau of Indian Affairs, names and addresses of agencies that provide information and pamphlets, and a list of booklets and recordings.

Overall, *Books about Indians* should probably be used with some caution, perhaps in connection with another list, since it is more comprehensive than selective.

> *Selected Media about the American Indian for Young Children K-3*, by Suzanne S. Cane, et. al. Commonwealth of Massachusetts, Department of Education, Division of Curriculum and Instruction, Bureau of Curriculum Innovation, December 1970. (Reprinted and distributed by the American Library Association, 1971.) 21pp. $1pb.

The title of this publication describes its contents: *selected* books and some audio-visual media dealing with Indians (mostly American with a few Canadian) for children in kindergarten to grade three. Overall, the intent of this compilation was to show Indians in nonstereotyped ways, with realistic portrayals of Indian life today and in the past, and Indian folk literature. The first section, Children's Materials, has two main parts: For Use by Children and For Use by Adults with Children. The first is an alphabetical listing of about fifty titles for children with a paragraph of descriptive and critical annotation. The most acceptable of both older and newer titles are included, but even these were regarded by the compilers as not always to be recommended in all their aspects. (As is so often the case in considering Indian materials, a plea is made for better publications showing Indians in more realistic ways.) The second part of this section provides resources for the adult working with children —history of Indians, crafts, stories for telling, poetry to read aloud, and so forth. No suggested age levels are given, and no textbooks were included. A short third section lists three museums in Massachusetts and Rhode Island which have extensive Indian exhibits.

The second section is Adult Background Materials, which has entries for books and audio-visual media about the history and current plight of Indians for the adult reader, which might be considered "consciousness-

Selected Media about the American Indian for Young Children

Beatty, Hetty Burlingame. LITTLE OWL INDIAN. Boston: Houghton Mifflin, 1951.
$3.40
The illustrations are the most appealing part of this book. Clear and
refreshing, they tell the story of a woodland Indian boy growing up, making
friends with the animals of his forest home, and saving them from the rushing
flames of a fire. In a "happily-ever-after" ending, Little Owl is rewarded
for warning the people of the village and the animals of the forest, and for
leading them to safety on the other side of the river.

Belting, Natalia M. THE LONG TAILED BEAR. Illus. by Louis F. Cary.
Indianapolis: Bobbs-Merrill, 1961. $3.25
Twenty-two short and amusing legends explaining how or why certain animals
acquired their distinctive spots, tails, colors, etc.; all are suitable for
reading or for storytelling. "How Terrapin's Shell Was Cracked," "How the
Cardinal Got His Red Feathers," and "How the Wildcat Got His Spots" are
especially delightful.

Brewster, Benjamin. THE FIRST BOOK OF INDIANS. Illus. by Ursula Koering.
New York: Franklin Watts, 1950. $2.95
A gold mine of pictorial and verbal information for young children.
Brewster's perceptiveness is exceptional, and his emphasis is on Indians as
people. Illustrations are small and full of detail, much of which is not
discussed in the text; many have explanatory captions. Chapters on "Indians
Today" and "Indians and White Men Together" are realistic but hopeful.

Bulla, Clyde Robert. INDIAN HILL. Illus. by James J. Spanfeller. New York:
Thomas Y. Crowell, 1963. $3.00
True-to-life portrayal of a Navajo family's decision to relocate in a city.
Kee Manygoats and his mother have a preconceived fear and dislike for the
white world. The story is not so much about preserving Indian identity in a
white man's world as about the first step in adjustment--openness to a new
life. Remarkable book that will stir feelings in both teacher and pupil.

CIRCLE OF THE SUN. Produced by the National Film Board of Canada. Distributed
by McGraw-Hill Text Films. 1960. 16 mm. 29 minutes. Color. Rental available
through the Audio Visual Library, Massachusetts Department of Education.
Purchase, $300.00; Rental, $8.50
An excellent film showing problems of adjustment as the old gives way to the
new on the Blackfoot lands in Alberta, Canada. Because of its length, we
recommend that the teacher preview the film and pick out the section or
sections which best suit his teaching unit. Two sequences stand out as
exceptional: the ceremonial opening of the beaver bundle, and the Sun Dance.

raisers." Section III, Selected Sources of Additional Materials, lists twenty-three government agencies, museums, companies, and organizations that supply other materials about Indians, ranging from printed publications to recordings of war chants to handicrafts. There is a brief description of the kind of material available; usually it will be necessary to write for exact descriptions and price lists. There is also a listing of publishers and addresses; most of these are well-known companies whose addresses are readily available, but a few might be hard to find elsewhere.

Although slightly out of date, this is a good source of Indian materials for younger children; books for upper elementary school children are not included. It is quite selective, since only about fifty of the several hundred children's books examined were selected, and it is suitable for use anywhere in the country, not just in Massachusetts.

In addition to these sources, the American Library Association is publishing a new book on this topic, *Selected Books on American Indians,* by Mary Jo Lass-Woodfin. For instructional audio-visual materials, consult *Bibliography of Nonprint Instructional Materials on the American Indian,* by the Instructional Development Program for the Institute of Indian Services and Research, Brigham Young University, Provo, Utah 84601. Although not designed specifically for children, a number of entries are designated Primary or Intermediate. All kinds of audio-visual media are included, but its aim is to be a comprehensive rather than a selective listing.

Girls and Women

Strong protest from various women's groups about the way girls and women in children's books are often shown in limited, stereotyped, and subservient roles has resulted in the publication of several lists of books depicting females who are strong main characters and who often act in nontraditional ways. Boys and men may also be shown in these books acting in ways not prescribed by the usual cultural norms. Contrary to some popular opinion, not all of these books necessarily have recent copyright dates or have anything specifically to do with the women's rights movement. Librarians and teachers are likely to find many books with which they are already familiar as well as some new titles.

A *Guide to Non-Sexist Children's Books,* compiled by Judith Adell and Hilary Dole Klein, edited by Waltraud Schacher. Academy Press, Limited, 176 West Adams Street, Chicago, Illinois 60603. 1976. 149pp. $7.95 ($3.95pb).

Fitzhugh, Louise
HARRIET THE SPY   Gr.4-7/$1.25P

Harper & Row, 1964

> There is nothing ordinary about Harriet who is
> convinced that in order to be a great writer she
> must write down all details about people's
> lives. While that is not the kind of activity
> which tends to endear her to everyone's heart,
> Harriet is nonetheless an appealing character.

Freeman, Barbara C.
LUCINDA   Gr.3-7

Grosset & Dunlap, 1967

> A 19th century child has the audacity to chal-
> lenge the despotism of her rich, penny-pinching
> uncle Prescott who is also her guardian. Their
> relationship ends, but it's only the beginning of
> Lucinda's trials.

Gauch, Patricia Lee
THIS TIME, TEMPE WICK?   Gr.3-7/$5.95H

Coward, McCann & Geoghegan, 1974

> A fictionalized story of a spirited and interest-
> ing historical character named Temperence
> Wick and of her adventures during the Revol-
> utionary War in New Jersey. Not only is she
> physically strong and a first rate horsewoman,
> but she also becomes more than a match for
> two Pennsylvania soldiers who try to steal her
> horse, Bonny.

This is an annotated bibliography of more than 450 books for children which show girls and women (and boys and men) in nontraditional roles, or which simply have a girl or woman as the main character. Both old and new stories are included, many with surprisingly "old" copyrights. Readers may be a little puzzled by the publisher's afterword which explains why some books were omitted—*Little Women*, for example, because it "shows girls and young women only as extensions of men" (p. 147) or all the *Babar* books because one of them is considered sexist. (*Little Women* is often regarded as an early book that is *not* sexist, and some of the *Babar* books could have been included, omitting only those that were adjudged to be sexist.) However, the intent was not to censor but to try to show nonstereotyped ways that girls and women can be portrayed.

The work is divided into Pre-School through Third Grade, Third Grade through Seventh Grade, Seventh Grade through Twelfth Grade, and All Ages. Each section has fiction and nonfiction entries, with simplified bibliographic information and one or two short sentences of annotation for some, a paragraph of annotation for others. There are suggested grade levels, but the compilers point out that these are only intended as a general guide. The front of the book has a conversion chart for ages and grades and there is one index by author and one by title.

This is a lengthy list that should be of help to anyone requiring nonsexist children's books even though a few of the omissions are surprising. It contains about three times as many recommendations as the following title, *Little Miss Muffet Fights Back*, and has a very recent publication date. Some libraries may find that they already have many of the books. *The Liberty Cap: A Catalogue of Non-Sexist Materials for Children*, by Enid Davis (Academy Press, 1977) contains reviews of recent children's books and audio-visual material from the nonsexist point of view.

> *Little Miss Muffett Fights Back, A Bibliography of Recommended Non-Sexist Books About Girls for Young Readers*, revised edition, by Feminists on Children's Media, compiled by Elizabeth Capelle, Susan Lewis, and Betty Miles. Feminists Book Mart, 162-11 Ninth Avenue, Whitestone, New York 11357. 1974. 62pp. $1.

There are critical annotations in *Little Miss Muffett* of about one hundred seventy children's books that show girls and women in nonstereotyped ways and in a variety of roles, varying in length from one sentence to a fairly long paragraph. There are also twenty illustrations from some of the books annotated, and references are sometimes made to other books by the same author. The work is divided into Picture Books, Fiction, Biography, and History of Women's Rights, with a short

Little Miss Muffet Fights Back

Welber, Robert, *The Train*.
Il. by Deborah Ray. Pantheon, 1972.
Elizabeth is a special person—a small black girl confronting the wide meadow she must cross to see the train go by—but her feelings are easy to share because they are so common: vague fear, hesitation, determin ation and finally the pleasure of success. Elizabeth's family and her feelings are brought to life with unusual insight in the illustrations.

Wellman, Alice, *Tatu and the Honey Bird*.
Il. by Dale Payson. Putnam, 1972.
Grandmother says, "And what do girls need to know? . . . to cook and plant the fields and birth the babies. School for girls is not the way things are. School is for getting smart." But Tatu and his sister, Lovala, who live in West Africa, know that *both* of them must go to school, and they find a way to do it.

Wells, Rosemary, *Benjamin und Tulip*.
Dial, 1973.
This small picture book, in which a daintily-dressed racoon called Tulip beats up an oppressed racoon named Benjamin time after time, is listed despite the risk of seeming to endorse bullying. It proves that meanness knows no sex distinctions, a lesson one might as well learn early as late, particularly when it is illustrated in a style as succinct and funny as this, with an outcome so equable.

Werth, Kurt, and Watts, Mabel, *Molly and the Giant*.
Parents, 1973.
Brave and clever Molly O'Shea outwits a wicked giant and wins the hands in marriage of three princes two for her sisters and one for herself.

Williams, Jay, *Petronella*.
Il. by Friso Henstra. Parents, 1973.
A smart and plucky princess rescues a prince from an enchanter by passing three dangerous tests with wit and bravery. Unfortunately, the prince is a fool, and the princess goes off with the enchanter instead—a wise choice, though so clever a princess might have questioned marriage itself. The illustrations are stylish and elegant, possibly more sophisticated than some young readers. This theme of traditional roles reversed also runs through *The Silver Whistle* and *The Practical Princess* by the same author and artist.

introduction to each section that explains how books were selected (or rejected). Arrangement is then alphabetical by author. There are no suggested usage levels, although Biography is divided into Younger and Older Readers. Some of the annotations contain a certain amount of criticism as well as praise, but all books included are recommended. Some annotations have quotations from the books.

The introduction explains that the books in *Little Miss Muffet* are *about* girls but not *for* girls only. Also, the titles included are drawn from ordinary children's books and do not relate particularly to the feminist movement with the exception of a few in the last section. Some old favorites as well as recent publications will be found. There are also appendixes on What Can I Do? (to encourage positive portrayals of girls and women), Publishing Your Manuscript, and Readings on Sexism in Children's Books (an annotated bibliography). Since its first edition in the early 1970's, *Little Miss Muffet* has sold 25,000 copies, which gives some idea of the concern in this area; a good many libraries may find that they already have a number of these titles and will want to add more.

> *Sexism and Youth,* edited by Diane Gersoni-Stavn. R. R. Bowker Company, 1180 Avenue of the Americas, New York, New York 10036. 1974. 468pp. $10.95.

Although *Sexism and Youth* is primarily a collection of articles about sex roles and behavior in adolescence, the third Section, Books: Propaganda and the Sins of Omission, should be of special interest to children's librarians. These articles deal with the ways girls and women are portrayed in children's and young adult books, and many discuss children's trade books and some texts. A number of well-known books are criticized in some of the articles; others offer suggestions for recommended books with a positive picture of girls and women. Common stereotyping and sex ratio (number of male characters compared to number of female characters) are shown. "Reducing the Miss Muffet Syndrome: An Annotated Bibliography" by Gersoni-Stavn, reprinted from *School Library Journal,* January 1972, has a bibliography of recommended nonsexist books for children arranged by categories. The entire book makes good background reading for this area of concern, with Part Three being particularly useful for evaluating individual books for whole collections.

There is also a study of the portrayal of girls and women in children's textbooks titled *Dick and Jane as Victims: Sex Stereotyping in Children's Readers,* by Women on Words and Images, 30 Valley Road, Princeton, New Jersey 08540, 1972.

Spanish Language/Chicano

Now that Spanish is used as a language of instruction in a number of elementary schools, and as the Chicano movement continues to grow, lists of recommended books in Spanish and/or about Mexican-Americans (Chicanos) will probably begin to proliferate. At the present time, however, many of these lists can be found only in journals such as *Booklist, Horn Book,* and others through their indexes. One problem in compiling lists on this topic has been that in some people's opinion there have been few books published that *can* be recommended, and good audio-visual materials are even harder to find. Several mimeographed lists of materials for and about Mexico, Mexican-Americans, or Spanish-speaking children have been prepared by Isabel Schon of Arizona State University for use in her classes or with exhibits of books. Three of these are "Books for and about Spanish-Speaking Children and Adolescents," "Libros de España," and "Libros de México." The first of these lists both recommended and not recommended books in English. The second two, which are in Spanish and are annotated, are expected to appear in *Booklist* in the near future. (See the bibliography for Schon's *Descriptive Study of the Literature for Children and Adolescents of Mexico.*)

For a discussion of some of the problems Chicano children may encounter in the classroom, and their possible solutions, readers might wish to send for *Para Los Niños, For the Children, Improving Education for Mexican Americans*, Clearinghouse Publication 47, U.S. Commission on Civil Rights, October 1974, by Frank Sotomayor. (Order from Superintendent of Documents, U.S. Government Printing Office, Washington, D.C. 20402.) This publication is also available in Spanish. The United States Committee for UNICEF also has some materials that could be useful in this area, both book and nonprint. Their address is 331 East 38th Street, New York, New York 10016. For a list titled *Spanish Language Books Published in Other Countries,* write to Martha V. Tome, Director, Projecto Leer, Organization of American States, Washington, D.C. 20006. Also, the International chapter of this book has some related material.

> *Libros en Español, An Annotated List of Children's Books in Spanish,* by Mary K. Conwell and Pura Belpré. New York Public Library, Office of Children's Services, 8 East 40th Street, New York, New York 10016. 1971. 52pp. $.50.

This is a unique tool in that the one-sentence annotations for each of the more than two hundred books are in both English and Spanish, although the texts of the annotations may not be exactly the same if the compilers deemed it advisable to vary them slightly. The bibliographic information is mostly in English, except for the titles, which are in

Libros en Español

Miguelín. By Joaquín Aguirre Bellver. Illustrated by Antonio Zarco. Afrodisio Aguado. 1965. $2.50.
The daily activities of a boy who lives in a small Spanish town with his grandmother. Made into a prize-winning film in 1965.

Las actividades diarias de un niño que vive con su abuela en un pequeño pueblo español. El libro filmado en una película para niños ganó un premio en 1965.

Mujercitas. By Louisa M. Alcott. Translated by Editorial Juventud. Juventud. 1952. $1.50.
The favorite story of Meg, Jo, Beth and Amy in nineteenth-century New England.

El cuento favorito de Meg, Jo, Beth y Amy en la Nueva Inglaterra del siglo diecinueve.

El mundo de las aves. By Jean Dorst. Translated by Montserrat Andreu and R. S. Torroella. Illustrated by Pierre Probst. Timun Mas. 1965. $7.95.
An illustrated book of birds of the world with information on their habits and habitats.

Un libro ilustrado de aves del mundo con información de sus costumbres y lugares donde viven.

Mundo sin geografía. By Carmen Alicia Cadilla de Ruibal. Illustrated by Frances del Valle. Departamento de Instrucción Pública de Puerto Rico. 1963. $2.00.
In this book, written by a distinguished Puerto Rican author, a peasant boy poetically describes the landscape of Puerto Rico.

En este libro, escrito por una distinguida autora puertorriqueña, un niño campesino describe poéticamente el paisaje de Puerto Rico.

Reprinted with the permission of the New York Public Library from *Libros en Español*, 1971.

Spanish, as are the books themselves, either originally or in translation from English to Spanish. They were published either here or abroad, in Mexico, Spain, or Puerto Rico, and other Spanish-speaking countries. The categories are: Picture Books (for the very young); Young Readers (for beginning readers); Books for the Middle Age; Books for Older Boys and Girls; Folklore, Myths, and Legends; Songs and Games; Bilingual Books (text in both English and Spanish); Books for Learning Spanish (some are texts); and Anthologies (two collections of Spanish-language children's literature). Arrangement is alphabetical within each category, and all titles were in print at the time of publication, with inclusion based on books in the New York Public Library. At the end is a list of publishers and distributors of Spanish-language children's books. The index is by author and title, but not by subject. No audio-visual materials are included.

This is an unusual and inexpensive tool that should be very useful to anyone who needs children's books in Spanish. Criteria for inclusion are not given, however, except that all the books were owned by the New York Public Library.

SEASONAL LISTS

For books for the many holidays, the best source may be *Children's Catalog* or *Elementary School Library Collection*. The three lists in this section all deal with Christmas, which rightly or wrongly has generally been the single holiday that has been most celebrated in public schools and libraries. Local libraries or large public libraries in major cities are also good sources of holiday lists.

> *And All the Dark Make Bright Like Day, Christmas Books, 1960-1972*, by Sidney D. Long. The Horn Book, Inc., 585 Boylston Street, Boston, Massachusetts 02116. 1972. 15pp. $1.50. *Light and Candles!*, by Marcia Dalphin, revised by Anne T. Eaton. Same publisher and address. $1.50.

All the Dark is a short bibliography (about sixty titles) of the best children's Christmas books, including collections, selected from books reviewed by the *Horn Book* since 1960, most of which are still in print. Each entry is annotated, and the list is divided into The Nights before Christmas, The Nativity, Miracles and Legends, Carols, Stories for Older Readers, Christmas Make-Believe, and Christmas Anthologies. A brief introduction discusses a few of the books and points out that many of the stories, perhaps significantly, are set in an earlier, rural, era. There are a few illustrations from the books.

Light the Candles! is a similar list which was originally published in

1960 and updated in 1970. It consists of Christmas books arranged by type, including games, songs, plays, and poems, as well as stories. Both are inexpensive lists that will help in selecting books to meet the usually large demand for Christmas titles.

> *Children's Books and Recordings, 19--, Suggested as Holiday Gifts.* New York Public Library, Fifth Avenue and 42nd Street, Room 58, New York, New York 10018. $2pb.

Every year the New York Public Library publishes a briefly annotated list of around four hundred books and recordings which are on display at the library at Christmas time. With the exception of a few new editions of older titles, only new books are included each year. The recordings, however, most of which are based on children's books, are not those from the past year only. The books are arranged in a number of interest categories and include fiction and nonfiction but do not have suggested age or grade levels. These are books or recordings that should make good suggestions for the parent or other adult who wants to give a child a book *for* Christmas, but these are not books *about* Christmas. There is an author-title index.

AUDIO-VISUAL

Many children in this television age respond better to audio-visual material, at least initially, than they do to books, and audio-visual media may be considered as a means in itself or as a way to lead children to books. The following aids combine (in most cases) lists of recommended media, some of one type only, some a combination of types, with suggestions on how to use these materials in programs with children.

For reviews of recent media, see the chapter on Keeping Up-to-Date, which includes media reviewing journals, and the *Notable Children's Films* list entry. As mentioned in the first chapter, *Elementary School Library Collection* includes annotations of recommended audio-visual items.

> *Films for Children, A Selected List.* New York Library Association. (Order from Carol Cox Book Company, P.O. Box 717, 20 Booker Street, Westwood, New Jersey 07675.) 1st edition, 1966; 2d edition, 1969; 3rd edition, 1972. $3pb.

This is an annotated bibliography, revised every three or four years, of around seventy good children's films. Each entry has the title of the film, number of minutes, designation of color or black and white, distributor, and price. The fairly long annotations usually include suggestions for a number of books on the same topic for children of various ages. (No age

CHRISTMAS IN AMERICA

RENFROE'S CHRISTMAS. By Robert Burch. Illustrated by Rocco Negri. Viking, 1968.
Renfroe suspects there is some truth in his sister's observation that he has a selfish streak, but he resents being made aware of it at Christmas time. The author re-creates with enjoyment and understanding the easy-going atmosphere of Christmas in a small north Georgia community.

A CERTAIN SMALL SHEPHERD. By Rebecca Caudill. Illustrated by William Pène du Bois, Holt, 1965.
The Christmas night that a blizzard engulfs Hurricane Gap brings a miracle to a small boy who has never been able to talk.

EVERETT ANDERSON'S CHRISTMAS COMING. By Lucille Clifton. Illustrated by Evaline Ness. Holt, 1971.
Since all little children don't live in the country come Christmas time, this story-poem of a little black boy's city Christmas is a welcome picture-book addition.

CHRISTMAS TREE ON THE MOUNTAIN. By Carol Fenner, Author-Illustrator. Harcourt, 1966.
The author-artist makes very believable the hard climbing, the frozen mittens, and the momentary feelings of despair that occur when two children — determined to find the perfect Christmas tree — take their little brother and a sled and venture up the mountain behind their house.

A GREEN CHRISTMAS. By Theodora Kroeber. Illustrated by John Larrecq. Parnassus, 1967.
A brother and sister, afraid that Santa will not be able to find them in their new home in California, are amazed when he not only finds them but leaves a letter thanking them for letting his reindeer feed on the clover and snow lilies in their yard. The illustrations, framed like colored slides, turn the story into a turn-of-the-century pastoral.

BIRD SONG. By Eleanor Frances Lattimore, Author-Illustrator. Morrow, 1968.
The chapters of the book which describe Christmas at Bird Song, a small South Carolina plantation, are filled with the special quality of life and feeling for place that all the best Christmas stories have.

Children's Books and Recordings Suggested as Holiday Gifts

PICTURE BOOKS

The Adventures of Obadiah. By Brinton Turkle. The Viking Press. $4.50. His family did not believe him because he had told falsehoods. A delightful story of Quaker Nantucket.

Alexander and the Terrible, Horrible, No Good, Very Bad Day. By Judith Viorst. Illustrated by Ray Cruz. Atheneum. $4.50. It was enough to make you want to go to Australia.

Apples. By Nonny Hogrogian. The Macmillan Company. $4.95. Over the years an orchard grows from apples stolen from a pedlar's cart. A wordless picture book.

Babar Visits Another Planet. Written and Illustrated by Laurent De Brunhoff. Translated from the French by Merle Haas. Random House. $3.95. The elephant hero meets space elephants with pointed heads.

Baby. By Fran Manushkin. Pictures by Ronald Himler. Harper & Row, Publishers. $3.50. A unique and childlike story about a mother who "was growing a baby."

Balarin's Goat. Story and Pictures by Harold Berson. Crown Publishers. $3.95. How a wife, jealous of her husband's pet goat, wins back his affection.

The Bear's Toothache. Written and Illustrated by David McPhail. Little Brown and Company. $4.95. The mournful midnight visitor needs medical attention in this amusing story.

Behind the Wheel. By Edward Koren. Holt, Rinehart & Winston. Paperbound. $1.25. Gadgets and dials for close perusal by young driving enthusiasts.

The Biggest Fish in the Sea. By Dahlov Ipcar. The Viking Press. $4.95. A tall tale with a moral — catch only what you can eat.

Birthday. By John Steptoe. Holt, Rinehart & Winston. $5.50. Javaka celebrates his eighth birthday and all of Yoruba comes to the party. A Black artist's fantasy.

Reprinted with the permission of the New York Public Library from *Children's Books and Recordings, 1972, Suggested As Holiday Gifts*, 1972.

or grade levels are given for the films, however.) The films may be animated, live action, puppets, fantasy, and so on. In the front there are suggestions for planning a film program, publicity ideas, instructions on how to set up the room and equipment for a program, and a bibliography for further reading. There are suggested programs on different themes and a subject index in the back.

This is a very selective list of films of high quality, all of which were well-received by children. The older editions, 1966 and 1969, are still used by many libraries, especially the 1966 edition; since these are classic films, they seldom go out of date. A similar publication, also by the New York Library Association, is *Films for Young Adults.*

> *Films Kids Like, A Catalog of Short Films for Children,* compiled and edited by Susan Rice, assisted by Barbara Ludlum. Published for the Center for Understanding Media, Inc., by the American Library Association, 50 East Huron Street, Chicago, Illinois 60611. 1973. 150pp. $5.50 pb.

Films Kids Like is a bibliography of about 220 short films for children, often fifteen minutes or less long. The paragraph-length annotations were written largely from the point of view of whether groups of children who viewed them liked them or not, and some reviews are rather critical both of the content and the children's response. In addition to the title and annotation, there is information on the type of film (animated, live action, iconographic, and so on) whether it is narrated or not, the length, whether color or black and white, the distributor, and country of origin—the list is very international. Some of the films were based on children's books, some were not; some are films usually considered to be for adults. Double-page spreads of black and white illustrations from the films are scattered throughout.

Films Kids Like is more than just a bibliography, however; the first section is a discussion of how to run a film theater, based on the experience of several such theaters in different parts of the country, and especially one in New York City sponsored by the New York State Council of the Arts and the National Endowment for the Arts. There are many practical suggestions for having a film festival or series of programs and conclusions as to what types of films children like. The compilers favor the involvement of children in activities related to films. There is also a short list of useful terms and their meanings.

This should be a good source for anyone with the resources to have a film festival; it could also be used as a purchasing guide in the usual fashion. It is very much based on what *children* like in films, and it is not curricula-related.

THE OWL AND THE PUSSYCAT

Edward Lear's well-known children's poem is translated into a simple animated film by John Korty. Unfortunately, the poem seems better known by adults than children, and the kids thus weren't too excited about it. Best for fours and fives, and a bit cloying even for them.
Animation   6 min.   color   C/McG   USA.

PADDLE TO THE SEA

Another classic; slow-starting, but worth the wait. This is the odyssey of a hand-carved boat that sets out in an inland stream and heads for the open seas. Beautifully photographed, often exciting, and appealing to a wide age range.
Live action   28 min.   color   C/McG   Canada.

PAINTINGS

A fantasy with animated paintbrushes, and a simple moral tale. The children were deeply engrossed in this film. The family of paintbrushes fascinated them, as did the inventive style of animation. Excellent for all age groups.
No narration   animation   10 min.   color C/McG   Czechoslovakia.

Reprinted by permission of the American Library Association from *Films Kids Like*, Susan Rice, ed., copyright © 1973 by the Center for Understanding Media.

Let's See It Again: Free Films for Elementary Schools, by J. A. Kislia. Pflaum Publishing Company, 2285 Arbor Boulevard, Dayton, Ohio 45439. 1975. 126pp. $2.95pb.

Based on her experiences trying to find free films that can be borrowed for school use, Kislia has selected, rated, and annotated two hundred films for elementary school-age children from about twice that number previewed. Many were produced by private industries and are not always directly available to show to children, and some were made by the government. Some may be borrowed from public libraries. (Several states were checked and found to have a number of the films in a large public library or state library.) Ratings were based mainly on reactions from children and adults who saw the films and are indicated as Poor, Fair, Low Good, Good, High Good, Very Good, and Excellent, or a combination of these. The Poor category was used for some films that were evaluated as poor in quality but are well known or well publicized; generally speaking, however, this is a selective list. Some films were also included in the Poor category because they are, in the compiler's opinion, inappropriate for children from kindergarten to eighth grade. Both the Poor and Fair ratings relied heavily on the film's lack of interest to children and adults. Low Good, Good, and High Good were used for films whose content was of interest; the three different ratings were mainly based on the originality of the film's treatment. A few films were rated Very Good or Excellent because of their outstanding qualities and appeal to both children and adults.

The arrangement is alphabetical by title and includes an indication of black and white or color, length in minutes, rating(s), suggested grade levels, subject headings and/or possible curricula units, abbreviation of the name of the producer/distributor, and date of release, if known. After the annotation itself (written by Kislia who viewed each film two to six times!) there are usually comments by students, identified by grades, and sometimes comments by teachers, also identified by grades taught. A double asterisk is used for films that are suitable for high school as well as elementary and junior high students. There is an alphabetical list of titles in the front and a subject index in the back. The names and addresses of distributors, also in the back, have a system of asterisks which indicates regional availability of films from that source.

According to the compiler, *Free Films* only lists a few of the very many free films usable with children that are available. A number of films are intended to sell a sponsor's product, either overtly or covertly, and some of the more blatantly commercial have been eliminated. It may also be necessary to use some ingenuity to obtain certain of the films, as sponsors may place restrictions on their use, such as not loaning them for viewing by children or only loaning in a certain geographical area. (Kislia

Let's See It Again

ELSA'S CUBS
(25 min)
Excellent
(1st - adult)
Animals
Library (Adamson) 1970

Less dramatic and more natural than Born Free; here the cubs leave Elsa, and Elsa dies. Elsa's death is simple, sad but not shattering. Wonderful shots of cubs, baby elephant. Everybody was satisfied with this splendid film.

ERUPTION OF KILAUEAU
1959-'60
(28 min)
Excellent
(6th - high school)
Earthquakes and Volcanoes
USGS 1961

The record of the approximately two-week-long eruption of Kilaueau volcano on Hawaii with magnificent photographs, and an excellent direct narrative that talks about what we see in the film as we are seeing it. Though the language is fairly technical and sometimes difficult, it does not explain phenomena such as lava fountains, cones and gases, ring of fire, etc., too analytically, and most ideas are comprehensible to older elementary children. The film records a spectacular story, but since it deals primarily with what took place day by day rather than rising to a dramatic crescendo, it becomes a little tedious for younger children (fourth grade — "we keep seeing the same pictures"), who were, however interested. With each higher grade, film was more appreciated.

mentions ways to obtain films even with these restrictions.) In spite of these drawbacks, some of the films are very good indeed and may not be available except from a sponsor. For situations in which little or no money can be spent for films, all of which are expensive, *Free Films* should be very helpful.

> *A Multi-Media Approach to Children's Literature: A Selective List of Films, Filmstrips, and Recordings Based on Children's Books,* compiled and edited by Ellin Greene and Madalynne Schoenfeld. American Library Association, 50 East Huron Street, Chicago, Illinois 60611. 1972. 262pp. $4pb.

Each of the more than one thousand entries in *Multi-Media Approach* is either for a children's book or for an audio-visual adaptation of what was originally in a children's book, except for a very few which began as audio-visual items and were then made into books. Only fiction for preschool to eighth grade is included. There is an entry, arranged alphabetically with bibliographic information and an annotation, for each original book (usually in hardback) and then one or more entries for the audio-visual version(s) of that book — filmstrip, recording, film, or a combination of these, usually called a set. The entries for audio-visual items also have bibliographic information and brief annotations, and Spanish editions of audio-visual items are noted. Selection for inclusion was based on both children's response and on quality; the audio-visual adaptation of a book had to be true to the spirit of the original book to be included. The Key to Abbreviations and sample entries in the front should be studied for familiarity with audio-visual terminology; since the names of publishers/distributors are abbreviated, the directory in the back must be consulted for complete names and addresses (WW for Weston Woods, for example). The indexes are by author, film title, filmstrip title, author or illustrator when he or she is featured in the work, record title, and subject arranged in broad groupings. There is also a brief introduction on how to use nonbook media and books in children's programs and a good bibliography for further reading.

This aid covers three of the most commonly used types of audio-visual media for children; it probably can be regarded as a basic collection of nonprint fiction for children, and the fact that in almost every case a book is also available makes it particularly useful. The items have also been rather carefully screened for quality. Note that nonfiction is not included.

> *Recordings for Children, A Selected List of Records and Cassettes,* 3rd edition. New York Library Association. (Order from Carol Cox Book Company, P.O. Box 717, 20 Booker Street, Westwood, New Jersey 07675. 40pp. $3pb.

318R   Books, Films, Filmstrips, Recordings

318R   Happy Birthday to You! and Other Stories, Caedmon, 196? (TC 1287) 2s 12in 33rpm $6.50; (CDL 51287) tape cassette $7.95. CAE (P)

Five Dr. Seuss stories read with verve by Hans Conreid. The electronic sounds of the Octopus, a sound machine with eight channels, are used to point up the action and give a suitably strange flavor to the nonsense. Includes: *Happy Birthday to You!* (no.130), *Scrambled Eggs Super, And to Think That I Saw It on Mulberry Street* (no.18), *Gertrude McFuzz,* and *The Big Brag.*

319   The Secret Garden, by Frances Hodgson Burnett; illus. by Tasha Tudor. Lippincott, 1962. 256p. $5.50 (I)

Three children find a garden and make it bloom again. The garden, in turn, changes the children. An attractive edition of an old favorite, illustrated with suitably sentimental pictures.

319F   The Secret Garden, M-G-M, 1949. 16mm 105min b/w $15 (rental only) FI (I)

Margaret O'Brien, Herbert Marshall, and Dean Stockwell star. Directed by Clarence Brown.

320   The Selfish Giant, by Oscar Wilde; illus. by Gertraud and Walter Reiner. Harvey House, 1967. unp. $3.50; lib. ed. $3.36 net (P)

It was always winter in the Giant's garden until he learned to share it with the children.

320F   The Selfish Giant, Reiner Film, Germany, 1971. 16mm 14min b/w $135. WW (P–U)

Based on the story by Oscar Wilde and illustrated with simple childlike drawings by Gertraud and Walter Reiner. Charles Cioffi's narration is accompanied by a bold musical score composed by Karl von Feilitzsch.

As its title indicates, this is a list of recordings for children, in both record and cassette form. It is a combination of an annotated and unannotated list of about four hundred recordings, divided into musical and nonmusical selections. The nonmusical entries are divided into Folk and Fairy Tales; Literature, subdivided into Prose, Poetry, and Of Professional Interest; Documentary, subdivided into People and Places; and Science and Technology. The musical section has Songs, Dance Music, Orchestral and Instrumental, Opera and Operetta, Ballet, and Musical Shows Soundtracks. (Holiday Recordings are in a separate section.) Overall, selections range from readings of familiar children's books by well-known actors and actresses to classical music to lesser-known ethnic sources, the latter often recorded by amateur groups. Many old favorites will be found here, including Caldecott books and selections from Newbery books. In the case of adaptations or cuttings from a book, the compilers tried to use only those that captured the flavor of the original. The foreword explains that all inclusions were carefully selected to avoid the "over-commercialized, patronizing, too exaggerated, slanted or ethnically stereotyped" (foreword, pp.iii-iv). The entry for some recordings only states who is performing, and has little or no description of contents. An asterisk before a title means it is suitable for very young children, although exactly what age is meant is not stated. Other than that, no age or grade levels are given. Order numbers are included as part of the bibliographic information, and there is a selective index by author-title-subject.

This seems to be a very good list with a wide range of types of recordings of both fiction and nonfiction. Note that only recordings are included and that the descriptions are brief.

> *Resources for Learning: A Core Media Collection for Elementary Schools,* edited by Roderick McDaniel. R.R. Bowker Company, 1180 Avenue of the Americas, New York, New York 10036. 1971. 365pp. $16.

Resources for Learning is a listing by subject and by title/author of recommended, nationally available, nonprint media for children from kindergarten to sixth grade, although many of the items are actually suitable for junior and senior high school use, according to the suggested grade levels. All types of nonprint media are included; transparencies, filmstrips, motion pictures (films), film loops, slides, pictures, records (phonodiscs), tapes, and so on. The introduction explains that preference was given to sound filmstrips over silent filmstrips, super 8 loops over standard 8mm. films, and filmstrips over slides. The first section is arranged alphabetically by subject, based primarily on *Sears List of Subject Headings,* with titles alphabetical under each topic. It is unannotated;

only title, distributor/producer, date, and collation (length, silent or sound, color or black and white, and physical description) are given. An asterisk by title indicates it is a "first purchase" title. McDaniel estimates the cost of this beginning collection at about $24,000 (1971 prices) or, if films are omitted, at about $4,600. The second section is alphabetical by title (or by author if there is a single, known author) interfiled. The title entry in boldface type is the main entry and is annotated. Each entry lists title; type of media, in parentheses after title; name of producer and/or distributor with order number, if any; date; length in minutes, number of frames, and so on; indication of sound or silent, if applicable; color or black and white; number of millimeters and other technical information; series, if any, in parentheses; price, in parentheses; suggested grade level; sources where the item was recommended; classification number; and annotations. In the case of a series or set, the individual items are given by title and length after the word "Contents." When the series is the main entry, cross-references are made from each individual title; these are in lightface type. There are main entries for more than four thousand items, but since a set or series is often entered as a unit, the number of individual items is even higher.

All the media were selected on the basis of their having been included on at least one of thirty-four lists of recommended media, which are shown in the introduction. These included several well-known lists such as *Elementary School Library Collection, School Library Journal,* American Library Association lists, and New York Public Library lists; some of the others are less well known, such as those prepared by local school districts. An abbreviation showing what list(s) the item was found on is included for each main (that is, title) entry in the title/author section. Selection for the basic collection (those entries with asterisks) was based on the item's having appeared on at least three lists, or on two lists combined with the editor's knowledge of its value. Both old and newer media are included, but generally speaking there are few pre-1961 items, the exception being some media in the fine arts or humanities which do not go out of date. All items are for use with children, not for the adult who works with children. There is a directory of producer/distributors and an index of subject headings used in the first section.

It is possible to select, order, classify, and catalog audio-visual items directly from *Resources for Learning.* Since it is based on lists of recommended media, it is selective; since full bibliographic information and addresses for distributors are given, ordering can be done directly (with the reservation that prices may have changed since 1971); since classification numbers based on a simplified Dewey Decimal System and subject headings are given, cards can be made directly—it is suggested that nonprint media be integrated with books. For an explanation of

NATIONAL CHARACTERISTICS.
 PEOPLE WE KNOW. (FILMSTRIP - SOUND) Guidance Associates, 1966. 2 filmstrips.
 color. 35 mm. and 2 phonodiscs: 4 s. 12 in. 33 1/3 rpm.

NATIONAL CHARACTERISTICS, AMERICAN.
 PEOPLE OF MIDDLE AMERICA. (FILM LOOP - CARTRIDGE). International Communication
 Films, 1965. 4 min. color. super 8 mm.

NATIONAL CHARACTERISTICS, INDIAN.
 INDIA'S POPULATION. (FILM LOOP - CARTRIDGE). International Communication Films,
 1963. 4 min. color. super 8 mm.

NATIONAL MONUMENTS - U. S.
 NATIONAL PARK SERVICE AREAS OF THE U. S. A. (FILMSTRIP). Society for Visual
 Education. 1966. 6 filmstrips. color. 35 mm.

NATIONAL PARKS AND RESERVES.
 NATIONAL PARK SERVICE AREAS OF THE U. S. A. (FILMSTRIP). Society for Visual
 Education, 1966. 6 filmstrips. color. 35 mm.
 ROCKY MOUNTAIN AREA: BACKBONE OF THE NATION. (MOTION PICTURE).
 McGraw-Hill, 1963. 16 min. sd. color. 16 mm.

NATIONAL PARKS AND RESERVES - U. S.
 GLACIER AND ROCKY MOUNTAIN NATIONAL PARKS. (FILMSTRIP). Eye Gate House,
 1960. 38 fr. color. 35 mm.
 MORE NATIONAL PARKS IN THE WEST. (FILMSTRIP). Eye Gate House, 1960. 38 fr.
 color. 35 mm.
 NATIONAL LANDMARKS, MEMORIALS & HISTORIC SHRINES. (FILMSTRIP). Eye Gate
 House, 1961. 9 filmstrips. color. 35 mm.
 NATIONAL PARKS IN THE EAST AND THE SOUTH. (FILMSTRIP). Eye Gate House, 1960.
 44 fr. color. 35 mm.
 NATIONAL PARKS IN THE WEST. (FILMSTRIP). Eye Gate House, 1960. 40 fr. color.
 35 mm.
 NATIONAL PARKS: OUR AMERICAN HERITAGE. (MOTION PICTURE). Released by Bailey
 Films, 1964. 15 min. sd. color. 16 mm.
 OTHER NATIONAL PARKS. (FILMSTRIP). Eye Gate House, 1960. 47 fr. color. 35 mm.
 OUR NATIONAL PARK SYSTEM. (FILMSTRIP). Eye Gate House, 1960. 38 fr. color. 35
 mm.

NATIONAL PARKS AND RESERVES - UTAH.
 THE NATIONAL PARKS OF UTAH. (FILMSTRIP). Eye Gate House, 1960. 40 fr. color.
 35 mm.

NATIONAL PARKS AND RESERVES - WYOMING.
 A VISIT TO YELLOWSTONE NATIONAL PARK. (FILMSTRIP). Eye Gate House, 1960.
 36 fr. color. 35 mm.

NATIONAL SOCIALISM.
 THE TWISTED CROSS. (MOTION PICTURE)Released by McGraw-Hill, 1958. 54 min. sd.
 b&w. 16 mm.

NATIONAL SONGS.
 AMERICAN PATRIOTISM IN POEMS AND PROSE, VOLUME 1. (PHONODISC). Caedmon
 CR 7001, 1968. 2 s. 7 in. 33 1/3 rpm. microgroove.
 ANTHEMS OF THE WORLD. (PHONODISC). Folkways Records FS 3881, FS 3882. 1959.
 2 albums (4 s.) 12 in. 33 1/3 rpm. microgroove.
 MARCHING ALONG TOGETHER. (PHONODISC). Decca DL 4450, n. d. 2 s. 12 in. 33
 1/3 rpm. microgroove.
 THIS IS MY COUNTRY; THE WORLD'S GREAT SONGS OF PATRIOTISM.
 (PHONODISC).Columbia ML 5819, 1963. 2 s. 12 in. 33 1/3 rpm. microgroove.

when a series was classified as a unit or as individual titles, see p. xiii of the introduction. Furthermore, the designation of a beginning collection extends the aid's usefulness even further. Some libraries might want to concentrate more on newer rather than older times, as 1961 is possibly too dated for some subject areas or for the methods of teaching used in some schools. Public library children's departments may find it of value also, although it appears to be mainly curricula-related. All in all, it is definitely a major selection tool for any children's library which plans to purchase media extensively, although not all libraries could afford the entire collection. Also, some children's librarians might want to use the list(s) from which items were selected as a guide. For junior and senior high school-age students, see *Core Media Collection for Secondary Schools,* by Lucy Gregor Brown (R.R. Bowker Company, 1180 Avenue of the Americas, New York, New York 10036. 1975. 221pp. $17.50.

> *World of Children, Films from the 1970 White House Conference on Children.* (Order from the Superintendent of Documents, U.S. Government Printing Office, Washington, D.C. 20402.) 18pp. $.40.

World of Children is an annotated bibliography compiled from hundreds of 16mm. films reviewed for the White House Conference on Children. The major portion is Films about Children and lists about one hundred films intended for the adult. The categories are Individuality, Creativity, and the Arts; Learning; Health; Families, Family Planning and Day Care; Communities, Media, and Prejudice; and Law, Rights, and Responsibilities. Each entry has the film title, indication of black and white or color, length, an annotation of several sentences, and the initials of the distributors. (A list in the back gives full names and addresses.) Section II, Films for Children, has a good short introduction which discusses some of the better producers of children's films and organizations which promote children's films. There are only twenty-two films in this section, intended as a "sampling" of good children's films. Several were made abroad, several are based on well-known children's books, and several utilize such techniques as puppets, slow-motion photography, or animated fantasy. Each one has title, type of photographic techique (animation or live action), black and white or color, length, country of origin, and the annotation. The third section, Films by Children, discusses some schools and organizations that have tried letting children make their own films! Four films by children are annotated as are several films and books about children's filmmaking. There are names and addresses for those interested in further information about children making their own films.

World of Children offers three different and very good approaches to films for, by, and about children. It could serve as a basis for workshops for adults interested in almost any area of children's education, as a small but very selective and international collection of films for children, and as a good starting point for anyone contemplating (or already involved in) children as filmmakers, an activity which is growing in importance.

One other place to look for children's films is *Films—Too Good for Words, A Dictionary of Nonnarrated 16mm. Films,* by Salvatore J. Parloto (Bowker, 1973, 209pp., $13.95) which has more than one thousand curricula-related films without words, but sometimes with other sound effects. This is an annotated bibliography arranged by subject, but it is not selective. Also, not all the films are for children; no suggested age or grade levels are given so it is necessary to determine which could be used successfully with children from the annotations, which is sometimes hard to do. It should be particularly useful when there is a specific need for nonnarrated films.

For a complete listing of a vast number of free audio-visual materials for libraries or classrooms, see *Educator's Guide to Free Films,* 36th edition, 1976, $12.75pb, edited by John C. Diffon and Mary F. Horkheimer; *Educator's Guide to Free Filmstrips,* 28th edition, 1976, $10pb, also edited by Diffon and Horkheimer; and *Educator's Guide to Free Tapes, Scripts, and Transcriptions,* 23rd edition, edited by Walter A. Wittich and James L. Berger, 1976, $10.50. All are published by Educator's Progress Service, Inc., 75 Moulton Street, Cambridge, Massachusetts 02138. There are also guides to free material in many subject fields in this series.

FOLK LITERATURE (FAIRY TALES)

An interest in the folk literature of European countries has its origins at least as far back as Perrault in the late 1600s; many of the well-known collectors such as the Grimm brothers, Joseph Jacobs, Andrew Lang, and Asbjornsen and Moe were working and publishing in the 1800s. Much scholarly research and writing is done about folk literature, and recently there has been a tremendous interest in the folk literature of Africa, native Americans (Indians), and Eskimos, to name only a few. Because of the very large number of folk tales, different titles for the same story, and variant versions of the same story, bibliographic control of this area is somewhat complicated. Furthermore, the practice of publishing folk tales in collections with one title for the entire collection adds even more complications. The aids which follow should help both in deciding which folk tale collections or single-volume editions to buy and in finding a particular story in the books the library already owns. Folk tales are especially popular with storytellers, and considering their sheer number and the interest in them today, some form of bibliographic control is necessary to save endless consultation of indexes or tables of contents of individual collections. *Children's Catalog* can be used to find folk literature in collections, but anyone needing more than this will probably want to consider some of the indexes described below.

The outstanding authorities on all kinds of folk literature are Peter and Iona Opie. Their definitive collections of various types of folk literature with scholarly comment are not particularly intended for children but are often purchased by children's libraries for adults to consult.

> *Index to Fairy Tales, Myths, and Legends,* 2d edition, by Mary Huse Eastman. F.W. Faxon Company, Inc., 15 Southwest Park, Westwood, Massachusetts 02090. 1926. 610pp. $11.

This is an index by title of what collection to consult to find individual folk tales. For each title the last name of the compiler and the name of the collection(s) are given, but not the page numbers within the collections. Several sources may be given for a single folk tale in case a particular collection is unavailable, and variant titles are in parentheses. More complete bibliographic information is given in the back of the book for collections used, listed by author. There is also a list for storytellers (geographical and racial) and a list of books for further reference. The whole work is intended primarily for storytellers, some of whom prefer to use folk tales exclusively, rather than as a selection aid. There are cross-references from subjects, but this is primarily a title index. Asterisks indicate stories suitable for small children.

The Index's Supplement I. (1937. 566pp. $11.) covers collections published since the original. The first supplement follows the same arrangement but adds a title list, in addition to the author list, and a brief subject index. References are made to the original *Index* so the supplement must be used in conjunction with it. A double asterisk means the material may need adapting for children. *Supplement II* (1952. 370pp. $11.) covers collections published since *Supplement I* up to 1948. It has the same arrangement as before.

> *Index to Fairy Tales, 1949-1972, Including Folklore, Legends and Myths in Collections,* by Norma Olin Ireland. F. W. Faxon Company, Inc., 15 Southwest Park, Westwood, Massachusetts 02090. 1973. 741pp. $18.

This tool is really a continuation of the previous three in spite of its slightly different title. The second *Supplement* stopped with 1948; this one indexes four hundred collections of folk tales published from 1948 to

A

Abbot of Innisfalen (poem).
Graves. Irish fairy tales.
See also Monk and the bird's song.
Abdallah. Cross and Statler. Story-telling. (Jew's tale.)
Field. Quest of the four-leaf clover.
Laboulaye. Fairy book.
Abdallah of the land and Abdallah of the sea. Arabian
nights, More tales (Olcott).
Abi Fressah's feast. Landa. Aunt Naomi's Jewish fairy
tales and legends.
See also Barmecide feast.
Aboo Mohammed the lazy. *See* Abou Mahomed the lazy.
Abou Hassan; or, The sleeper awakened.
Gibbon. Reign of King Cole. (Abu-l-Hasan the wag.)
Arabian nights (Dodge ed.).
Marshall. Fairy tales of all nations. (Caliph for one day.)
Olcott and Pendleton. Jolly book. (Abul Hassan the wag.)
Scudder. Children's book.
See also Death of Abu Nowas and his wife.
Abou Mahomed the lazy. Arabian nights (Colum. Abu
Mohammad the lazy.)
Arabian nights. More tales (Olcott).
Gibbon. Reign of King Cole. (Aboo Mohammed the lazy.)
About angels. Richards. Golden windows.
About Leviathan, king of the fish. Friedlander. Jewish
fairy book.
About the real and unreal devils. Wenig. Beyond the gi-
ant mountains.
Abraham. Landa. Aunt Naomi's Jewish fariy tales and
legends. (Star child; Higgledy, piggledy palace.)
Abraham and the old man. Scudder. Book of legends.
Abraham's tree. Friedlander. Jewish fairy book.
Abu-l-Hasan the wag.
See Abou Hassan; or, The sleeper awakened.
Abu-Mohammad the lazy. *See* Abou Mahomed the lazy.
Abudah and the search for the talisman of Oromanes,
History of. Olcott. Tales of the Persian genii.
Abused boy. *See* Hong Kil Tong.
Accommodating circumstance. Stockton. Queen's museum.
Accomplished and lucky tea kettle. Griffis. Japanese fairy
tales. (Wonderful tea-kettle.)
Hearn. Japanese fairy tales. (Tea-kettle.)
James. Green willow. (Tea-kettle.)
Lang. Crimson fairy book. (Magic kettle.)

1

Reprinted from *Index to Fairy Tales, Myths and Legends*, 2nd ed., © 1926, by Mary
Huse Eastman, by permission of the publisher, F. W. Faxon Company, Inc., Westwood, Massachusetts.

Index to Fairy Tales, 1949-1972

Reprinted from *Index to Fairy Tales, 1949-1972, Including Folklore, Legends and Myths
in Collections,* © 1973, by Norma Olin Ireland, by permission of the publisher, F. W.
Faxon Company, Inc., Westwood, Massachusetts.

1972. It differs from the Eastman indexes in that it has subject entries, which they do not, interfiled with the title entries, which are still the main entries. The title entries have the name of the compiler, the title of the collection, and the page numbers. Subject entries give only the title, so it is then necessary to refer to the title entry to obtain the name of the compiler, the name of the collection, and the page numbers. Often, one must also refer to the List of Collections at the front of the books for full bibliographic information. Like Eastman, it has no entries by compiler and no single-story editions; There are some entries by what are often thought of as "authors" — Grimm or Perrault, for example.

This set of indexes is not as hard to use as it may seem if one remembers that the title entry is the main entry. It is possible, since so many new editions of folk tale collections have appeared in recent years, to use only the Ireland volume and still have rather good access to many folk tales and related material, including some from ethnic groups and countries not found to any great extent in Eastman. This may be necessary if funds do not permit buying the whole set. Also, the List of Collections in the front of the Ireland volume is a good buying guide in itself.

> *Folklore: An Annotated Bibliography and Index to Single Editions,* by Elsie B. Ziegler. F. W. Faxon Company, Inc., 15 Southwest Park, Westwood, Massachusetts 02090. 1973. 213pp. $12.

While several other folk literature indexes and bibliographies concern themselves with *collections* of folk tales and related literature, this title indexes and annotates *single-story* editions. The first section, Stories by Title, gives the name of the story, its adaptor, illustrator (if any), publisher, date, the number of pages, a short description of its contents, a list of subjects found therein, the country of origin, motifs (that is, themes) in the story, and the type of folk literature (folk tale, fable, myth, and so on). There may be several editions of the same story, and these are listed together under a uniform title heading, with cross-references from the various titles. There are five indexes; the first of these, Stories by Subject, lists a title or titles for each subject with the entry number (not page number). Stories by Motifs, the third section, is in the same format, with titles listed by a number of themes commonly found in folk literature. Stories by Countries lists titles by ten areas, subdivided into countries; Stories by Type of Folklore divides the titles into Epics, Fables, Folk Songs and Ballads, Folk Tales, Legends, Myths, and Nursery Rhymes. Finally, Stories by Illustrator lists the titles by their illustrator. For all five indexes it is necessary to refer to the annotated bibliography section, Stories by Title.

The introduction explains that its purpose is to help in selecting stories for storytelling, for curricula-related purposes, or simply to help children

STORIES BY TITLE

0542 ALADDIN

0404 Aladdin, The Story of

Reteller, Naomi Lewis
Illus. Barry Wilkinson
New York, Henry Z. Walck, Inc., 1971. 48p.

Aladdin finds himself buried alive in an underground vault with an old lamp. As he raises his arms for prayer, he touches a magic ring an evil sorcerer had lent him and a magic genie appears who does his every wish.

SUBJECTS —	Allah	COUNTRY — Iran
	Aladdin and the Lamp	
	Geni and the Lamp	
	Lamp, Magic	
	Ring (Magic)	
	Sultan	
	Magician	

MOTIFS —	Magic Objects	TYPE OF
	Trickery	FOLKLORE — Folk Tales
	Wit Prevails	
	Magic Transforma-	
	tion	
	Religion	

0402 ALADDIN AND THE WONDERFUL LAMP

Reteller, Jean Hersholt
Illus. Fritz Kredel
New York, George Macy Companies, Inc., 1949. 39p.

Similar to title no. 0404 Aladdin, The Story of.

SUBJECTS —	Allah	COUNTRY — Iran
	Aladdin and the Lamp	
	China	
	Geni and the Lamp	
	Lamp, Magic	
	Ring (Magic)	
	Sultan	
	Magician	

MOTIFS —	Magic Objects	TYPE OF
	Trickery	FOLKLORE — Folk Tales
	Wit Prevails	
	Magic Transformation	
	Religion	

16. Thompson, Stith, *ed.*

TALES OF THE NORTH AMERICAN INDIANS. Bloomington, Indiana
University Press [1966] 386 p. fold. map. (Midland books, MB–91)
E98.F6T32 1966

Contents.—Mythological stories.—Mythical incidents.—Trickster tales.
—Hero tales.—Journeys to the other world.—Animal wives and hus-
bands.—Miscellaneous tales.—Tales borrowed from Europeans.—
Bible stories.—Notes (Comparative notes; List of motifs discussed in
the notes; Sources arranged by culture areas and tribes).

"Full, well-told" examples of the better known tales of the Indian
and Eskimo, selected from the extensive body of available material, are
given as they originally appeared in government reports, folklore journals, and publications of learned societies; changes are always indicated. The introductory survey describing the varied character of this
body of folklore, the comparative notes (p. [271]–360) showing
the extent of distribution of tales and motifs, and the bibliography
(p. [373]–386) make this a valuable guide to important source materials for each of the culture areas and tribes.

Children's Anthologies

17. Hooke, Hilda M.

THUNDER IN THE MOUNTAINS, LEGENDS OF CANADA. Illustrations by
Clare Bice. Toronto, New York, Oxford University Press [1947]
223 p.   E98.F6H6 1947

Bibliography: p. 221–223.

Eleven of these 14 folktales, some of which are stories of the new
settlers, are based on Indian sources and represent many sections of
Canada including Labrador. A brief introduction giving the local setting leads directly into each tale. The compiler states in her preface
that these stories "are based upon legends gathered up in a variety of
ways. Some are taken from authentic source material such as the
Anthropological series issued by the Canadian Department of Mines;
others embody parts of legendary cycles . . . such as the Hiawatha,
Glooscap and Nanna-Bijou stories; . . . some were picked up by word
of mouth, and some were adapted from existing versions of familiar
legends."

The stories are treated "freely" in an informal narrative style, colored
with modern embellishments, as in the descriptions of the new coats
Wesukechak makes for the animals. "Lynx, had a coat of butter-yellow,
with little tufted ear-muffs," "Kakwa the Porcupine, who wanted to

find stories to read on their own. The annotations are descriptive rather than critical and do not usually give much information on the illustrations beyond the name of the illustrator. Neither this nor the Eastman/ Ireland volumes is selective.

> *Folklore of the North American Indians: An Annotated Bibliography,* compiled by Judith C. Ullom. Library of Congress, 1969. (Order from the Superintendent of Documents, U.S. Government Printing Office, Washington, D.C. 20402.) 126pp. $2.25

Folklore of the North American Indians consists of lengthy selective annotations and many illustrations about Indian and Eskimo folk tales. Unlike the Eastman and Ireland indexes, which merely tell where to look to find the folk tale, this work has considerable information about each entry. The first short section is General Background, which has information on anthologies, bibliographies, and indexes. The main body of the work is titled North American Culture Areas and has these categories: Eskimo; Mackenzie; Plateau; North Pacific; California; Plains; Central Woodland; Northeast Woodland; Iroquois; Southeast; and Southwest. Each section has a paragraph of introduction and is usually divided into Source Books and Children's Editions. Overall, although not restricted to children's books, the work places considerable emphasis on them, and the frequent illustrations add a great deal. It is indexed by author-title-subject. This is probably a "must" for anyone who is working at all extensively with native American folk tales. It is interesting and useful itself even without all the books discussed.

POETRY

Children's poetry has enjoyed something of a renaissance in the past few years. Almost gone are the sentimental, singsong poems of the past, although this is not to say that *all* old poems are bad poems by any means. Today's poetry for children is fresh and vigorous and speaks to today's child. Librarians and teachers are faced with the task of selecting the best of the old and of the new, refusing to compromise on poorly written poetry, no matter how fondly it may be remembered from their own childhoods, but not falling prey to the idea that because a poem is new it must be good. Since there are thousands upon thousands of children's poems, it is quite possible to be very selective. The following tools provide some access to this vast body of literature which, like folk tales, would be overwhelming if there were no guides in the form of indexes. The subject approach to poetry is very popular at the moment with good reason. It enables librarians and teachers to select peoms in regard to some topic, such as a program in the library or a curriculum unit, rather than by poet, title, or grade level.

Children and Poetry, A Selective, Annotated Bibliography, compiled by Virginia Haviland and William Jay Smith. Library of Congress, 1969. (Order from the Superintendent of Documents, U.S. Government Printing Office, Washington, D.C. 20402.) 67p. $.75.

This is a bibliography by author of poetry for children, divided into Rhymes, Poetry of the Past, 20th-Century Poetry, and Anthologies. About 250 poets from the United States and other countries are included; for each one the compilers have recommended one or more titles (often collections) and provided a brief critical and descriptive analysis of the poet's work, usually with quotations from well-known critics and often with examples from the poet's writings. Full bibliographic information is given, including a suggested Library of Congress catalog number, rarely used for childen's books except in an academic library. A number of black and white illustrations from the works discussed add interest. There are no Mother Goose rhymes or other folk literature, but the works included range from Shakespeare to Dr. Seuss. There is a good introduction to what children like in poetry and why, written by Smith. The index is by author and title, but not by subject.

This is a good, inexpensive buying guide to the best children's poets and their poetry. It could also be used somewhat in reference work. It is a little dated perhaps (1969), but not unduly so, and there is likely to be something for everyone.

Childhood in Poetry, A Catalogue, with Biographical and Critical Annotations, Of the Books of English and American Poets Comprising the Shaw Childhood in Poetry Collection in the Library of The Florida State University, by John Mackay Shaw (volumes 1-5). Gale Research Company, The Book Tower, Detroit, Michigan 48226. 1967. $135. *First Supplement,* 3 volumes, 1972. $87.50. *Second Supplement,* 2 volumes, 1976. $87.50.

The first five volumes of this work, published in 1967, are based on the catalog of the collection at Florida State University of books of American and English poetry *about childhood* and/or *read by children,* prepared by the donator and curator of the collection. Each of the first four volumes describes and often critically analyzes the ten thousand volumes in the collection, arranged in alphabetical order. Often there are quotations of poetry from the books and from their prefaces or introductions. Each entry has very full bibliographic information and a complete contents analysis. Sometimes there are remarks by the compiler, who states that his intent was to be comprehensive (that is, to include the entire collection) rather than to be selective. All together, more than 100,000 poems are included. Volume 5 is an index to the first four volumes by Short Title List and Key (an alphabetical by author arrangement with titles under each author and a referece to the entry by item

Austin, Mary H.

THE CHILDREN SING IN THE FAR WEST. With drawings by Gerald Cassidy. Boston, Houghton Mifflin, 1928. 187 p.   PS3501.U8C5   1928

The poet began the collection many years ago when the West was "so new that there were no songs about it that children could have for their own." A number of these poems, like "The Sandhill Crane" and "Grizzly Bear," children can claim, through anthologies, for their own. While many of the poems sound stiff and old-fashioned to the modern ear, others are worthy of note, especially those dealing with the flora and fauna and landscape of the mountains and the desert. The final section of translations and adaptations of Indian songs and chants is especially valuable.

Behn, Harry.

THE WIZARD IN THE WELL; POEMS AND PICTURES. New York, Harcourt, Brace [°1956] 62 p.   PZ8.3.B395Wiz

Along with *All Kinds of Time, The Little Hill,* and *Windy Morning,* this small volume is by an American writer who looks at things clearly from the point of view of childhood. Dealing in musical rhythms, gay words, and simplicity of forms with the out-of-doors and child play and imagining, most of the poems are brief and appeal to the very young. The poet himself illustrates his work with small, lively designs.

> Once a wizard wondrous wise
>   Lived in a deep dark well,
> His store of lore was more than vast,
>   Too vast for words to tell.

Louise Bechtel called attention to this "distinguished" little book's "moments of special joy caught in lovely words, its mixture of cosy reality and poetic magic. He is taking an important place among contemporary poets who write especially for children."

26

BOURNE, JANE

568. A COMPANION TO THE NOAH'S ARK, being conversations between a mother and her children, on the animals contained in the ark, interspersed with pieces of poetry, and remarks on heathen mythology, particularly that of the Egyptians. By Mrs. Bourne, authoress of 'The fisherman's hut,' 'Conversations on the church catechism,' 'The crooked sixpence,' &c. &c. Swaffham: printed for F. Skill. Sold in London by Simpkin and Marshall, and all other booksellers, M.DCCC.XXXIII. First edition. iv,165p. 14.2x9.2cm. Marbled boards, morocco back.

Preface, (Coventry, July, 1833): "The following little work was commenced as a Sunday recreation for some of my own children, who found much pleasure in searching the Bible for the different animals mentioned in it, and in reading or enquiring their histories."

Typical Passages: Our Saviour and our Shepherd: Since thou art ever near and kind,/Why should I fear or want or woe,/Thy wisdom hath my lot assigned,/Thou wilt whate'er is right bestow. On the insufficiency of human wisdom: Then trust not learning, reason, skill,/They could not guide to Heaven;/But humbly strive to do His will,/By whom they all are given. Noah and his family: Gently the tiger laid him down,/Meekly the tame hyena stood/And food was as a welcome boon,/Ta'en by the monarch of the wood. The ark: The furious winds came rushing wild,/The tempest raved against its side;/Yet safely as a cradled child,/The ark rose on the rising tide.

Volume Also Contains: Think not that numbers can protect; Arouse thee, O Israel; Forgive me that temptation slight; The subsiding of the waters; The raven and the dove; Our Saviour our ark.

569. NOAH'S ARK, being conversations between a mother and her children, on the animals contained in the ark, interspersed with pieces of poetry, and remarks on heathen mythology, particularly that of the Egyptians. By Mrs. Bourne, authoress of "The fisherman's hut," "Conversations on the church catechism," "The crooked sixpence," &c. &c. London, T. Allman, 1841. 165p. 13.9x9cm.

Editor's Note: Except for the revised title-page and the omission of the preface, conforms exactly to the 1833 edition, apparently printed from the same plates.

BOURNE, Margaret   See 6313

BOURNE, S. K.   See 6315

— 252 —

number) and a Key Word index.

The first supplement consists of three additional volumes that incorporate the sixty thousand poems in about eight thousand books that have been added to the collection since the first five volumes were published in 1967. The same two kinds of indexes are used. The second supplement consists of one volume that again updates the new additions to the collection since 1972 and provides an index volume to the entire work including a book title index.

This is a very impressive work, but it must be pointed out that its cost may place it beyond the reach of a good many small school and public libraries. Furthermore, a number of the poems and poets may be of more importance to the student or scholar interested in the historical development of children's poetry than to a children's librarian concerned with day-to-day use. Certainly, it should be considered if funds permit, especially in a larger public library or academic library.

> *Index to Children's Poetry, A Title, Subject, Author, and First Line Index to Poetry in Collections for Children and Youth,* by John E. Brewton and Sara W. Brewton. H. W. Wilson Company, 950 University Avenue, Bronx, New York 10452. 1942. 965pp. $20.

The title is descriptive of the contents of this work: It is possible to look up in it any of fifteen thousand children's poems, listed alphabetically by author, title, subject, or first line. The reference tells where a particular poem may be found in 130 collections of poems for children and young adults from preschool to high school. The entries by title for each poem have the full name of the author of the poem, the translator, if any, and an abbreviation. This abbreviation can be deciphered by using a key to collections in the front, which gives full bibliographic information for each work. (An individual poem may have several references since it may appear in more than one collection.) There are also many subject entries for most of the poems. These entries have the title of the poem, the author's first initial and last name, and the abbreviation for the name of the collection. Author entries have the full name of the author (no translator), the title of the poem, and the abbreviation for where it may be found. Any of these types of entries can be utilized merely by looking up the abbreviation for the collection in the front. First-line entries, on the other hand, merely refer to the title entries so it is necessary to look in two places. The list of books indexed gives grade level and analyzes the contents of each collection.

Obviously, the primary use of *Index to Children's Poetry* is for reference work by providing an approach in any of the four ways indicated. It may seem hard to use at first but can be easily figured out, and it provides a comprehensive listing—a citation to almost any poem published before 1942 should be here, and the range is wide. It indexes only collections, not individual poems.

The *First Supplement* (1954, $12) covers sixty-six collections published from 1938 to 1951, and the *Second Supplement* (1965, $12) does the same for the eighty-five collections from 1949 to 1963. In all three volumes there are thirty thousand poems by more than five thousand authors! See the next entry for an updating from 1963.

Index to Poetry for Children and Young People, A Title, Subject, Author, and First Line Index to Poetry in Collections for Children and Young People, 1964-1969, by John E. Brewton, Sara W. Brewton, and G. Meredith Blackburn, III. H. W. Wilson Company, 950 University Avenue, Bronx, New York 10452. 1972. 575pp. $20.

This is actually an updating of the previous work for the years 1964 to 1969, adding eleven thousand poems by two thousand authors. The title was changed slightly to reflect the increase in poems for young adults in grades seven to twelve. It covers 117 collections for the years indicated as well as a few volumes for earlier years omitted in the original work. The arrangement is the same. *Supplement I* (1972) further updates the work.

Subject Index to Poetry for Children and Young People, by Sell and Smith, American Library Association (1957) is currently too out of date to be very useful, but an updating of this work titled *Subject Index to Poetry for Young People, 1957-1975,* appeared in the summer of 1977.

STORIES AND PLAYS

The following three books provide access to stories and plays that have been published either in collections or individually. They are primarily indexes to the material. The *Science Fiction Story Index* is rather old and not particularly directed toward children, but it has been included because of the intense interest in science fiction that sometimes develops in older elementary school children, coupled with the fact that these children will often read far beyond their usual reading level if they have become addicted to "sci fi." *Young People's Literature in Series* is a new and much-needed index to the better fiction series for children, while *Index to Children's Plays in Collections* should be useful because of the growing need for plays suitable for children to perform, an activity which seems to be growing in popularity.

FOR CHILDREN AND YOUNG PEOPLE

Index to Children's Plays in Collections, by Barbara Kreider. Scarecrow Press, Inc., 52 Liberty Street, P.O. Box 656, Metuchen, New Jersey 08840. 1972. 138pp. $6.

This work provides an index by author, title, and subject to about five hundred plays suitable for children, published between 1965 and 1969. The author entry is the main entry and has title(s) of play(s) by that author and collections where works may be found, by author, title, and the number of characters. The subject entries, distinguished by capital letters, give only the author and titles of individual plays (not the collections where they may be found); title entries give only the author. For the last two types of entries it is then necessary to refer to the author entry. There is full bibliographic information for each collection at the end under the heading Bibliography-Collections Indexed. The bibliography also has a section on professional aids that lists other sources of plays for children. Another section at the back called Cast Analysis arranges plays by the number of characters in the cast, divided by female, male, or mixed characters. Puppet shows are also included, and there is a directory of publishers.

Obviously, Index to Children's Plays is intended to be used for finding plays, published between 1965 and 1969, for children to present, but the list of collections could also be used for purchasing. It is a comprehensive rather than a selective listing and only plays in collections are included. The second edition was published in 1977.

Science Fiction Story Index, 1950-1968, by Frederick Siemon. American Library Association, 50 East Huron Street, Chicago, Illinois 60611. 1972. 274pp. $4.50pb.

This is an index to more than 3,400 science fiction stories in collections. It is not really intended for children or young adults, but is included here because an interest in science fiction will often carry an older elementary school-age child far beyond his or her usual reading level. The Author-Title section gives, in alphabetical order, the name of the science fiction author, a list of titles for that author in alphabetical order, and a symbol, consisting of one letter and three numbers, for the collection where each title can be found. The user must then check the second part of the book, Bibliography of Indexed Anthologies, to find full bibliographic information for the collection, looking it up by the code number. The third part is a listing of all stories and authors by title of individual story. It is also possible to look up the name of a collection in this section; these last two are necessary if the name of either an individual story or collection of stories is known but the author is not, since the main listing in the work is by author.

Science Fiction Story Index can be considered for purchase in any chil-

COLUMBUS, CHRISTOPHER

    Bakeless, K.   Most memorable voyage

    Bennett, R.   The plot

    Boiko, C.   Spaceship Santa Maria

    Dias, E.   The ghost from Genoa

    MacLellan, E.   Return of the Nina

    Peterson, M.   Beyond mutiny

    Roberts, H.   For the glory of Spain

COMEDY

    Boiko, C.   The book that saved the earth

    _____ .   Cupivac

    _____ .   The Franklin reversal

    _____ .   Scaredy cat

    _____ .   Terrible Terry's surprise

    Brydon, M.   The reluctant ghost

    Chisholm, J.   A prince is where you find him

    _____ .   Shades of ransom

    Grahame, K.   The reluctant dragon

    Hale, L.   The lady who put salt in her coffee

    Hark, M.   Father keeps house

    _____ .   Our own four walls

    _____ .   Too many kittens

    _____ .   When do we eat?

    Irving, W.   The legend of Sleepy Hollow

    Jarvis, S.   Supper with the queen

    Lawrence, J.   Inside a kid's head.

AUTHOR–TITLE	ANTHOLOGY

Hasse, Henry.
 The Eyes. F700
 He Who Shrank H430
Hatcher, Jack.
 Fuel for the Future G805
Hawkins, Peter.
 Circus C290
 Life Cycle. C295
Hawkins, William.
 The Dwindling Sphere J330
Hawthorne, Nathaniel.
 The Birthmark L885
 Rappaccini's Daughter. C770 M940
Healy, Raymond J.
 Adventures in Time and Space [J.F. McComas] H430
 Famous Science Fiction Stories [J.F. McComas] H430
 The Great Devon Mystery H440
 New Tales of Space and Time [Editor]. . . . H435
 Nine Tales of Space and Time [Editor]. . . . H440
Heard, Gerald.
 B M—Planet 4 . . . . H435
Heard, Henry Fitz-Gerald.
 The Collector M190
 Cyclops C965
 The Great Fog C870
 Wingless Victory D425
Heinlein, Robert A.
 "All You Zombies—" M230 M655
 And He Built a Crooked House C640
 Assignment in Eternity H470
 The Black Pits of Luna . . C795 G225 .H475 H490
 Blowups Happen . . . . A875 .C935 H490
 By His Bootstraps . . . . . . A510 .H485 M330
 Columbus Was a Dope A835 H485
 Coventry . . . . C850 .H490 K690

dren's library where there is a strong interest in science fiction among the patrons — and an interest in science fiction, once acquired, can be very strong indeed. It is rather out-of-date, but many classic science fiction stories remain popular.

> *Young People's Literature in Series: Fiction, An Annotated Biblio-graphical Guide,* by Judith K. Rosenberg and Kenyon C. Rosen-berg. Libraries Unlimited, P.O. Box 263, Littleton, Colorado 80120. 1972. 176pp. $7.50.

This is an alphabetical listing, by author, of fiction series books (that is, those with the same characters from one story to another). For each author there is a title, publisher, and date for every book in a series. (Some authors have more than one series, of course.) There is also a sum-mary of the whole series, not usually of individual titles, although this may happen when the quality varies from title to title. The remarks range from commendatory to critical. No symbols or other designations are used to show whether a whole series (or individual titles in a series) is recommended or not; it is necessary to read and evaluate each entry it-self. Occasionally, only certain books in a series but not the entire series will be recommended. Some books are evaluated as being for one sex or the other, which some people may criticize. Suggested age range levels are given; the work covers primarily books for third to ninth graders and includes books published since 1955 only. There are two indexes, one by series title and one by individual title, but no subject index.

Some libraries do not buy very many (or any) of what are usually thought of as series books, such as Nancy Drew or the Hardy Boys, be-cause of the poor quality of the writing, but these and their like have been omitted from the Rosenberg work. Extremely well-thought-of series like the *Little House* books can be found here. Some others are question-able but in fact are not evaluated very highly. Series books are something of a recurring problem for libraries, with the children asking for them and the librarian hesitating to commit the money, time, and shelf space. *Young People's Literature in Series: Fiction* should help give some idea of the quality and content of a series and aid in deciding whether some or even all of the series should be purchased.

BIOGRAPHIES

Children's interest in biography has increased somewhat over the past few years, largely due to the better quality of biographies for children be-ing written. Some children read biographies on their own, but others will do so only when required to for an assignment. Teachers need good bio-graphies to suggest as supplemental reading in this situation, and li-

Young People's Literature in Series: Fiction

DUNSING, Dorothy

> 442. War Chant.
>> New York, Longmans, 1954.
> 443. The Seminole Trail.
>> New York, Longmans, 1956.

This series is historical fiction, set in Florida in the 1830s against the backdrop of the Seminole wars. This unusual setting should be especially of interest due to the resurgence of interest in Indians and their history.

EAGER, Edward

> 444. Magic or Not?
>> New York, Harcourt, 1959.
> 445. The Well-Wishers.
>> New York, Harcourt, 1960.

The first volume of this series with Laura and James as the chief characters is very well done, with a fresh plot, and a lively mystery. Unfortunately, the second suffers from a mixed-up plot, too much preaching, and adult philosophy, as well as literary allusions not in the field of a young reader's knowledge.

> 446. Half Magic.
>> New York, Harcourt, 1954.
> 447. Knight's Castle.
>> New York, Harcourt, 1956.
> 448. Magic by the Lake.
>> New York, Harcourt, 1957.
> 449. The Time Garden.
>> New York, Harcourt, 1958.

This is by far the most successful series of the two. It is a delightful fantasy spoof, again about a group of children who discover many magic devices, including a coin that only grants half their wish. All show imagination and humor and can be read on more than one level.

ANNE CARROLL MOORE
1871–1961

Pioneer in children's library work

The library profession was largely dominated by men when Anne Carroll Moore began her long career as a children's librarian. Ms. Moore truly loved children and books, and with her imagination and determinism, made children's literature an important part of the library system. She single-handedly shaped the present practices and philosophies of the New York Public Library children's rooms.

For ten years she was in charge of the children's room in the Pratt Free Library in Brooklyn, and for thirty-five years she administered the children's department of the New York Public Library. During this period her ideas and practices were widely emulated by libraries throughout the world. Even after her retirement she continued to lecture, write, and serve as a consultant to the world of children's books.

*** *Sayers, Frances Clark* ANNE CARROLL MOORE: A BIOGRAPHY Illus. with photographs. Atheneum, 1972. (grade 9 and up)
   Fascinating, skillfully written biography incorporates excerpts from Anne Carroll Moore's writings and letters, offering a warm, informative view of her life. Young adults considering library work as a career or those attracted to children's literature will find this adult biography particularly interesting for it chronicles the history of children's libraries as well as telling the story of Ms. Moore's life—a wise approach, for it is impossible to separate the two.

brarians need to be able to recommend books that will capture the interest of the child who would otherwise simply select the smallest book on the biography shelves! In either case, it is heartening to know that there are now so many good children's biographies.

> *Her Way, Biographies of Women for Young People,* by Mary-Ellen Kulkin. American Library Association, 50 East Huron Street, Chicago, Illinois 60611. 1976. 449pp. $25.

The first section of *Her Way* consists of one or two paragraphs of biographical information for 260 women, entered alphabetically. For each entry the woman's birth and death dates and field of endeavor are given. In addition to the biographical information, however, each entry has from one to three or four references to full-length biographies about the woman. Each of these consists of author, title, publisher, date, grade levels, and a short paragraph of annotation. Entries are rated Acceptable (one asterisk), Recommended (two asterisks), Highly Recommended (three asterisks), or Unacceptable (two daggers — ††); the compiler was especially concerned with sexism and racism as well as with literary merit and accuracy. Thus the first section is both a source of information about the women themselves and an index to biographies, with an indication of the merits of the books indexed.

The second section provides information on about three hundred collective biographies of women, entered by the name of the compiler with long annotations of their contents. At the end of the work, women included are classified by country and by profession; the index is by name of biographee.

Her Way fills an important gap in the area of the biographies about women. Note that it is comprehensive of all in-print biographies as of 1975 for children and to some extent for young adults but is not selective. The ratings make it possible to use it for selection, however, or for evaluating books already owned. Its emphasis on nonsexist and nonracist biases and its recent copyright date make it a very contemporary work.

> *Index to Young Readers Collective Biographies, Elementary and Junior High Level,* 2d edition, by Judith Silverman. R. R. Bowker Company, 1180 Avenue of the Americas, New York, New York 10036. 1975. 322pp. $14.95.

This is an alphabetical index to more than five thousand biographies about famous (and not so famous) people from all over the world, written for children and young adults. All the biographies indexed are those found in more than seven hundred collections, not in individual biographies. One section is arranged by the name of the biographee and one is by specific topics associated with that person. Each entry gives the

Index to Young Reader's Collective Biographies

Addams, Jane (1860-1935). Social worker.
BOC; COG; COKA; CUC; DEDA; DOD;
FEC; FOH; FOJ; GIBA; LEZC; MAN;
MASA; MAT; MEA; NAB; PA; STJ;
STLA; WECB; WIC

Adderley, Herb. Football player. JOA

Addison, Thomas (1793-1860). English
physician. POB

Ade, George (1866-1944). Humorist, play-
wright. BEE

Adenauer, Konrad (1876-1967). German
chancellor. WEA

Adler, Felix (1851-1933). Educator, ethical
reformer, born Germany. BEA

Adler, Felix (d. 1960). Clown. KIB

Adler, Kurt Herbert (1905-   ). Conductor,
chorus master, born Austria. STM†

Adler, Peter (1899-   ). Conductor, born
Czechoslovakia. STM†

Adrian, Edgar Douglas (1889-   ). English
physiologist. RIF

Affonso I (1506-1545). King of Kongo. DOA;
MIC

Agassiz, Alexander (1835-1910). Ocean-
ographer, zoologist, born Switzerland.
COR

Agassiz, Louis (1807-1873). Naturalist,
born Switzerland. HYB; MIB

Agatha, Saint (d. 250?). QUA

Ager, Milton (1893-   ). Song writer.
MOA

Agganis, Harry (1930-1955). Football
player. HIE

Agnes, Saint (291-304). ONA; QUA; WIB

Agnew, Spiro Theodore (1918-   ). Ex-
vice-president of U.S. FEA

Agnon, Shmuel Yosef (1888-1970). Israeli
author. ROGA

Agricola, Georgius (1494-1555). German
mineralogist. SHFB

Agricola, Gnaeus Julius (37-93). Roman
general. COM

Agrippa, Cornelius Heinrich (1486?-1535).
German philosopher. COEA

name of the person; birth and death dates, if known; nationality, if other than American; profession or field of endeavor; and an abbreviation of the author and title of the collection where the biography can be found. It is then necessary to consult the key to symbols in the front of the book to decipher the author and the name of the book; a list in the back gives full bibliographic information for each title. The inclusions are not necessarily recommended, since the intent was to be comprehensive, not selective. A daggar beside an entry means there is very little information about that person in the source. There is an index by subject headings.

This tool is primarily a key to finding a biography about a specific person without looking in the indexes of each book of collective biography in a library. Some children, however, may prefer or need individual biographies, which are not included. Since it is not selective, it should not be looked on as a list of recommended biographies.

> *Index to Short Biographies for Elementary and Junior High Grades,* compiled by Ellen J. Stanius. Scarecrow Press, Inc., 52 Liberty Street, P.O. Box 656, Metuchen, New Jersey 08840. 1971. 348 pp. $8.50.

This tool differs from *Index to Young Reader's Collective Biographies* in that it is an index to *short* biographies in collections only, whereas the former primarily indexes biographies that provide more information on each individual (but still in collections). *Index to Short Biographies* has for each entry the name of the biographee, his or her profession, nationality if other than American, and a reference to book(s) where information may be found about that person by the last name of the author, the title, and page number(s). Many biographees have more than one reference. For full bibliographic information refer to the title list which has the name of the author of the biography, the title of the collective biography, and the place, publisher, and date of the work. The symbols E or J are used for elementary (third, fourth, and fifth grades) or junior high (sixth, seventh, and eighth grades). There is no subject arrangement or index, but none is really needed. Inclusion was comprehensive rather than selective.

The introduction points out that this work may be used by an individual student or a whole class, or for interlibrary loan (which is not used much in most children's libraries). The choice between this and the previous tool, if one must be made, is between an index that provides access to a moderate amount of material for each biographee (often about a chapter) in the former tool, or one that provides access to a smaller amount (about a page perhaps) in the latter. See the Hotchkiss books in the next section for recommendations of single biographies.

HODGES, GILBERT RAY (American baseball player)
    Daley, Kings of the Home Run, pp. 149-157.
    Fitzgerald, Champions in Sports, pp. 1-25.

HOFER, ANDREAS (Austrian patriot)
    Mabie, Heroes and Patriots, pp. 207-208.

HOFFENSTEIN, SAMUEL G. (American poet)
    Benet, Famous American Humorous Poets, pp. 53-60.

HOFFMAN, MALVINA (American sculptress)
    Clymer, Modern American Career Women, pp. 48-60.
    Coffman, Twenty Modern Americans, pp. 221-234.
    Stoddard, Famous American Women, pp. 225-233.

HOGAN, BEN (American golf champion)
    Fox, Little Men in Sports, pp. 187-196.
    Hollander, Great Athletes, pp. 59-61.
    Schoor, Courage Makes the Champion, pp. 9-20.
    Silverman, More Sports Titans, pp. 73-89.

HOGARTH, WILLIAM (English artist)
    Chase, Famous Artists, pp. 64-67.
    Kales, Masters of Art, pp. 65-67.
    Ruskin, 17th and 18th Century Art, pp. 140-143.

HOGG, HELEN SAWYER (American scientist)
    Yost, Women of Modern Science, pp. 31-47.

HOHEMUT, GEORGE (German explorer - South America)
    Chapman, Search for El Dorado, pp. 44-51.

HOKUSAI, KATSUSHIKA (Japanese engraver, painter)
    Chase, Famous Artists, pp. 26-29.

HOLBEIN, HANS "THE YOUNGER" (German artist)
    Kales, Masters of Art, pp. 38-40.
    Kielty, Masters of Painting, pp. 95-99.
    Turngren, Great Artists, pp. 45-51.

HISTORY AND HISTORICAL FICTION

For many people, both children and adults, their concept of history is formed at least as much from reading historical fiction as it is from school courses. Often centering around some historical conflict such as a war or a transitional period when an old order gives way to a new one, these books usually contain stirring action and daring deeds. Today's history books (neither texts nor fictionalized treatments of history but simply nonfiction accounts of historical events) are also reflecting a more pluralistic society and a diversity of opinion that was unheard-of a few years ago. The inclusion of treatment of minority groups and of women increases the appeal of history for many children.

> *American Historical Fiction and Biography for Children and Young People,* by Jeanette Hotchkiss. Scarecrow Press, Inc., 52 Liberty Street, P.O. Box 656, Metuchen, New Jersey 08840. 1973. 318pp. $8.50.

This is a selective annotated bibliography of more than fifteen hundred books for children and young adults in the area of American historical fiction and biography. The entries were selected for accuracy, literary quality, and good taste, and both old and new books are included. Each entry has bibliographic information, a well-written sentence or two of descriptive annotation, and recommendations by symbols: E for elementary through the second grade; I for intermediate, through fifth or sixth grade; YA for young adult, in junior high; YA and Up for senior high; and A for adult but suitable for various ages. The books are divided chronologically in the first section and subdivided in each section by topic; most relate to United States history: Early Exploration and Conquests; Colonial Period;. Revolutionary Period; New Nation; Expanding Frontier; Closing Frontiers; First Quarter of the 20th Century; and Second Quarter of the 20th Century. In the second section the books are arranged by subject: Alaska and Hawaii; Arctic and Antarctic; Arts; Canada; Education and Social Service; Folklore; Indians, the Native Americans; Industry and Technology; Latin America and the West Indies; Medicine; Mexico; Presidents and their Families; Sailing, Ships and Seamen; Science; Slavery, Civil Rights, and Black History; Spies and Secret Service; Sports; and Women. This section covers much of the western hemisphere besides the United States, especially North and South America. The author explains that the first section is primarily for those who already know and like history, the second for those who need to be enticed. There are indexes by author, by title, and by biographee, and even a special index for horse lovers!

This index would be good for history units, for children's "pleasure

193 Sutton, Felix. Sons of Liberty. Ill. by Bill Barss.
       Map of the Thirteen Colonies by Barry Martin.
       Julian Messner, 1969. Short biographies of the
       following: Samuel Adams, John Hancock, Patrick
       Henry, Paul Revere, and Joseph Warren. (I)
194 Todd, A. L. Richard Montgomery, Rebel of 1775.
       Ill. and maps by Leonard Vosburgh. David McKay,
       1966. A solid, factual book about the 1775 expedi-
       tion into Quebec in which Montgomery (1736-75) took
       St. Johns and Montreal but was killed in the unsuc-
       cessful attempt to take Quebec. His conversion
       from English çitizen to Continental rebel is described
       and his responsibility for securing the colonies
       against attack from the north is shown to be a de-
       cisive factor in the Revolution. A monument to him
       can still be seen in New York City where Broadway
       meets Fulton, Church and Vesey Streets. (YA and
       Up)
195 Wagner, Frederick. Patriot's Choice: The Story of
       John Hancock. Ill. with photographs of paintings and en-
       gravings. Dodd Mead, 1964. This biography of the
       wealthy merchant (1737-93) whose name appears first
       on the Declaration of Independence, provides a
       pleasantly readable and authoritative history of the
       causes and results of the American Revolution. (YA)

REVOLUTION IN THE NORTH

196 Albrecht, Lillie. The Grist Mill Secret. Ill. by
       Lloyd Coe. Hastings House, 1962. A story about a
       young Massachusetts girl entrusted by her father
       with a vitally important secret concerned with the
       Committee of Safety and the Minute Men; also a
       story of the intolerance and suspicion which develop
       in violent times. (I)

reading," or for purchasing. Children and young adults could use it themselves because the annotations are easy to read and interestingly written.
The only criticism might be that it is sometimes hard to tell which books
are biography and which historical fiction, if this matters in a particular
case.

> *European Historical Fiction and Biography for Children and
> Young People,* 2d edition, by Jeanette Hotchkiss. Scarecrow
> Press, Inc., 52 Liberty Street, P.O. Box 656, Metuchen, New Jersey
> 08840. 1972. 272pp. $8.50.

The same general format as the previous work, also by Hotchkiss, is
used for *European Historical Fiction and Biography.* The arrangement is:
British Isles; Central Europe; France and the Lowlands; Greece and the
Balkans; Italy (Rome) and Switzerland; Russia and Poland; Scandinavia;
and Spain and Portugal. Each section usually has categories of general
history and folk literature, then a chronological arrangement, with more
than thirteen hundred entries in all. The age levels are slightly different
from the preceding work — E for beginners and just beyond; E and I for a
little more advanced; I for ages eight to twelve; I and YA for age ten and
up; YA for ages twelve to fourteen; YA and A for up to college level; and
A for adult. As before, each entry has bibliographic information, a short
annotation, and recommended age levels for each entry. The indexes are
by author, by title, and by biographee.

This is a companion volume to *American Historical Fiction and Biography* and can be used, as that book can, for supplemental reading in
history and social studies or for a student who enjoys historical writing.
As it is a selective list it can be used for purchasing. In either volume, the
annotations are so pleasantly written that they might well interest a child
who usually does not care for historical fiction or biography.

> *American History in Juvenile Books, A Chronological Guide,*
> 1966. 329pp. $10. *World History in Juvenile Books, A
> Geographical and Chronological Guide,* 1973, 356pp. $12. Both
> by Seymour Metzner, H. W. Wilson Company, 950 University
> Avenue, Bronx, New York 10452.

The first of these two titles, *American History in Juvenile Books,* is a
sometimes annotated bibliography of *all* books for children (up to grades
six or seven) in the area of American history. It is not intended to be selective and includes both fiction and nonfiction titles, but no texts. It differs
from the Hotchkiss volumes on these two points: Hotchkiss is selective
and includes historical fiction and biographies but not nonfiction history
books. The division is chronological with subdivisions of smaller units of
time. Within each of these there are categories titled Fiction, Biography,

European Historical Fiction and Biography
for Children and Young People

Part IV
Greece and the Balkans

1. Prehistory (Archaeology, Myth and Legend)

Berry, Erick (Best, Allena)---<u>The Winged Girl of Knossus</u>
---Appleton, 1933---ill. with decorations redrawn
from murals and decorations of Knossus and other
Minoan cities. A novel of Inas (daughter of Daedalus),
Princess Ariadne, and Theseus and the final destruc-
tion of Knossus.   YA

Capon, Paul---<u>Kingdom of the Bulls</u>---Norton, 1962---
ill. by Lewis Zacks. A novel about a young girl of
Sarum, England, who is stolen by Cretan traders to
be taken as a sacrifice to the Minotaur in the Knossus
of King Minos. Great suspense.   YA

Coolidge, Olivia---<u>Greek Myths</u>---Houghton Mifflin, 1949
---ill. by Edouard Sandoz.   YA

   <u>The King of Men</u>---Houghton Mifflin, 1966---ill. by
   Ellen Raskin. A novel based on the Agamemnon leg-
   end about his struggle for power and the conquest of
   Helen.   YA

   <u>The Trojan War</u>---Houghton Mifflin, 1952---ill. by
   Edouard Sandoz. The Homeric legend, with a helpful table of characters.   YA

D'Aulaire, Ingri and Edgar Parin---<u>D'Aulaire's Book of</u>
   <u>Greek Myths</u>---Doubleday, 1962---ill. by the authors.
   A beautiful book.   I

de Selincourt, Aubrey---<u>Odysseus the Wanderer</u>---Cri-
   terion, 1956---ill. by Norman Meredith. A fine retelling of Homer's epic, with excellent format.   I

Faulkner, Nancy---<u>The Traitor Queen</u>---Doubleday, 1963.
   A well-constructed novel about Mycenean plots
   against Crete and its King Minos, with a useful map.
                                                        YA

71

GROWTH AND CONFLICT: 1821-1861

OTHER NONFICTION

Level One

BRYANT, WILL. Kit Carson and the Mountain Men. (3-7) Grosset, 1960. 60p. illus.

McCALL, EDITH. Heroes of the Western Outposts. (3+) Childrens Press, 1960. 126p. illus. map

McCALL, EDITH. Hunters Blaze the Trails. (3+) Childrens Press, 1959. 128p. illus.

McCRACKEN, HAROLD. Winning of the West. (3-7) Doubleday, 1955. 63p. illus. maps

Level Two

AMERICAN HERITAGE. Trappers and Mountain Men. (5+) Am. Heritage, 1961. 153p. illus. maps

BUEHR, WALTER. Westward With American Explorers. (4-6) Putnam, 1963. 93p. illus.

CAMPBELL, MARJORIE. Nor'westers: The Fight for the Fur Trade. (5-9) St. Martin, 1956. 176p. illus.

CHILTON, CHARLES. The Book of the West. (5+) Bobbs, 1962. 320p. illus. maps

PLACE, M. T. Buckskins and Buffalo: The Story of the Yellowstone River. (5-7) Holt, 1964. 128p. illus.

Level Three

DAUGHERTY, JAMES. Trappers and Traders of the Far West. (7-8) Random, 1952. 181p. illus. maps

REINFELD, FRED. Trappers of the West. (7+) Crowell, 1957. 153p. illus.

F. Settling the New Lands

1. Westward the Trails

FICTION

Level One

CARR, M. J. Children of the Covered Wagon; a Story of the Old Oregon Trail. (3-7) Crowell, 1957. 302p. illus. map and Other Nonfiction. Each of these is further divided into Level One (grade three or lower), Level Two (grades four and five), and Level Three (grades six and seven). Some of the levels have no entries if no material for that category and grade level could be found. (Chapter 10 consists of those books that did not fit into any of the nine chronological chapters.) For each entry there may be only bibliographic information and a suggested grade level (in addition to the division into levels); books for which the title is not explanatory have a brief sentence of description. The author notes that books about Indians are included only as they relate to relations with Indians and white settlers, as he feels that materials about Indians belong in their own separate listing. There are indexes by author, biographical subject, and title. The work is rather out-of-date (1966).

World History in Juvenile Books has the same style and format, but covers the entire scope of world history rather than just American history. It has more than 2,700 entries.

In using either of these companion volumes, remember that the good, the bad, and the indifferent are all here. However, the fact that non-fiction books are included extends the range beyond the Hotchkiss books. In fact, the author intends the user to look elsewhere (such as in *Children's Catalog, Junior High Catalog, Adventuring with Books, The ACEI Bibliography, and others)* for recommendations, or the lack of them, before deciding to buy or use a book from these bibliographies. The volumes can be used by adults or by students.

> *Creating Independence, 1763-1789: Background Reading for Young People, A Selected Annotated Bibliography,* compiled by Margaret N. Coughlan. Children's Book Section, General Reference and Bibliographic Division, Library of Congress, 1973. (Order from the Superintendent of Documents, U.S. Government Printing Office, Washington, D.C. 20402.) 62pp. $.75.

Prepared for the Bicentennial, this publication is a fascinating combination of illustrations and sample pages from old books as well as a bibliography of recommended books for both adults and young adults, arranged by broad chronological topics. A few of the entries are suitable for small children; some could be used by older elementary-age children, but many are definitely for older users. (No recommended age levels are given.) The annotations are lengthy and penetrating, often with quotes from the book itself. Most entries are in the areas of history and biography, but there are some fictionalized accounts. All entries were selected on the basis of being books that still have revelance to today's concerns.

This is a very interesting and inexpensive publication, but may not be as useful for everyday children's library use as some of the others in this

Ethiopia

FICTION

BRADLEY, DUANE. Meeting With a Stranger. (4-6) Lippincott, 1964. 128p. illus.
>Ethiopian boy's ways clash with American ideas.

COATSWORTH, ELIZABETH. The Princess and the Lion. (3-7) Pantheon, 1963. 88p. illus.
>Abyssinian princess sets out to rescue her imprisoned brother.

NONFICTION

KAULA, E. M. The Land and People of Ethiopia. (7-9) Lippincott, 1965. 160p. illus. maps

NOLEN, BARBARA. Ethiopia. (4-6) Watts, 1971. 96p. illus.

Glubok, Shirley.

THE ART OF COLONIAL AMERICA. Designed by Gerard Nook. [New York] Macmillan [1970] 48 p. illus. (part col.), facsims. (part col.), ports. (part col.) N6507.G6

A description of paintings, buildings, and household objects reflecting the culture of the Colonies. A profusion of well-produced illustrations make the volume attractive.

Graham, Shirley.

YOUR MOST HUMBLE SERVANT. New York, J. Messner [1949] 235 p. QB36.B22G7

"Notes on sources": p. 227-235.

An emotional, fictionalized account of the life of Benjamin Banneker, an "Ethiopian" mathematician, surveyor, and astronomer "who helped lay out Washington." Although there are minor inaccuracies (the use of "Lord Calvert" for Lord Baltimore, for example), and although Banneker's contribution to America was made after the Revolution, the book is included here for its representation of the conditions under which free Negroes lived at the time.

presidency. "Here you will find a great deal on social and economic development; horses, ships, popular sports, and pastimes; eating, drinking, and smoking habits. Pugilists will be found cheek-by-jowl with Presidents; rough-necks with reformers, artists with ambassadors. More, proportionally, than in other histories, will be found on sea power, on the colonial period in which basic American principles were established. . . ." (Preface)

Plate, Robert.

CHARLES WILLSON PEALE; SON OF LIBERTY, FATHER OF ART AND SCIENCE. New York, McKay Co., 1967. 276 p. illus., ports. E207.P4P55

Bibliography: p. 265-269.

A vigorous portrayal of an "energetic citizen," artist, and "painter of patriots" who found time to participate in the Revolution, dabble in the sciences, run a museum of natural history, and experiment with "illumination" and "moving pictures."

Russell, Francis.

Coughlan, Margaret N., compiler. *Creating Independence, 1763-1789; Background Reading for Young People.* A selected annotated bibliography. Washington, D.C., Library of Congress, 1972. 62 p.

section. It is a good addition to further enrich a collection in the American history area and can even be used to some extent by itself without the books it recommends, because of the many illustrations and extracts from the books.

PAPERBACKS AND OTHER INEXPENSIVE MATERIAL

There is little doubt that paperbacks are here to stay in children's libraries. Their relatively low cost, frequently small size, and attractive, colorful covers make them very appealing to both librarian and child. The heavy use sometimes accorded library books must be taken into account, however, when making the decision to purchase paperbacks. In the long run it may actually be cheaper to purchase a hardback copy of a book that will receive heavy use, because the cost of replacing the paperback, perhaps several times, will soon outweigh the cost of the hardback. The point is that so many children's titles are now available in both editions that one has a choice of bindings in many cases. Some libraries even buy both a hardback and one or more paperback copies of a title — the hardback for permanent use and the paperbacks to be loaned as long as they last. This can be especially useful when the librarian knows there will be heavy but temporary demand for a title. Some children's libraries, of course, may have funds that limit them almost solely to paperbacks for the time being. It has also been found that paperbacks may appeal to the child who dislikes reading or is reluctant to read. The titles in this section encompass both lists of recommended books and discussions of how to utilize paperbacks to their fullest extent.

For paperback reference books, see the Wynar book in the reference book section. Also, the *RIF Guide* in the multiethnic section is a list of books for a paperback giveaway program for children.

> *Good and Inexpensive Books for Children,* by Catherine Boules. Association for Childhood Education International, 3615 Wisconsin Avenue, N.W., Washington, D.C. 20016. 1972. 62pp. $2.

Formerly titled *Children's Books for $1.50 or Less,* this is an annotated bibliography of about six hundred books for children, nearly all of which are paperbacks. Entries were selected for quality as well as for cost. Each entry has bibliographic information and a short descriptive annotation, and there are a few illustrations from the books. Entries are divided in Picture Books; Fiction, Easy; Fiction, Intermediate; Fiction for Older Boys and Girls; Rhymes and Verses; Fairy Tales and Legends; Biography; Social Studies; Science; Recreation and Hobbies; and For Parents and Teachers. There are indexes by author and by title, but no subject index, which would have been helpful.

The purpose of this aid is obvious — to provide a list of good children's books that are also inexpensive. It can be useful subject to the qualifications that obtain when buying any paperbacks. Many old favorites, familiar in the hardback editions, will be found here in paperback.

> Growing Up with Paperbacks, compiled by Eleanor B. Widdoes. R. R. Bowker Company, 1180 Avenue of the Americas, New York, New York 10036. 1975. 32pp. (See Growing Up with Books for rates.)

Similar in style and format to the other titles in this series (Growing Up with Books and Growing Up with Science Books, which have entries elsewhere), Growing Up with Paperbacks lists and briefly annotates about 175 paperback books for children, some of which have sample illustrations in black and white. There is a good balance of the old and new, and some titles are very well known, while others are not. It is divided into For the Very Young (Ages 3 to 6 — Picture Books); Ages 5 to 9 (Stories and Poetry); Animal Stories; Fantasy (Age 7 Up); Stories for Boys and Girls (Age 8 Up); Adventure, Mystery and Historical Fiction (Age 10 Up); Novels for Girls and Boys (Age 12 Up); History and Geography (Age 10 Up); Science and Nature (Ages 5 to 9 and Age 10 Up); Social Issues (Age 12 Up); Sports (Age 9 Up); Mystery and Science Fiction (Age 9 Up); Just for Fun (All Ages); and For All Ages (Old Favorites, Classics and Poetry). The last two categories have books for children of all ages. The arrangement may seem rather complicated, but because of the pamphlet's small size, it is not especially hard to use. Arrangement is random in each category, not alphabetical by either author or title. There are no indexes.

As before, the small size and attractive cover make this booklet useful for promotional purposes. It is actually intended as a guide for adults buying gift books for children, as well as for librarians or teachers. It can be used for parents and other relatives asking for just that — a list of good inexpensive books to buy to give to children. Children could conceivably use it themselves to purchase books, as most of the titles listed are not very expensive.

> Paperback Books for Children, edited by Beatrice Simmons, compiled by the Committee of the Paperback Lists for Elementary Schools, American Association of School Librarians, American Library Association. Citation Press, 50 West 44th Street, New York, New York 10036. 1972. 130pp. $.95.

This is very similar to several of the tools in Building the Basic Collection, and is, in fact, a small but comprehensive book-selection aid of more than seven hundred recommended titles available in paperback, although seven hundred books could not be counted a complete basic collection for even a very small library. The arrangement is very simple; there are five main divisions: Picture Books; Fiction; Nonfiction; Myths, Folklore, and Fairy Tales; and Poetry, Rhymes, Riddles, and Jokes. The nonfiction is divided into six topics: Animals and Pets; Biography—Individual and Collective; History; Language; Leisure Activities—Games, Sports, and Hobbies; and Natural History and Science. There are more fiction than nonfiction titles, but overall it has a fairly good balance. Each category has an alphabetical author listing, with title, illustrator, paperback distributor, price, and grade levels, the latter usually quite broad; each entry also has a short annotation. *Children's Catalog, Books for Elementary School Libraries, The Elementary School Library Collection, School Library Journal, Booklist,* and *Horn Book* were primarily used for selecting the books, although choice was not limited to these. In each case the paperback version of a title had to be basically the same as the hardcover edition. There is a directory of paperback publishers (harder to find than hardback publishers' lists), and indexes by author and by title. This is a good source of a fairly large number of inexpensive books; it is easy to use and fairly up to date.

> *Paperback Books for Young People: An Annotated Guide to Publishers and Distributors,* by John T. Gillespie and Diana L. Sprit. American Library Association, 50 East Huron Street, Chicago, Illinois 60611. 1972. 177pp. $5pb.

Part 1 of *Paperback Books for Young People* is a directory of paperback publishers. The arrangement is alphabetical by the name of the publisher (not the name of the paperback series). Each entry gives quite a lot of information on each company, a discussion of what series of paperbacks each publishes for adults and for young people, any special services, and ordering information. Part 2 is a directory of paperback distributors (since many paperbacks are sold through a middleman known as a jobber rather than directly from the publisher). It is arranged alphabetically by states. Part 3, Selection Aids, lists and describes rather fully some aids to purchasing and using paperbacks.

This will be useful for anyone needing information on obtaining paperbacks; a library that already has such channels may not need it. Also, it could be used for determining what company publishes what series if this information is not known. The bibliography could be helpful for anyone planning an extensive paperback program. There are no recommended children's books.

> *The Young Phenomenon: Paperbacks in Our Schools,* American Library Association Studies in Librarianship no. 3, by John T. Gillespie and Diana L. Sprit. American Library Association, 50 East Huron Street, Chicago, Illinois 60611. 1972. 140pp. $5pb.

This is a report on the use of paperback books in the schools, based on surveys sent out to a number of schools. Two sets of questionnaires were used, one in 1967 and one in 1970, and this data is analyzed with many charts and tables. Other chapters cover a listing and description of various research papers relating to paperbacks, some case studies on paperback use, how to select paperbacks (many of these suggestions could be applied to selecting hardbacks as well), how to administer a paperback collection, and the promotion and sale of paperbacks directly to students. There is a selected bibliography (unannotated) and samples of the surveys used in an appendix, as well as a binder's directory and names and addresses of manufacturers of paperback book racks; either of the latter two might be hard to find elsewhere. (For information on how to order paperbacks themselves see *Paperback Books for Young People,* discussed previously.)

There are a number of useful ideas for using paperbacks in this work, as well as background reading for the development of the popularity of paperbacks. It, too, does not have lists of recommended children's books.

Horn Book also has two lists, *Recommended Paperbacks, 1968-1971* and *Recommended Paperbacks, 1971-1973.* These are $.50 each and may be ordered from The Horn Book, Inc., 585 Boylston Street, Boston, Massachusetts 02116. Teachers especially may be interested in a series called *Educators Guide to Free* — — — — which lists all the available free material in the various subjects. Much of this information may be more suited to young adults but some will be useful for children.

MISCELLANEOUS

The following are books which should be useful to children's librarians but do not fit into separate categories of their own.

> *Books that Help Children Deal with a Hospital Experience* by Anne Altshuler. U.S. Department of Health, Education, and Welfare, 1976. (Order from Superintendent of Documents, U.S. Government Printing Office, Washington, D.C. 20402.) 24pp. $.55.

This publication is primarily an annotated bibliography of about fifty-five books to help preschool and elementary school-age children who must face a hospital stay. The compiler, a pediatric nurse, selected the books on the basis of their accuracy and literary and artistic quality. Each entry has full bibliographic information, with a description of the illustrations, suggested grade level, and ratings of excellent, very good, good, fair, poor, or a combination. The annotations, arranged by author, are critical as well as descriptive and some criticize the books very sharp-

Books that Help Children Deal with a Hospital Experience

*Kay, Eleanor. The Clinic. New York: Franklin Watts, Inc. 1971. 51 pp. Illustrated with black and white photos. Grades 4 to 6. $3.75. Good to very good.

The story takes a small black boy through his first visit to a clinic, explaining history taking, the physical setup, and general routines of clinics.

Kay, Eleanor. The Emergency Room. New York: Franklin Watts, Inc. 1970. 63 pp. Illustrated with black and white photos. Grades 5 to 7. $3.75 Excellent.

The experiences of an 11-year-old boy, injured while playing at a construction site, are followed from arrival at a hospital emergency room through examination and treatment. The way the hospital staff handles many types of emergencies and the use of equipment are described in detail.

Kay, Eleanor. Let's Find Out About the Hospital. New York: Franklin Watts, Inc. 1971. 48 pp. Illustrated in green, black, and white by William Brooks. Grades k to 3. $3.75. Fair.

This book introduces hospital staff, departments, routines (oral medications, siderails on beds, wheelchairs, play, visiting hours, etc.). Emphasis is placed on cleanliness of the hospital. There is no preparation for unpleasant experiences; instead, a child is shown reacting unnaturally with a smile as his finger is stuck for a blood test.

12

Published by U.S. Department of Health, Education, and Welfare, Public Health Service, Health Services Administration, Bureau of Community Health Services, Rockville, Maryland 20857.

ly. An asterisk shows those books suggested for a hospital library. The annotations explain just what operation or procedure the book focuses on, as almost all books about children's hospitalization use a particular illness, accident, or medical condition as a topic — only a few deal with the general workings of a hospital. The introduction explains that many books about children's hospital experiences are very poor, unrealistic portrayals of hospital procedures that do not adequately prepare the child for what he or she can expect. The index is by title.

Although the title of *Books that Help Children Deal with a Hospital Experience* gives the impression that it is a list of recommended books, a number of those included were rated rather poorly. It should probably be used with selectivity as much as possible, choosing those books that received better ratings. Also, some of the books are rather old and hospital procedures have changed, as the compiler is careful to point out. There is a great need for good books of this nature.

> *Music Books for the Elementary School Library,* compiled by Peggy Flanagan Baird. Music Educators National Conference, 11202 Sixteenth Street, N.W., Washington, D.C. 22091. 1972. 48pp. $3.

Music Books is an annotated bibliography of nearly two hundred music books for children from preschool through junior high and occasionally high school. By "music books," the compiler means books about the history of the development of music, about famous musicians, composers, or directors; lyrics and scores; dictionaries; and the like. Each entry consists of the author, illustrator, title, place and publisher, date, number of pages, descriptive annotation, and suggested grade levels by a wide range. Baird included only those books with which she herself was familiar so the list is not necessarily inclusive. Although there are no indications of the relative quality of different books in the annotations and no system of ratings, the list appears to have been at least somewhat selective, with an asterisk to indicate those titles that are particularly outstanding. There is an index by subject which gives an indication of the scope of the contents: Biography; Books in Spanish or Related to that Culture; Dictionaries, Encyclopedias, and References; Easy Readers — Picture Books (which includes such old favorites as *Lentil* and *Frog Went A-Courtin'*); Ethnic Music (including the American Negro); Instruments; Jazz; Music and Related Arts; Music History and Appreciation; Opera and Operetta; Science and Music; Songs and Collections; Sounds of Listening; and Noise Pollution! Several blank pages in the back are headed New Listings so users can keep the list up-to-date on their own.

Unfortunately, music books do not always comprise the strongest part of a children's library collection; *Music Books* should be very valuable in

*Arnold, Elliott. Illus. by Lolita Granahan. *Finlandia, The Story of Sibelius.* New York: Holt, Rinehart and Winston, 1950, 24 pages.

> Fictionalized account of the life of Sibelius with facts confirmed by the composer. Each chapter ends with a quotation from *The Kalevala.* Discography included. Upper elementary, junior high school.

Attaway, William. Illus. by Carolyn Cather. *Hear America Singing.* New York: Lion Press, 1967, 187 pages.

> Following an introduction by Harry Belafonte, folk music of America is traced from its roots in European, African, and American traditions. Lyrics of many familiar and unfamiliar ballads, hymns, marches, and blues. Grades 5-9.

*Bakeless, Katharine Little. *Story-Lives of American Composers.* New York: J. B. Lippincott Co., 1962, 292 pages.

> Following the introductory chapter on general aspects of America's music, the book is devoted to certain American composers and their music, including Stephen Foster, John Philip Sousa, W. C. Handy, Charles Ives, Jerome Kern, Roy Harris, Walter Piston, Deems Taylor, Richard Rogers, and William Schuman. Portraits of some of the musicians included. Grades 5-8.

Baker, Laura Nelson. Illus. by Nicolas Sidjakov. *The Friendly Beasts.* New York: Parnassus Press, 1957, 22 pages.

> The old English Christmas carol beautifully illustrated. Piano score with six verses of the song. Early primary grades.

Balet, Jan. Illus. by author. *What Makes an Orchestra.* New York: Henry Z. Walck, Inc., 1951, 41 pages.

> This amusing book is illustrated to give an accurate, yet entertaining, picture of the instruments of the orchestra. The subject of chamber music also is developed with the illustrations and explanations of the duet, quartet, quintet, and sextet. The conductor is introduced with the full orchestra. Grades 3-6.

rectifying this omission. Only books, not suggested phonodiscs or cassettes, are included.

> *Young People's Literature in Series: Publishers and Non-Fiction Series, An Annotated Bibliographical Guide,* by Judith K. Rosenberg and Kenyon C. Rosenberg. Libraries Unlimited, Inc., P.O. Box 263, Littleton, Colorado 80120. 280pp. $10.

The main body of this work is an evaluative directory by series name to more than six thousand series of books of two types: those known as publishers' series which have a number of different authors for the various books (whether fiction or nonfiction), and nonfiction series that have only one author. (The distinction is made since fiction series by one author are found in the Rosenbergs' other work, *Young People's Literature in Series: Fiction.*) Each entry starts with the name of the series followed by an alphabetical listing of every author who writes for that series, with his or her titles and publication dates alphabetically underneath. The evaluations, which are well written and often give suggestions for classroom use, are for the entire series, not usually for individual titles. Not all included books are necessarily recommended—one must read each annotation and decide individually. There are author and individual title indexes (in case a single title in the series is known but the name of the series is not). References are by item number, not page number.

Considering the great proliferation of series books, this should be a very useful guide. There is sometimes a temptation to buy all or most of the series simply because it is convenient to do so; series books are often given a great deal of promotion and may seem to be an easy way to fill a large gap in the collection. The two Rosenberg titles together cover almost all series books (except a few very well-known ones) and provide an evaluation of the series as a whole. Some series of books in the nonfiction area especially are excellent, while some are terrible; it is difficult to find evaluations for many series books because the standard reviewing journals or basic collection aids do not often review or evaluate them, or do so only for individual titles. No other similar works devote themselves entirely to series books. Series for the reluctant reader are also included.

Since many children's libraries, especially those with a number of preschool patrons, are adding toys and other realia to their collections, readers may be interested in a new book edited by Faith H. Hektoen and Jeanne R. Rinehart, *Toys to Go: A Guide to the Use of Realia in Public Libraries* (American Library Association, 50 East Huron Street, Chicago, Illinois 60611. 1976. 24pp. $2.50). *Matters of Fact* by Margery Fisher (Thomas Y. Crowell, 666 Fifth Avenue, New York, New York 10019. 1972. $11.95) is an excellent work on using nonfiction books with children, but its orientation is essentially British and for young adults.

Young People's Literature in Series

HERE IS YOUR HOBBY SERIES —Putnam (cont'd)
> Neumann, Bill
>> 3796. Here Is Your Hobby: Model Car Building (1971)
> Powers, William
>> 3797. Here Is Your Hobby: Indian Dancing and Costumes (1966)
> Roth, Bernhard
>> 3798. Here Is Your Hobby: Archery (1962)
> Wels, Byron G.
>> 3799. Here Is Your Hobby: Amateur Radio (1968)
>> 3800. Here Is Your Hobby: Magic (1967)
> Young, Helen
>> 3801. Here Is Your Hobby: Doll Collecting (1964)

All facets of a hobby are presented in this series: the history, the rules for collecting or making the items involved, the type and cost of equipment necessary, and information on displaying items. Each book also provides a glossary and an index, and some of them offer lists of the publications, clubs, and manufacturers of supplies pertinent to the hobby.

HISTORICAL CHARACTERS SERIES —McGraw-Hill
> Bellis, H.
>> 3802. Admiral Nelson (1970)
>> 3803. Captain Cook (1970)
> Purton, R. W.
>> 3804. Captain Scott (1970)
>> 3805. Doctor Livingstone (1970)

These are short, easy-to-read biographies of people who are not the usual subjects of such series. Although the authors sometimes invoke fiction, using a story format, these are nonetheless presentable introductory biographies. Glossaries and bibliographies are provided. For ages 10 on up.

HISTORICAL EVENTS SERIES —McGraw-Hill
> Gray, Peter
>> 3806. D-Day (1970)
>> 3807. The Battle of Hastings (1968)
>> 3808. The Invincible Armada (1970)

Another easy-to-read historical series from McGraw-Hill. This one introduces readers to important individual events in history. The incidents are related with a verve that should capture the imagination of the casual reader as well as the student of a particular event. For ages 9 through 13.

4

Illustrators, Authors, and Awards

Children are often interested in the lives and experiences of authors or artists whom they have come to know about though their books. Sometimes it will be a personal favorite, other times it will be someone another child has mentioned. Occasionally, a brief biographical sketch may be required by a teacher as part of a project, although hopefully the written book report complete with tedious plot summary has died a natural death. Children are also surprisingly interested in the various awards in children's literature, especially the two best-know ones, the Newbery and Caldecott.

With interest in children's literature growing among adults, there is a need as well for sources that the student or parent, for example, can consult for more in-depth analysis of the person's literary or artistic style than would probably be useful to children. Several of the sources in this section are somewhat more for the adult than the child; however, works of literary or artistic criticism solely for the adult are in the bibliography, as are books relating to the theory of children's book art and its production. Several of the books in the author section also deal with illustrators.

ILLUSTRATORS

> *Illustrators of Children's Books, 1744-1945,* compiled by Bertha E. Mahony, Louise Payson Latimer, and Beulah Folmsbee, 1947. 527pp. $20; *Supplement 1, 1946-1956,* compiled by Ruth Hill Viguers, Marcia Dalphin, and Bertha Mahony Miller, 1958. 299pp. $20; *Supplement 2, 1957-1966,* compiled by Lee Kingman, Joanna Foster, and Ruth Giles Lontoft, 1968. 205p. $20. All published by The Horn Book, Inc., 585 Boylston Street, Boston, Massachusetts 02116.

Probably the definitive work on children's artists, the original volume of *Illustrators of Children's Books* has a lengthy discussion of the de-

ELLIOTT, ELIZABETH SHIPPEN GREEN

Born in Philadelphia. Studied at Pennsylvania Academy of Fine Arts, and with Howard Pyle at Drexel Institute. Also studied six years abroad.

MANY people remember the charming interiors in color which appeared in the *Ladies' Home Journal* in the late nineteenth century. From 1902 to 1911 Elizabeth Shippen Green worked exclusively for *Harper's Magazine*. For four years — 1924, 1928, 1932 and 1936 — she designed the Elizabethan Programmes for the Bryn Mawr May Day Fete. Her illustrations for books, magazine covers and magazine drawings are well known. She has been the recipient of a number of medals and prizes. On June 3, 1911, Elizabeth Shippen Green married Huger Elliott. Her home is in the Mt. Airy section of Philadelphia. This information was obtained in part from *Who's Who in America.*

EMERSON, SYBIL

Born 1895 in Worcester, Massachusetts. Childhood was spent first in Chicago, and then in Columbus where Ohio State University was attended. Also studied at art schools in New York and Paris.

" I STARTED to travel at the age of two when my parents moved from Worcester, first to Chicago and then to Columbus, Ohio," Sybil Emerson says. " It was at Ohio State University that I first became interested in art. After graduating, I went to New York and entered a drawing class at the Art Students League and at an evening school. My family moved to California three years later, so I studied painting in San Francisco and Monterey. From there I went to Paris and continued painting and drawing for ten years. My stories grew out of experiences in France. Mural decorations for kindergarten rooms in the American church, and elsewhere, led me to make the sketches of children in Paris and these suggested the theme of the books. My paintings have been exhibited in the Salon d'Automne and Salon des Tuileries, Paris; the Art Institute, Chicago; the San Francisco Art Association; the Academy, Philadelphia, as well as in New York and other cities. At various times I have taught art and am at present teaching at the Pennsylvania State College." Miss Emerson lives at State College, Pennsylvania.

velopment of English and American children's art from Newbery (in 1744) to 1945, including numerous black and white examples of the work of many artists, and one chapter on books from countries other than the United States and England. This takes up the first half of the work; the second half is biographical sketches of more than four hundred living (in 1947) artists, also with examples of work for some. A number of artists can be found both in the historical discussion and the biographical listing.

Part III, Bibliography, is a list of artists, their dates of birth and death, nationalities, and a representative list of their works, also with some illustrations. In addition, there is a Bibliography of Authors with names and titles, a long Bibliography of Sources, Notes and References, a List of Artists Represented by Illustrations, and an Index to Part I. (Part II is alphabetical and needs no index.) The supplements bring the work up to date for the years indicated.

This is a monumental, scholarly work that is indispensible to any adult seriously interested in children's book art, its development, or its artists. It is far too difficult to be used by children, and for that reason should be supplemented by one of the other tools in this chapter intended for their use.

> *Illustrators of Books for Young People,* 2d edition, by Martha E. Ward and Dorothy A. Marquardt. Scarecrow Press, Inc., 52 Liberty Street, P.O. Box 656, Metuchen, New Jersey 08840. 1975. 223pp. $8.

Illustrators of Books for Young People is an alphabetical listing of brief (usually a fairly short paragraph) biographical sketches of 750 illustrators of books for children. The artists included are of many different nationalities, but almost all have had books published in English. Each entry has the illustrator's name and dates, a simply written summary of the person's career, including where he or she was born and has lived and studied, and several representative titles for children; it is not an attempt to be a complete listing of the person's work. There is no analysis or description of style or technique, as in the preceding work. All the Caldecott winners may be found here, and most entries have one or more notations at the end which refer the user to one of the three volumes of *Illustrators of Children's Books* (above) or to *Authors of Books for Young People,* also by Ward and Marquardt. It is therefore a kind of index as well as providing information. There is a title index. This book can be used directly by children, as it is quite easy to use. Each entry is brief but has enough information to be sufficient in many instances.

McDERMOTT, Gerald. A filmmaker and artist, he was
    born in Detroit, Michigan. Mr. McDermott and his
    artist wife have lived in France. He was the recipi-
    ent of the Blue Ribbon at the American Film Festival
    for the film version of his book <u>Anansi the Spider</u>,
    adapt. and illus. by G. McDermott (Holt, 1972).

MacDONALD, James. Born in Scotland, he later lived in
    Roslyn, New York. He studied art in both Scotland
    and the United States. He has worked in advertising
    in addition to illustrating books and book jackets,
    maps, and title pages. Mr. MacDonald has enjoyed
    travel and painting (watercolors) in Maine. For young
    people he illustrated C. Rourke's <u>Davy Crockett</u> (Har-
    court, 1934) and O. Hall-Quest's <u>Jamestown Adventure</u>
    (Dutton, 1950).

McDONALD, Ralph J. Naturalist-painter. He has made his
    home in Madison, Tennessee. In addition to illustrat-
    ing books for boys and girls, he has also painted por-
    traits including one for a state governor. His work in-
    cludes B. Carlson's <u>Let's Pretend It Happened to You</u>
    (1973), M. Ward's <u>Ollie, Ollie Oxen-Free</u> (1969), and
    <u>Spooky Tales about Witches, Ghosts, Goblins, Demons,</u>
    <u>and Such</u>, comp. by M. Luckhardt (1972), all for Ab-
    ingdon.

McENTEE, Dorothy, 1902- . She was born in Brooklyn,
    New York where she later attended Pratt Institute.
    She also studied in Chester Springs at the Pennsylvan-
    ia Academy of the Fine Arts. Ms. McEntee has taught
    in a Brooklyn high school in addition to creating water-
    colors which have been exhibited. She also has done
    wood engraving. For boys and girls she illustrated
    her sister, Fran Martin's books, <u>Nine Tales of Raven</u>
    (Harper, 1951) and <u>Pirate Island</u> (Harper, 1955).
    ICB-2

MACHETANZ, Frederick, 1908- . Artist-writer, he was
    born in Kenton, Ohio. He and his wife, author Sara
    Dunn Machetanz have lived in Alaska and Ohio. Fred-
    erick Machetanz studied at Ohio State University and at
    the American Academy of Arts and the Art Institute in
    Chicago. He served with Naval Intelligence during
    World War II. He has been a filmmaker and lecturer
    in addition to a book illustrator. For children he
    wrote and illustrated <u>On Arctic Ice</u> (Scribner's, 1940),

AUTHORS

> *Authors of Books for Young People,* 2d edition, by Martha E. Ward and Dorothy A. Marquardt. Scarecrow Press, Inc., 52 Liberty Street, P.O. Box 656, Metuchen, New Jersey 08840. 1971. 579pp. $17.

Similar in style to Ward and Marquardt's *Illustrators of Books for Young People,* its companion volume, this work has more than two thousand entries for authors of children's books. They are arranged alphabetically and each entry has a brief paragraph of information about the person: where he or she was born and educated; other fields of endeavor (in addition to writing for children); present place of residence; interests and hobbies; and several titles published, with publisher and year of publication. These are merely examples of the person's work and are not intended to be inclusive. Frequent personal touches make the authors seem more real. A symbol at the end of most entries refers the user to entries in *Contemporary Authors* or *Junior Book of Authors, More Junior Authors,* or *Third Book of Junior Authors.* Lists of the Caldecott and Newbery winners are in the back, and biographies of all the recipients of these awards are included. However, the preface explains that preference was given to those authors whose biographies are hard to find elsewhere. Accordingly, some less well-known authors of children's books can be found here. Note that this is an updating of the authors' previous work of the same name which was published in 1964 and supplemented in 1967.

Like its companion volume, *Authors of Books for Young People* can easily be used by children. Considering that there are two thousand entries, children are likely to find information on many of the authors that interest them. Since each entry is a fairly short paragraph, another source will have to be used if more lengthy or in-depth information is needed.

> *Books Are by People, Interviews with 104 Authors and Illustrators of Books for Young Children,* 1969. 349pp. $6.95 ($4.95pb.). *More Books by More People: Interviews with 65 Authors of Books for Children,* 1974. 410 pp. $8.95 ($4.95pb.). Both by Lee Bennett Hopkins. Citation Press, 50 West 44th Street, New York, New York 10036.

As the title suggests, these are interviews with authors and illustrators of children's books, all conducted by Hopkins. Each is usually about two or three pages long and has an illustration of the person interviewed and a sample from the person's work if an illustrator. A list titled Some Other Books at the end of the interview includes the titles of books other than

Authors of Books for Young People

A

ABRAHAMS, Robert David 1905-
Attorney and author, Robert Abrahams has been on
the staff of the Law School at Temple University in
Philadelphia and has also been associated with a
prominent law firm in that city. He has been a
Trustee of the School of Law at Dickinson College
in Carlisle, Pennsylvania. Mr. Abrahams has written prose and verse for magazines, and for young
people he wrote Bonus Of Redonda, Macmillan, 1969.

ACHESON, Patricia Castles 1924-
She was born in New York City and attended Bryn
Mawr College in Pennsylvania. She has been a history
teacher in Boston and has also taught at the Madeira
School in Washington. She and her attorney husband
have lived in Washington, D. C. Her books for young
people include: America's Colonial Heritage, Dodd,
1957; Our Federal Government: How It Works, Dodd,
1969. CA-3

ACKER, Helen
Born in Niagara Falls, New York, she received her
B. A. and M. A. degrees from the University of Min-
nesota. She has taught in Puerto Rico and at the
University of Minnesota. She married Arthur B.
Anderson, and they have lived in Minneapolis. She
wrote Five Sons Of Italy, Nelson, 1950.

ADAMS, Ruth Joyce
Author and teacher, she has made her home in San
Pedro, California. Mrs. Adams has been a music
teacher in the schools of Los Angeles. Her poetry
and stories have been published. Her first book for
children was Mr. Picklepaw's Popcorn, Lothrop, 196

ADAMS, Samuel Hopkins 1871-
He graduated from Hamilton College where he

5

those discussed in the article. The tone is quite informal, and both books are easy to read and were written for children's use. They are not intended to provide complete biographies. Many anecdotes and personal glimpses of the person's life are included.

The first volume is limited to authors and illustrators for children from preschool to grade three, of fiction and poetry, not nonfiction; obviously, since it is based on interviews, the book is confined to living authors and illustrators. The second volume adds sixty-five more people, and the articles tend to be rather longer.

The informal tone of these books may appeal to some children; however, a number of interviews verge on the coy in an effort to be personal. There is more information than in *Authors of Books for Young People*. A similar work is *Junior Book of Authors* and its two supplements.

> *Famous Author-Illustrators for Young People*, by Norah Smaridge. Dodd, Mead and Company, 79 Madison Avenue, New York, New York 10016. 1973. 160pp. $3.95.

This is a group of fairly short articles (usually eight to ten pages) about nineteen authors and/or illustrators of books for children. The approach is biographical rather than critical and has a generally laudatory tone. (It may be even too inclined to show lives in a rosy light; the statement that Beatrix Potter was never "unhappy or bored" as a child has been contradicted by other biographers, for example.) Some of the entrants may be hard to find elsewhere, however—Lenski, Turkle, Ungerer, and Anglund, for instance, although inclusion of the latter may be somewhat questionable. (Brief biographical sketches can be found of most of these people, but not longer articles.) It is unfortunate that women are almost always referred to by their first names and men by their surnames or a combination of first and last name. The index is by author-title-subject.

The work is easy to read and could be used by older children, but it is not the best source for this type of information; it could be used to supplement other collective biographies. The photographs of some of the people add interest but, unfortunately, there are no sample illustrations of artists' work.

> *Junior Books of Authors*, 2d edition, edited by Stanley J. Kunitz and Howard Haycraft, 1951. 309pp. $10. *More Junior Authors*, edited by Muriel Fuller, 1963. 235pp. $10. *Third Book of Junior Authors*, edited by Doris de Montreville and Donna Hill, 1972. 320pp. $12. All published by H. W. Wilson Company, 950 University Avenue, Bronx, New York 10452.

The *Junior Book of Authors* series has the distinctive quality of having biographies written as often as possible by the authors themselves.

Eleanor Estes

May 9, 1906-
AUTHOR OF
*The Moffats, The Hundred Dresses,
Rufus M., Etc.*

Autobiographical sketch of Eleanor Estes:

THE town of West Haven, Connecticut, where I was born, is in a hollow with hills behind it, the New Haven harbor and Long Island Sound lapping against two sides, and a small river meandering along its eastern margin. It was a perfect town to grow up in. It had everything a child could want, great vacant fields with daisies and buttercups, an occasional peaceful cow, and even a team of oxen with whose help cellars for new houses were dug.

There were marvelous trees to climb, woods where there were brooks, and springs, and wild flowers growing. There were swimming and building in the sand and fishing and clamming in the summertime, and ice and snow and sliding down hill in the wintertime, with rowboat exploration of the small river for eels and killies in the betweentime. It had all the joys of a small New England town and yet it was near enough to New Haven for special excursions and occasions, such as the circus, or Santa Claus in Shartenberg's.

In this town I was born, and went to school, and learned to spell, and add two to two. When I graduated from the high school there, I went to work in the children's department of the New Haven Free Public Library. In 1928 I was made head of it. The Caroline M. Hewins scholarship for children's librarians was awarded to me in 1931 and I came to New York to study at the Pratt Institute library school. In 1932 I married Rice Estes, then a student and now a professor of library science.

' As a children's librarian I worked in various children's rooms of the New York Public Library until 1940 when my first book, *The Moffats,* was accepted. I scarcely remember when I did not have the idea I wished to be a writer.

Due to my mother's and father's fondness for and interest in them, books have always been an important part of my life. My mother could quote profusely from all the great poets. She had an especial love for Tennyson, Shakespeare, and Heine. And

Arni

ELEANOR ESTES

for the old folk tales. She was very dramatic in her presentation of these and I still shudder when I recall the way she told "Great Claus and Little Claus," which I have never since heard told so well. She had an inexhaustible supply of songs, stories, and anecdotes, fictitious and remembered ones, with which she entertained us as she went about her housework. She took a great joy in painting and drawing, and wrote quantities of light verse, to fit any special occasion, having had herself a wish to become a writer.

Of my father it was said he could add a column a mile long and a mile wide in his head. His name was Louis Rosenfeld and he was born in Bridgeport, Connecticut, of Austrian and Scotch-Irish parents.

My mother was born Caroline Gewecke, in New York City. Her father was of French descent and her mother German, and there were many musicians in the family. "Little old New York," because of our mother's stories, seemed like our second home. Washington Square and University Place, Greenwich Village, the East River and the North River, the Palisades, masquerades in old Madison Square Garden, the Metropolitan Opera House, the dreadful *Slocum* disaster, these, because of her vivid re-creation of them, were extremely real to me, my two brothers, and my sister.

Consequently when, in 1931, I came to live in New York the sensation was rather

(Naturally, some of the authors were no longer living when the volumes were compiled.) Some articles are a combination of the person's own autobiographical remarks and material written by the editors. The length of each biography varies, but is usually at least half a page to several pages long. There is almost always a photograph of the author and often, in the case of illustrators, examples of their work. Dates and some titles are given at the beginning of the entry. Usually, the article includes in the author's or illustrator's own words why she or he writes or illustrates for children. The overall tone of most articles is modest but not critical, and the articles are easy to read and can be used by children or adults. Entries are alphabetical by pen name.

Each of the first two volumes has about three hundred entries, the third has about 250. Some very well known people whose biographies could easily be found elsewhere are omitted. The third volume is slightly different: each entry consists of the biographee's own remarks followed by information provided by the editors. it has an index to all three volumes by name of biographee, but since the arrangement is alphabetical, this is seldom used. There is a longer list of each author or illustrator's works at the end of each entry rather than the short list at the beginning in the other two volumes. Also added is a reference to where other biographical material for that person may be found.

Like *Authors of Books for Young People* or *Books Are by People,* the *Junior Book of Authors* series can be used directly by children. Altogether there are about 850 entries compared to about two thousand for *Authors of Books for Young People.* However, there is considerably more information about each person and the illustrations add much. *Books Are by People* and *More Books by More People,* on the other hand, consist of interviews with about 170 authors and illustrators and are similar in that they provide photographs and follow an informal style.

> *Something About the Author: Facts and Pictures About Contemporary Authors and Illustrators of Books for Young People,* edited by Anne Commire. Gale Research Company, Book Tower, Detroit, Michigan 48226. Volumes 1-9: vols. 1 and 2, 1971; vol. 3, 1972; vols. 4 and 5, 1973; vol. 6, 1974; vol. 7, 1975; vols. 8 and 9, 1976. $25 each.

There are entries in the nine volumes in this set for about 1,800 authors or illustrators of books for children. Each entry includes such categories as Personal, Career, Writings (both for adults and for children), and Sidelights (comments by or about the biographee). There is usually a photograph of the person, and often a sample illustration from a book or from its movie version. For some entries categories titled Work in Progress and Avocational Interests are also included. Sources are given at the end of

NESS, Evaline (Michelow)   1911-

PERSONAL: Born April 24, 1911, in Union City, Ohio; daughter of Albert and Myrtle Woods (Carter) Michelow; married Eliot Ness (associated with F.B.I.), 1938 (deceased); married Arnold A. Bayard, 1959. *Education:* Studied at Ball State Teachers College, 1931-32, Chicago Art Institute, 1933-35, Corcoran Gallery of Art, Washington, D.C., 1943-45, Academia Della Belles Artes, Rome, Italy, 1951-52. *Home:* 45 Sutton Pl. South, New York, N.Y. 10022.

CAREER: Artist, tapestry designer, illustrator and author of children's books. *Member:* Society of Illustrators (New York, N.Y.). *Awards, honors:* First prize for painting, Corcoran Art Gallery, Washington, D.C.; *All in the Morning Early*, *A Pocketful of Cricket*, and *Tom Tit Tot* have been runners up for the Caldecott Medal; Caldecott Medal for *Sam, Bangs and Moonshine*, 1967.

WRITINGS: Josefina February, Scribner, 1963; *A Gift for Sula Sula*, Scribner, 1963; *Exactly Alike*, Scribner, 1964; *Pavo and the Princess*, Scribner, 1964; *A Double Discovery*, Scribner, 1965; *Sam, Bangs and Moonshine*, Holt, 1966.

Illustrator: *Story of Ophelia*, by Mary J. Gibbons, Doubleday, 1954; *Bridge*, by Charlton Ogburn, Houghton, 1957; *Lonely Maria*, by Elizabeth Jane Coatsworth, Pantheon, 1960; *Where Did Josie Go?*, by Helen E. Buckley, Lothrop, 1962; *All in the Morning Early*, by Sorche Nic Leodhas, Holt, 1963; *A Pocketful of Cricket*, by Rebecca Caudill, Holt, 1964; *Tom Tit Tot: An English Folk Tale*, by Virginia Haviland, Scribner, 1965; *Favorite Fairy Tales Told in Italy*, by Virginia Haviland, Little, 1965; *Pierino and the Bell*, by Sylvia Cassedy, Doubleday, 1966; *Josie's Buttercup*, by Helen E. Buckley, Lothrop, 1967; *Mr. Miacca*, Holt, 1967; *The Truthful Harp*, by Lloyd Alexander, Holt, 1967; *Kellyburn Braes*, by Sorche Nic Leodhas, Holt, 1968.

SIDELIGHTS: "On a small island, near a large harbor, there once lived a fisherman's little daughter (named Samantha, but always called Sam), who had the reckless habit of lying." Thus begins the story of Sam and Bangs, the cat, related along with the delicate fantasies, the "Moonshine," that Sam spins. "You get so mixed up when you're little," Miss Ness told Ann Durell. "You make up what you want to be true, be real, and then you say it's so, and you believe it. Then you're absolutely

165

each entry for biographical and critical information about the person. Each volume has alphabetical entries for A to Z—the set is *not* divided like an encyclopedia with certain letters in certain volumes. There is an index in each volume by illustrator, but no author index is needed since the entries are alphabetical. Also, volume 2 has an index to volumes 1 and 2, by author and by illustrator; volume 5 has a cumulative index for volumes 1 to 5, also by illustrator and by author, and each subsequent volume (6, 7, 8, and 9) has cumulative indexes for the entire set up through that volume.

Something About the Author was written for children to use. It is a large set, both in physical size and in the number of authors and illustrators included. Naturally, it is more expensive than some smaller volumes which may either have fewer entries or less information about each person. It is necessary to purchase all nine volumes, of course, to have a complete set; the cost and advantages of this should be weighed against how much use children in a particular library will make of it. Where use will be heavy, it will probably be well worth the cost. Where use of authors' and illustrators' biographies is slight, a smaller volume might be acceptable, or could serve until the library can afford this set. It is an ongoing work with a new volume approximately every year.

> *The Who's Who of Children's Literature,* compiled and edited by Brian Doyle. Schocken Books, Inc., 200 Madison Avenue, New York, New York, 10016. 1968. 380pp. OP.

The Who's Who of Children's Literature consists of biographical essays on mostly British and American children's writers and illustrators. Many of them are important in American children's literature today for their historical influence but are not perhaps still read a great deal by most children. Overall, the book is fascinating reading and could be used by children, but was not intended primarily for them. Each essay is a critical as well as descriptive evaluation of the person's work with many black and white illustrations of authors and illustrators, examples from their books, samples of early magazine covers, and so on. The range is 1800 to the present (1968), and only writers of fiction are included. The first section has about three hundred authors, the second about one hundred illustrators. There are lists of the Carnegie, Kate Greenaway, Newbery, and Caldecott Medal winners. An excellent and lengthy bibliography lists further sources of information on authors and illustrators of children's books and magazines, both collective and individual works.

Although there are a great many sources of information on authors and illustrators of children's books, this is one of the best written and most scholarly. Unfortunately, most children will find it too difficult to use. Adults will probably find it very useful.

1972
A DAY IN THE COUNTRY by Willis Barnstone (Harper) C
AMERICAN PAINTER IN PARIS: A LIFE OF MARY CASSATT by Ellen Wilson (Farrar) YA

International Board on Books for Young People (IBBY) Honor List

Every two years since 1956, on the occasion of the Congresses of the International Board on Books for Young People, an IBBY Honor List is announced. In its early days, books selected for the Honor List were identified by the same jury that selects the recipients of the Hans Christian Andersen Awards. At the present time, each National Section of IBBY selects two books (one for text and one for illustration), published in a two-year period before the year in which they are selected, for an IBBY biennial Congress. Those titles are the Honor Books on the List. In the United States, the books are selected by a committee of the Children's Services Division of the American Library Association. Important considerations in selecting the Honor List titles are that the books chosen be representative of the best in children's literature from each country, and that the books be recommended as suitable for publication throughout the world, thus furthering the IBBY objective of encouraging world understanding through children's literature. The listing below includes only United States Honor List titles. For a listing including all titles, write Children's Book Council (175 Fifth Ave., N.Y., NY 10010). (Certificate) See also Hans Christian Andersen Award.

1956
CARRY ON, MR. BOWDITCH by Jean Lee Latham (Houghton)

MEN, MICROSCOPES AND LIVING THINGS by Katherine Shippen (Viking)
PLAY WITH ME by Marie Hall Ets (Viking)
1958
THE HOUSE OF SIXTY FATHERS by Meindert DeJong (Harper)
1960
ALONG CAME A DOG by Meindert DeJong (Harper)
THE WITCH OF BLACKBIRD POND by Elizabeth George Speare (Houghton)
1962
ISLAND OF THE BLUE DOLPHINS by Scott O'Dell (Houghton)
1964
THE BRONZE BOW by Elizabeth George Speare (Houghton)
1966
WHERE THE WILD THINGS ARE by Maurice Sendak (Harper)
1968
VALLEY OF THE SMALLEST by Aileen Fisher (Crowell)
1970
UP A ROAD SLOWLY by Irene Hunt (Follett)
1972
TRUMPET OF THE SWAN by E. B. White (Harper)
1974
Text: THE HEADLESS CUPID by Zilpha Keatley Snyder (Atheneum)
Illustration: THE FUNNY LITTLE WOMAN retold by Arlene Mosel, ill. by Blair Lent (Dutton)

AWARDS

Children's Books: Awards and Prizes, 1975 Edition, compiled and edited by Catherine Stawarcki. The Children's Book Council, 67 Irving Place, New York, New York 10003. 156pp. $5.95.

Awards and Prizes is a listing by the name of the award of virtually all the American and the important international and foreign (English language) children's book awards, about sixty in all. For each award there is a brief description of its history (when founded and by whom) and the criteria for selection (why the award is given). The form of the award (for example, plaque or citation) is also explained. All the recipients of an award since its inception are listed in chronological order, with the runners-up, if any, and the address for its sponsor. Names of illustrators are included only if the award was for the artwork. Awards that are no longer given are mentioned in the front, as are other sources of information about awards. There is an index by title and one by author/illustrator. A new edition comes out approximately every two years; the price for the 1977 edition is $6.95.

This is the best source of all the winners of many of the well-known and little-known children's book awards. It is simple and easy to use; children could use it as well as adults. The most recent edition should always be purchased, even though it will be slightly out of date near the end of each two-year period.

History of the Newbery and Caldecott Medals, by Irene Smith. Viking Press, Inc., 625 Madison Avenue, New York, New York 10022. 1957. 140pp. OP.

This book discusses John Newbery, Randolph Caldecott, and Frederick Melcher (founder of the two medals), how the Caldecott and Newbery Medals came into being, how they are selected, changes in the selection process over the years, the importance and influence of the medals, and the winners (up to the date of publication), often from a comparative point of view. There is an index by author-title-subject.

This is an easy-to-read and informative little book that should be useful to anyone needing background information on the two medals.

Caldecott Medal Books: 1938-1957, with the Artists' Acceptance Papers and Related Material Chiefly from the Horn Book Magazine, edited by Bertha Mahony Miller and Elinor Whitney Field, 1957. 329pp. $10. *Newbery Medal Books, 1922-1955, with their Authors' Acceptance Papers and Related Material Chiefly from the Horn Book Magazine,* edited by Bertha Mahoney Miller and Elinor Whitney Field, 1955. 458pp. $10. *Newbery and*

Caldecott Medal Books, 1956-1965, with Acceptance Papers, Biographies and Related Material Chiefly from the Horn Book Magazine, edited by Lee Kingman, 1965. 300pp. $12.50 *Newbery and Caldecott Medal Books, 1966-1975, with Acceptance Papers, Biographies and Related Material Chiefly from the Horn Book Magazine,* edited by Lee Kingman, 1975. 321pp. $15. All published by The Horn Book, Inc., 585 Boylston Street, Boston, Massachusetts 02116.

Each volume in this set consists primarily of the speeches made by recipients of the Caldecott or Newbery awards and describes the awards and years covered. Before the text of each speech, there is some background information about the book: for the Caldecott books, information about the format from a technical point of view and a short descriptive paragraph are given; for the Newbery books, there is a longer descriptive annotation including excerpts. The speeches themselves usually deal with how the person writes or illustrates for children, either in general terms or for the book that won the award. In addition to the acceptances, there are biographical or autobiographical sketches for each person, and sections of illustrations from the books, in color for the more recent volumes. Also, the last volume (1966-1975) has a section on the Honor Books, those that are runners-up for the awards. Each volume also has some discussion of the Caldecott and Newbery Awards, and of the writing and illustrating of children's books by authorities other than the award winners.

Since the Newbery and Caldecott are far and away the best-known children's book awards in this country, there may be considerable interest in the acceptance speeches in some libraries, from adults primarily. The biographical sketches are well written and penetrating, but biographical information can be found elsewhere. The acceptance speeches can also be found in individual issues of *Horn Book Magazine.* There is an index by title and one by authors in each volume.

5

Using Books with Children

CURRICULA-RELATED (CLASSROOM)

Today's elementary school teachers often try (or would like to try) to integrate children's library books into classroom use, frequently as part of the language arts program. While publications that deal with the technique of using children's trade books in the classroom are largely outside the scope of this book, a few are included here, with a brief description of their contents, for those who need some assistance. All are written from the point of view of the teacher and generally reflect recent strategies in teaching. These are intended as a few suggestions only and are in no way a complete bibliography on the topic.

> *The Child as Critic: Teaching Literature in the Elementary School,* by Glenna Davis Sloan. Teachers College Press, Columbia University, 1234 Amsterdam Avenue, New York, New York 10027. 1975. 133pp. $4.95pb.

This gives an analysis of the types of literature for children and elements found therein with a strong case for teaching literature as literature for its own sake and for its importance in helping children develop imagination. Many specific examples and some classroom activities are provided.

> *Children's Literature in the Curriculum,* by Dewey W. Chambers. Rand McNally and Company, P.O. Box 7600, Chicago, Illinois 60680. 1971. 227pp. $10.95.

Chambers stresses the qualities in children's library books that can enrich any curricula area and the love of children's books for their own sake. Some titles are suggested in the text, as well as some activities. It is a strong and convincing plea for using chldren's library books in the classroom.

> *Children's Literature in the Curriculum,* by Mary S. Montebello.

William C. Brown Company, 2460 Kerper Boulevard, Dubuque, Iowa 52001. 1972. 158pp. $3.95pb.

Each chapter in this book discusses children's trade books that can be used in teaching units in language arts, the sciences, or aesthetics, with suggested activities based on the entries. There is a bibliography in the back divided by curricula units.

Children's Literature: Strategies of Teaching, by Robert White-head. Prentice-Hall, Inc., 301 Sylvan Avenue, Englewood Cliffs, New Jersey 07632. 234pp. $4.95pb.

Whitehead supplies ideas for using children's library books, particularly in the language arts. Many activities from arts and crafts to games and puzzles to oral and dramatic presentations, all based on children's books and reading, are described. (Forms for written book reports and contests based on the number of books read are included; these are no longer used by some teachers and librarians.) Each chapter has suggestions for further reading. There is a wealth of ideas here.

Enjoying Literature with Children, by Alice M. Meeker. Odyssey Press (Distributed by Bobbs-Merrill Company), 4300 West 62nd Street, Indianapolis, Indiana 46206. 1969. 152pp. $2.96pb.

This is for teachers and parents. There are chapters titled Looking and Listening, Home and Nursery School Years, Culturally Deprived Children, The Library, Book Reports, Storytelling, Poetry, Holidays, and Bulletin Boards. The bibliographies are good, but some ideas seem a little dated by today's standards, such as those for book reports and some of the library usage procedures.

Enrichment Ideas, by Ruth Kearney Carlson. William C. Brown Company, 2460 Kerper Boulevard, Dubuque, Iowa 52001. 1970. 109pp. $3.95pb.

Carlson includes many suggestions (and much information about the books themselves) for ways to use children's books and related activities in the elementary school literature program. Many of the ideas could also be used in teaching science, art, and other subjects.

Literature with Children, edited by Monroe D. Cohen. Association for Childhood Education International, 3615 Wisconsin Avenue, N.W., Washington, D.C. 20016. 1972. 64pp. $2.05pb.

This aid is excellent and inexpensive. Its chapters list very practical suggestions for many ways to use children's books, mostly in the classroom. There is also a list of other ACEI publications for teachers and librarians inside the back cover.

Poetry and Children, by Helen Painter. International Reading Association, 800 Barksdale Road, Newark, Delaware 19711. 1970. 94pp. $4.

There are ways to select and use poetry with contemporary children. The chapters include the actual texts of many poems.

Storytelling and Creative Drama, by Dewey W. Chambers. William C. Brown Company, 2460 Kerper Boulevard, Dubuque, Iowa 52001. 1970. 92pp. $2.50pb.

Approximately half of this book is on storytelling in the classroom, and half is on creative drama for children. Some books are suggested but the concentration is mostly on methods. Ways to integrate both methods into the curriculum are suggested.

Read to Write: Using Children's Literature as a Springboard to Writing, by John Warren Stewig. Hawthorn Books, 260 Madison Avenue, New York, New York 10016. 1975. 263pp. $9.95.

This lists all kinds of ways to teach the usual elements of writing via children's library books *and* audio-visual materials. Creativity in children's writing and modern methods of teaching are stressed.

Also, see the fall 1975 issue of *Reading Teacher* for a list of trade books for use in the classroom, and *El-Hi Textbooks in Print* for all available textbooks.

CURRICULA-RELATED (LIBRARY)

No firm line can be drawn, of course, between classroom and library use of trade books. However, the books in this section are largely written from the point of view of the librarian or for library use, rather than for the classroom teacher. What use is made of them or the books they recommend is, of course, up to the librarians and teachers involved.

A Guide to Subjects and Concepts in Picture Book Format, by the Yonkers Public Library Children's Services. Oceana Publications, 75 Main Street, Dobbs Ferry, New York 10522. 1974. 166pp. $7.50.

This is a listing, not annotated, of children's picture books, divided into more than fifty topics, most of which are further subdivided into smaller topics. Subjects range from concrete items such as fish or toys to concepts such as fear or shape and sizes. There is also a special section on wordless books and a short bibliography for adults.

The preface explains that this is not intended as a buying guide but rather to supplement the card catalog subject headings; some books are listed under a subject or concept that is actually a minor theme in the book. The work was based on questions asked at the Yonkers Public Library, and includes books owned by the library.

Guide to Subjects and Concepts should be used with certain reservations. Enjoyment of picture books should not, in the opinion of many, depend solely on whether a particular subject or concept is exemplified. However, more and more adults, especially parents, are asking for books on specific topics, particularly for small children, so there is probably a need for something of this type. it may be desirable for each individual library to make its own file of subjects and concepts in picture books based on the collection; these can be kept separately or added to the card catalog as additional subject headings. Ordinarily, catalog cards do not include a heading for every possible subject or concept in a picture book, only for perhaps three or four at most.

> *Independent Reading Grades One Through Three: An Annotated Bibliography with Reading Levels,* by Gale Sypher Jacob. Bro-Dart Publishing Company, 1609 Memorial Avenue, Williamsport, Pennsylvania 17701. 1975. 86pp. $3.95pb.

Each entry in *Independent Reading* has full bibliographic information and an annotation. The overall arrangement is by subject (some are further subdivided into smaller subjects) and by author's last name within each category. What makes this aid unusual is that each entry also has the reading level by grade and by first half or second half of that grade (such as 2.1 or 3.2), based on the Spache formula. There are entries for about 850 trade books for use in the classroom or library; many are recent publications (since 1970) although there are quite a few older books as well. They are intended for use in teaching reading or for "independent reading." In addition to reading level, the inclusion of books was based on the probable appeal to children in grades one through three in terms of format. Some well-known selection aids such as *Elementary School Library Collection,* published by the same company, and some journals were consulted in selecting books for inclusion, although some titles were evaluated by the author or by members of the advisory committee. Fiction and nonfiction titles are included.

It is not, of course, common practice to assign such precise reading levels to children's library books, although it is laudable to encourage small children to select books that help them have a feeling of success in reading and to encourage teachers to use trade books to teach reading instead of relying solely on a basal reader. The author herself points out that *Independent Reading* is not intended to tell a child what he or she may or may not read but merely contains suggestions for teachers or possibly librarians who need some guidance in helping children select books. Also, different formulas for computing reading levels sometimes give rather different results, although the Spache formula is one of the best known and most widely used. Some librarians may feel that encouraging individual classroom collections, as suggested in this book, takes away from the centralized library staffed by a professional librarian that many have worked so hard to achieve.

> *Reading Guidance in a Media Age,* by Nancy Polette and Marjorie Hamlin. Scarecrow Press, 52 Liberty Street, P.O. Box 656, Metuchen, New Jersey 08840. 1975. 267pp. $10.

There are all kinds of activities here to help encourage children's love of books. Some are suggestions for home or classroom use, but most are school-library oriented. A section in the back lists annual workshops and conferences about children's literature.

> *Subject Index to Books for Intermediate Grades,* 3rd edition, 1963. 308pp. OP. *Subject Index to Books for Primary Grades,* 3rd edition, 1967. 113pp. OP. Both compiled by Mary K. Eakin. American Library Association, 50 East Huron Street, Chicago, Illinois 60611.

Each volume lists topics likely to be useful for children in the intermediate grades (fourth to sixth) or the primary grades (kindergarten to third) for supplementary material for teaching units. After each subject there is a list of books by author's last name, with title and page numbers if necessary, for that subject. (If there are no page numbers, the entire book will be useful.) An asterisk indicates *fiction.* In the primary volume, the designation RA for Read Aloud followed by a grade level in parentheses indicates the level at which children can understand a book if it is read to them. The symbol IN for Independent Reading, followed by a grade level in parentheses, is the level at which children can read the book themselves, and many books have a combination symbol. In the volume for intermediate grades, only the usual grade levels are given. There are about one thousand entries for the Primary volume and eight hundred for the Intermediate one. It is necessary to refer to the list of books indexed to find full bibliographic information for each book; this is alphabetical by author and has usage levels by grade range and suggested simplified Dewey Decimal Numbers. The books indexed are almost all trade books, but a few texts were included, especially if no good trade books could be found; all entries were chosen for accuracy as well as for literary quality. Generally speaking, the books are nonfiction and realistic fiction rather than fantasy, poetry, or folklore.

These two volumes are badly out of date; they have been included here partly in the hope that they will stimulate teachers and librarians to utilize trade books as part of the curriculum. They should be supplemented with more current materials in most units of study.

STORYTELLING AND RELATED ACTIVITIES

Storytelling is a very worthwhile activity that continues to grow in popularity. Children very much enjoy hearing stories, and it gives them an appreciation of oral language. Originally, folk literature of different kinds, with its rich heritage of oral tradition, was used almost exclusively for storytelling, but today almost any story is used for storytelling. (If it is a picture book, it should be held so all children can see the illustrations.) Many books and pamphlets have been published for storytellers that explain techniques of storytelling and/or give lists of suggested books. An excellent discussion of how to tell stories is in Arbuthnot and Sutherland's *Children and Books*. If at all possible, those planning to do storytelling should see *The Pleasure Is Mutual* (younger children) and *Something About a Story* (older children), two movies which have long been used in storytelling-training workshops and children's literature courses. The pamphlet which accompanies the former, "How to Conduct Effective Picture Book Programs, a Handbook," is one of the best guides to procedure and lists a few suggested books; it can be used even without the movie. It may be ordered from The Children's Book Council, 67 Irving Place, New York, New York 10003.

Following are a few books and pamphlets on storytelling with a brief indication of whether they contain lists of stories to tell, suggestions on how to do storytelling, actual stories, or a combination. Some are reprints of books originally published fifty or sixty years ago, but children like the same stories year after year when they hear them. There are a great number of books on storytelling, so this list is not in any way inclusive.

Children's Stories and How to Tell Them, by Woutrina A. Bone. Gale Research Company, Book Tower, Detroit, Michigan 48226. 1975. (Reprint of 1924 edition) 200pp. $9.

This aid generally concentrates on folk literature as the basis of storytelling. There is a good deal of scholarly information on folk tales and even a discussion of the argument in 1924 of whether folk and fairy tales are bad for children! The texts of several stories and a long annotated bibliography of stories to tell are included. It is British but useful in this country.

Guide to Story Telling, Arthur Burrell. Gale Research Company, Book Tower, Detroit, Michigan 48226. 1971. (Reprint of 1926 edition) 336pp. $13.

This *Guide* provides a long combination of stories to tell (complete texts), background information on stories, techniques of storytelling, and accounts of the author's experiences telling stories to children. It is British but useful in this country with children or young adults.

> *Once Upon a Time,* 2d edition, by the New York Library Association, 60 East 42nd Street, New York, New York 10036. 1964. 16pp. $2.

Here are suggestions on how to plan story hours for young children and a bibliography of recommended books.

> *The Ordinary and the Fabulous, An Introduction to Myths, Legends, and Fairy Tales for Teachers and Storytellers,* 2d edition, by Elizabeth Cook. Cambridge University Press, 32 East 57th Street, New York, New York 10022. 1976. 182pp. $5.95pb.

This is another British publication that focuses on folk literature for storytelling. There is much discussion of different versions of the same story and an annotated bibliography of sources for storytelling. This aid is probably as much for the student of folk literature as for the storyteller.

> *Pre-School Story Hour,* 2d edition, by Vardine Moore. Scarecrow Press, 52 Liberty Street, P.O. Box 656, Metuchen, New Jersey 08840. 1972. 174pp. $6.

Moore mostly deals with planning and implementing a story hour for the youngest children. Some lists of books and related activities are given.

> *Stories, A List of Stories to Tell and to Read Aloud,* 6th edition, compiled by Ellen Greene. New York Public Library, Fifth Avenue and 42nd Street, Room 58, New York, New York 10018. 1968. 78pp. $3pb.

This is a frequently revised, annotated list of about four hundred stories and a few recordings. For each story, several places may be given where it can be found, since many are in collections. There is an index by country of origin of the stories. The original list was one of the earliest lists of stories to tell children, and the New York Public Library has long been known for its storytelling activities. A revision is expected soon.

> *Stories to Tell to Children, A Selected List,* 8th edition, by Laura E. Cathon, Marion McC. Hausholter, and Virginia Russell. University of Pittsburgh Press, 127 North Bellefield Avenue, Pittsburgh,

Pennsylvania 15260. 1974. 145pp. $3.50pb.

This is an unannotated list of stories to tell to children of different ages with a special section on holiday programs. There are also aids for the storyteller (a list of sources) and a very complete subject index. The first edition of this list came out in 1916.

Storyteller's Choice, A Selection of Stories, with Notes on How to Tell Them, by Eileen Colwell. Henry Z. Walck, Inc., 750 Third Avenue, New York, New York 10017. 1964. 223pp. $6.50

Here is a collection of the texts of twenty stories to tell with special instructions in the back for each one and an indication of which are easy and which more difficult. The book was followed in 1965 by Storyteller's Second Choice, also by Colwell.

The Way of the Storyteller, revised edition, by Ruth Sawyer. Viking Press, 625 Madison Avenue, New York, New York 10022. 1962. 350pp. $4.50 ($3.45pb).

Originally published in 1942, this is one of the best-known books on storytelling. Background information on folk tales and techniques of storytelling is included.

In addition, a new Handbook for Storytellers, by Caroline Feller Bauer, appeared in the spring of 1977, published by the American Library Association, and Telling Stories to Children, by Sylvia Ziskind, was published by H.W. Wilson Company too late in 1976 for inclusion.

EXHIBITS, FAIRS, AND PROMOTIONS

Good promotion of books and reading should be an integral part of the library's function. It can stimulate interest among both children and adults—there is something special about owning a book of one's own even to the child who has access to many library books. Adults often like to buy gift books for children, and almost everyone enjoys looking at a new, attractive display of books, even if no purchases are actually made at that time. For the disadvantaged child, owning a book may be the beginning of untold wonders.

In addition to the sources listed below, many companies or jobbers (middlemen between publishers and libraries) offer preselected book fairs. Also, the RIF Program, in the section on Multiethnic Sources, is a very good promotional activity.

Children's Book Showcase, by Children's Book Council, Inc., 67 Irving Place, New York, New York 10003. Prices as described.

The Children's Book Council is a nonprofit organization of publishers devoted to the furthering of children's books and reading. One of their many activities is an annual showcase of children's books which a panel of judges selects every year primarily for the excellence of their graphic artistry. Usually, about twenty-five books are selected each year, including picture books, and fiction and nonfiction for older boys and girls. Anyone can sponsor a showcase — libraries, community organizations, or individuals. The list of books for each year and a pamphlet on how to organize a showcase can be obtained by sending a self-addressed, stamped envelope to the address above. A catalog of the current (1977) showcase, which gives a sample illustrated double-page spread from each book, and technical information on the book's format and the judge's opinion, is $9.95. The catalogs are interesting even without the books to display, and anyone planning a showcase should have one or more catalogs for patrons to look through. (Because of their rather technical nature and small type, adults rather than children will be most likely to read them.) Posters and bookmarks to promote the showcase are also available. The showcases began in 1972, and catalogs for past years are available for $5.95.

Anyone interested in having a showcase must make her or his own arrangements for getting the books, as Children's Book Council does not provide them. Sometimes a local library or state library will have most or all of the titles and will loan them, or a local bookstore may agree to provide them for exhibit. (Books are not usually sold at a showcase exhibit, but it can be done; arrangements would have to be made with the bookseller if someone were to take orders or actually sell copies of the books on the spot.) The books could also be purchased outright through the usual channels and then added to the collection after the exhibit. Some schools or public libraries cooperate with other libraries in the area, with each individual library buying some of the books, to be retained after the exhibit. Many who come to the showcase will be amazed at the quality children's books can achieve, especially if they are only familiar with inexpensive "variety store" types of children's books. This is all to the good.

For more information on the wealth of other services and materials provided by the Children's Book Council, see the entries for *Calendar* and *Recipe for a Book Fair,* or write to CBC directly at the above address for a brochure of publications and materials.

> *Guide to Better Bulletin Boards, Time and Labor-Saving Ideas for Teachers and Librarians,* by Kate Coplan and Constance Rosenthall. Oceana Publications, Inc., 75 Main Street, Dobbs Ferry, New York 10522. 1970. 232pp. $17.50

Guide to Better Bulletin Boards consists of instructions on how to make several hundred bulletin boards for children, many of which are based on books. Each has an illustration, sometimes in color, of how the finished bulletin board should look, plus a list of materials and instructions. In the back are patterns for drawings which provide plans for many of the needed objects and which may be copied as is or enlarged via the instructions. There are a list of suppliers if all the materials are not available locally (they often will be) and some related readings. The index is by subject in the back and there is an alphabetical list of illustrations by the "title" of the bulletin board in the front.

There are many good ideas for bulletin boards here, and readers are encouraged to use their own creativity to make others of their own. Children love bulletin boards, especially if they are changed often! Coplan also has two other, earlier books on bulletin boards: *Effective Library Exhibits: How to Prepare and Promote Good Displays* (Oceana Publications, 1958); and *Poster Ideas and Bulletin Board Techniques: For Libraries and Schools* (Oceana Publications, 1962).

> *Planning a School Book Fair,* by Sarah Chokla Gross. Children's Book Council, Inc., 67 Irving Place, New York, New York 10003. 1970. 24pp. OP.

This little pamphlet explains in very practical terms exactly how to plan and run a successful book exhibit or fair. It is written for parents or others who wish to sponsor a fair, but could certainly be used by librarians or teachers as well. A section at the back shows sample press releases, order forms, and an organization chart. An earlier publication also by the Children's Book Council, *Recipe for a Book Fair* (1962, 47 pp., O.P.), also has some good suggestions.

FOSTERING A LOVE OF BOOKS

While many of the aids already discussed may encourage a love of books in one way or other, there are some books expressly designed to do this. These are written for adults, especially parents, to help them foster a love of books in their children. Any librarian or teacher who has worked with children who come from homes where books are a part of everyday life will know what a joy this can be. Every library should have some of these for those parents or other relatives who ask for ways to help their children learn to love books; some librarians and teachers might do well to read them themselves.

> *Bequest of Wings, A Family's Pleasure with Books.* 1944. 207pp. OP. *Longer Flight; A Family Grows Up with Books.* 1955. 269pp.

OP. Both by Annis Duff. Viking Press, Inc., 625 Madison Avenue, New York, New York 10022.

When Annis Duff wrote *Bequest of Wings,* television was yet to come into general usage, and childhood had an innocence and lack of conflicting activities that few children know today. Nevertheless, her books stand as an inspiration to anyone who believes, or does not yet know, how much children can enjoy books and how easy and natural the process of bringing this about can be. Duff relates how she and her husband encouraged their two children to love books and includes some mistakes they made. It is written in the style of personal reminiscence and is easy and enjoyable to read. *Longer Flight* carries the story on through the children's adolescence. These two books will probably be most suitable for the family of good educational background, with parents who are themselves familiar with many children's books.

Best-Selling Children's Books, by Jean Spealman Kujoth. Scarecrow Press, Inc., 52 Liberty Street, P.O. Box 656, Metuchen, New Jersey 08840. 1973. 305pp. $8.50.

Best-Selling Children's Books is an annotated listing by author of nearly one thousand children's books that have sold the most copies (100,000 or more) and are still in print. There is also an unannotated list of the books by title, as well as others by illustrator; year of publication; number of copies sold; and type, subject, and age level.

This title should be used for an indication of the popularity of a book only in situations where sheer numbers sold is important. It might, however, give some indication of books that might appeal to children, keeping in mind that most children's books are not actually purchased by children. Another selective aid used in conjunction with *Best-Selling Children's Books* should give a better picture of a book's literary and artistic merit as well as popularity.

The Calendar, published by the Children's Book Council, Inc., 67 Irving Place, New York, New York 10003. $5 for life.

The *Calendar* is a twice-a-year publication of the Children's Book Council. (See *Children's Book Showcase* above.) It is packed full of all kinds of information about happenings in the children's book world, artists, authors, critics, speakers, publishers and publications, news of free and inexpensive materials, ideas for using books and other media with children, special annotated bibliographies, and more. There is a one-time charge of $5 to be placed on the mailing list for Calendar; Also, the brochures listing and describing all CBC publications will come twice a year. These materials, in addition to the Showcase Catalog and Prelude (discussed later) are generally promotional material related to children's books and reading. The council sponsors summer reading programs and National Children's Book Week (always the third week in November) and cooperates with many other organizations in developing special booklists and programs. Many posters, bookmarks, friezes, and other materials are available to advertise such events. Newbery and Caldecott Medal bookmarks may be purchased for $4.25 per hundred.

It is well worth the $5 fee to keep up with what is going on in children's books and to have access to purchasing display material. Good public relations should form an integral part of children's library work.

> *In What Book?*, by Ruth Harshaw and Hope Harshaw Evans. Macmillan Publishing Company, Inc., 866 Third Avenue, New York, New York 10022. 1970. 130pp. $5.95.

This entire book consists of sets of questions and answers based on children's books. It is divided into For the Very Young (three to six), For Young Readers (four to eight), For Readers in the Middle Years (eight to twelve), and For Older Readers (twelve up). For each question the answer is the name of a book and its author or the name of a character in a book. (Most are simply the title of a book.) Children with a wide knowledge of books will probably enjoy playing with this sort of thing; it should not be used as a form of examination, nor did the authors intend it to be, because it is based almost totally on simple recall. The child who has little knowledge of children's books will simply be baffled by it. There is an index by author-title.

> *Introducing Books: A Guide for the Middle Grades,* by John J. Gillespie and Diana L. Lembo. R.R. Bowker Company, 1180 Avenue of the Americas, New York, New York 10036. 1970. 318pp. $12.50.

Introducing Books is intended for "teachers and librarians who are giving reading guidance and book talks to children and young adults between the ages of nine and fourteen" (preface, p. xv). It is arranged by broad topics: Getting Along in the Family; Making Friends; Developing Values; Understanding Physical Problems; Forming a World View; Respecting Living Creatures; Evaluating Contemporary Problems; Identifying Adult Roles; Learning to Think Abstractly; Appreciating Books; and Reading for Fun. Each section has eight books on its topic. There is a synopsis of the plot (usually several pages long), thematic material (explanations of the theme of the book), book talk material (suggestions on what to include in the talk, points to stress, and passages to read aloud), and additional suggestions (other similar books, filmstrips, films, and so on). The work was based to some extent on the results of questionnaires sent to children, teachers, and librarians and partly on the quality of the books. Therefore, it has a good many books that are popular with children and young adults. Various reading levels are covered in each chapter, but no age or grade levels are given; the user must decide which books will appeal to which ages, although the terms "younger," and "older" readers are sometimes used. Fiction only is included. (Nonfiction books, except for biographies, are rarely used for book talks.)

Unfortunately, many of the books are recommended for boys or for girls; this is true in all the sections, not just in Identifying Adult Roles. Some books, on the other hand, are recommended for both boys and girls, and some have no gender designated and are presumably for either sex. The statement will sometimes be found that the book is recommended for boys but also enjoyed by girls! In the chapter titled Identifying Adult Roles, six of the eight books have boys as the main characters and the two that feature girls show them accepting traditional roles. While the book's intention is probably merely to suggest which books will appeal mostly to which sex (a topic of much bitter debate among librarians in recent years), overall the book seems very sexist for something published in 1970. Two things must be pointed out, however: books talks are particularly designed to encourage children to read books solely on their own volition, so the gender designations may be justified, and the labels can be omitted in practice.

There is an author and title index, with an asterisk for those books fully discussed and a subject index arranged by more specific topics than the eight chapter headings. Girls' stories but not boys' stories are listed.

This book and its companion volume *Juniorplots* (see below) are for anyone inexperienced in giving book talks who needs to know where to begin. It is also perfectly possible to give book talks simply from one's own knowledge of and love of books. Using either of these titles could be a good starting point and the librarian and teacher could branch out after getting an idea of what to include. One word of warning: some librarians do not allow children access to these books because they fear children will copy the plot summaries in lieu of written book reports! This is not a problem where written book reports have been superceded by other and better methods of teaching.

> *Juniorplots: A Book Talk Manual for Teachers and Librarians,* by John T. Gillespie and Diana L. Lembo. R.R. Bowker Company, 1180 Avenue of the Americas, New York, New York 10036. 1967. 222pp. $10.95.

This book preceded *Introducing Books* (above); it also is a book guide to giving book talks for children and young adults from nine to sixteen, a slightly different range from *Introducing Books*. (*Introducing Books,* however, has somewhat more material for fifth and sixth graders than does *Juniorplots.*) The same format is followed, and the categories are: Building a World View; Overcoming Emotional Growing Pains; Earning a Living; Understanding Physical Problems; Making Friends; Achieving Self-Reliance; Evaluating Life; and Appreciating Books.

Introducing Books may be preferred to *Juniorplots* because it is slightly more up to date and somewhat more geared to children rather than young adults. Some titles in *Juniorplots* seem a little dated.

> *Let's Read Together, Books for Family Enjoyment,* selected and annotated by a Special Committee of the National Congress of Parents and Teachers and the Children's Services Division of the American Library Association, 3rd edition. American Library Association, 50 East Huron Street, Chicago, Illinois 60611. 1969. 103pp. $2.

Let's Read Together is an annotated bibliography of nearly six hundred children's books, designed primarily for parents to use with their children. The books are arranged by categories and by age ranges within categories. Some reference books and books for parents' use are also included. The latter are activity books to use with children, sex education books, and books about children's books. There is also a list of series books (fiction), some of which are annotated in the body of the work. There is a title and author index, but no subject index. Parents are encouraged to either buy these books for their children or to borrow them from libraries. It is a good standard list of titles, but may be overwhelming to some parents who do not really want so lengthy a list.

> *A Parent's Guide to Children's Reading,* 4th revised edition, by Nancy Larrick. Doubleday and Company, Inc., 245 Park Avenue, New York, New York 10017. 1975. 432pp. $8.95 (Bantam Books, Inc., 666 Fifth Avenue, New York, New York 10019. $1.95pb.)

This book differs from others in this section in that it includes not only suggested books, but also much information on how parents can help their children to read and enjoy reading. The chapters are generally a combination of information about reading skills, reading interests, what parents can do, and suggestions of recommended books that are likely to be popular with children (with descriptive discussions). There are about fifty sample illustrations (in black and white) interspersed throughout the text. More than seven hundred popular children's books are discussed in all, and the influence of television on children's reading is considered. Many kinds of audio-visual materials are also discussed. There is a bibliography in the back, Books They Like, which has annotations and reading age levels as well as an audio-visual bibliography and one of materials for the adult.

Parent's Guide to Children's Reading stresses how much parents can help children with reading by getting them involved in reading (and in the spoken language). Since many parents are very much concerned with their children's lack of ability to read well, they will welcome this guide. The patron who merely wants some brief suggestions for a good children's book should probably be given a shorter, simpler list. Note the very inexpensive price for the paperback edition.

> *Reading Interests of Children and Young Adults,* compiled by Jean Spealman Kujoth. Scarecrow Press, Inc., 52 Liberty Street, P.O. Box 656, Metuchen, New Jersey 08840. 1970. 449pp. $11.

This is a collection of articles, fifty-five in all, which were originally published in various journals such as *Publishers Weekly* or *Elementary English* (now *Language Arts*) in the 1940s, 1950s, or 1960s. Some appeared in British journals. They are divided into sections by ages from the youngest children through high school, with one section on the exceptional child. All the authors have worked with children and books in some capacity, and they give their observations, sometimes by relating experiences with individual children, sometimes by charts showing the interests of groups of children, of what children *like* to read. There are author and subject indexes.

Any attempt to use accounts of children's reading interests must take into consideration that individual children vary widely in what they like, based on their backgrounds and experience, as well as their facility with reading. In using the Kujoth book, it should also be remembered that many of the articles are rather old, and children today are somewhat different from children of the 1950s and 1960s. (Television has had a large influence on reading habits.) Nonetheless, some books go on being popular for generations. See *Proof of the Pudding* in the bibliography for more information on this topic. Some of the old "rules" of what children like and don't like are no longer considered valid.

> *Prelude: Mini-Seminars on Using Books Creatively,* by the Children's Book Council, 67 Irving Place, New York, New York 10003. Series 1 (three cassettes of six talks), $42.40. Series 2 (three cassettes of six talks), $47.50. Includes five supplementary booklets per set. Additional booklets are $1.95 for 1-4, $1.50 for 5-10, $1.10 for 11-100, and $.75 each for more than 100.

The *Prelude* sets are unlike any other of the aids in this book. Each set, designed for librarians, teachers, and other adults who work with children and books, consists of thirty-minute talks by six well-known children's literature specialists on an aspect of using books with children. The first series has these topics and speakers: Bringing Books to Life

Through Drama, by Virginia Reid; Reading Books and Asking Questions, by Jack Fraenkel; Reading Poetry Aloud, by Sam Sebesta; Reading Prose Aloud, by Zena Sutherland; Science Books and Young Children, by Glenn O. Blough; and Storytelling, by Augusta Baker. Series 2 consists of: Children's Responses to Books, by Charlotte S. Huck; Encouraging Families to Read Together, by Lavinia Russ; Enjoying Poetry with Children, by Leland B. Jacobs; Fantasy and the Human Condition, by Lloyd Alexander; Good Science Teaching Develops the Whole Child, by Roma Gans; and Using Folklore as an Introduction to Other Cultures, by Anne Pellowski. The tapes feature suggestions on how to use books with children, how to evaluate different types of children's literature, or the values to children in various types of children's books. The supplementary booklets have summaries of the tapes and lists of related books.

This is an excellent set of tapes, which should have something of interest for almost anyone, from prose to poetry, from fantasy to science. They are undeniably expensive, but any library that can possibly afford it should definitely consider purchasing one or both sets.

In addition to the books and cassettes already mentioned, the following pamphlets make good giveaway material:

> Choosing a Child's Book, Children's Book Council, 67 Irving Place, New York, New York 10003. 1973. 50 copies for $2.95.

> Reading Aloud to Children, American Library Association, Children's Services Division, 50 East Huron Street, Chicago, Illinois 60611. 1967. 20 copies for $1, 125 copies for $5, 500 copies for $15.

> Reading Begins at Home, American Library Association, Children's Services Division, 50 East Huron Street, Chicago, Illinois 60611. 1974. $.05.

Always send a self-addressed, stamped envelope for a single free copy of this type of material.

6

Technical Processes

ORDERING

Obtaining the exact information needed for filling out the order forms or purchase orders in a particular library sometimes causes difficulties, although many schools or public libraries now have a centralized system. There may be complete bibliographic information in the reviewing journal or, more rarely, in a comprehensive book-selection aid. If not, these tools should help. Many libraries today prefer to order from a jobber rather than directly from book and/or audio-visual companies.

> *Children's Books in Print, An Author, Title and Illustrator Index to Children's Books.* R. R. Bowker Company, 1180 Avenue of the Americas, New York, New York 10036. Annual. $25.

This tool is simply a listing of all the children's books in print, that is, available for purchase from publishers or distributors in the United States. Each entry consists of complete bibliographic information only. The key to abbreviations in the front and the section on how to use *CBIP* will explain any unfamiliar symbols or numbers. Note that there is *no* indication of quality or content of a book. It should *not* be used for selection except in unusual cases, as good, bad, and indifferent books are all listed, about forty thousand titles in all. Each book is entered by author, title, and illustrator; it can be found if any one of these three facts is known. The publishers are abbreviated by initials, but the listing in the back gives complete names and addresses; this is the best place to find correct addresses for more than five hundred publishers of children's books. Many children's libraries find that they need *CBIP* for verifying ordering information. There is also a *Subject Guide to Children's Books in 7000 Categories,* published by the same company. This uses the same titles as *CBIP* but arranges them by subject headings. It can be helpful in cases where the title has been forgotten but will be recognized when seen or when all the available children's books on a subject are needed, not a normal procedure for most children's libraries; selecting books from *Subject Guide* would only be done in very unusual circumstances.

Audio-Visual Market Place, A Multimedia Guide, edited by J. A. Neal. R. R. Bowker Company,1180 Avenue of the Americas, New York, New York 10036. 1976. 394pp. $19.95.

Audio-Visual Market Place is primarily a guide to the names and addresses of producers and distributors of audio-visual software (the actual media) and hardware (basically, the machines on which the software is used). The type(s) of media or machines each company makes and/or sells is also given. No individual titles of any media are listed, however. The arrangement is alphabetical by name of company for producers and distributors, with indexes by type of media and by subject area. There are also names and addresses for production companies who do not do audio-visual programming or distribution themselves but produce material written by others. There are some other related materials such as reference books and journals about media and funding sources. *Audio-Visual Market Place* is useful for verifying names and addresses; it is not a selection aid.

Index to Instructional Media Catalogs, A Multi-Indexed Directory of Materials and Equipment for Use in Instructional Programs. R. R. Bowker Company, 1180 Avenue of the Americas, New York, New York 10036. 1974. 272pp. $21.50.

This is a subject index to the catalogs of companies which produce media for schools in various curricula areas. It is arranged by broad subject areas, and subdivided into smaller ones. Suggested grade levels are given, but there are no individual media titles. There is also a directory of producers of hardware and related equipment and a complete name and address directory. After finding a citation in this *Index*, one must look in the catalog of the appropriate company. In no way is this a selection tool, as there is no evaluation of the media.

NICEM Index to Educational Audio Tapes, 4th edition, 1977, $47pb. *Index to Educational Overhead Transparencies,* 5th edition, 1977, $75.50pb. *Index to Educational Records,* 4th edition, 1977, $47pb. *Index to Educational Slides,* 3rd edition, 1977, $42.50pb. *Index to Educational Video Tapes,* 4th edition, 1977, $29.50pb. *Index to 16mm. Educational Films,* 6th edition, 1977, $109.50pb. *Index to 35mm. Filmstrips,* 6th edition, 1977, $86.50pb.

All these tools furnish bibliographic information with annotations of the indicated type of media. The arrangements are alphabetical by title with subject indexes, and both individual title and series entries are used.

There are, however, no prices, so that information must be obtained elsewhere, such as from a review, a publisher's catalog, or by writing directly to the distributor. NICEM also publishes an *Index to Producers and Distributors*, 4th edition, 1977, $21.50pb, or see the previous entry. The address is: University of Southern California National Information Center for Educational Media (NICEM), University Park, Los Angeles, California 90007.

CATALOGING

Some children's libraries today still do what is known as original cataloging, that is, they make their own sets of cards to go in the card catalog. They must decide what information to put on the card and its correct form, assign a Dewey Classification Number, and reproduce in some form the appropriate number of cards to make up a complete set for a given book. At least one course in cataloging and classification at a library science school is the best background for this, but this is not always possible. Some libraries, on the other hand, rely almost entirely on sets of printed cards which they purchase from a supplier. Three sources of these printed cards are Baker and Taylor Company, *Library Journal/ School Library Journal,* and the Library of Congress. The latter, although produced by the Library of Congress, have Dewey Decimal Numbers, not Library of Congress Classification Numbers for children's books. (For many years the H. W. Wilson Company also provided catalog cards, but no longer does so.)

A few sources that may be of help to a librarian faced with doing original cataloging and classification are: *Commonsense Cataloging, A Manual for the Organization of Books and Other Materials in School and Small Public Libraries,* by Esther J. Piercy, 2d edition revised by Marian Sanner (H. W. Wilson Company, 950 University Avenue, Bronx, New York 10452. 1974. 229pp. $8) which includes directions for dealing with both books and audio-visual materials; *Abridged Dewey Decimal Classification and Relative Index,* 10th edition, by Melvil Dewey (Forest Press, Inc., 85 Watervliet Avenue, Albany, New York 12206. 1971. $12); *Sears List of Subject Headings,* 10th edition, edited by Barbara M. Westby (H. W. Wilson Company, 950 University Avenue, Bronx, New York 10452. 590pp. $12), and *Typewritten Catalog Cards: Manual of Procedure and Form,* 2d edition, by Russell E. Bidlack and Constance Rinehart (Campus Publications, 713 Ellsworth Road, Ann Arbor, Michigan 48104. 1970, $5.25pb.). For ideas on ways to utilize volunteer help, see *The School Library Volunteer,* by Lillian Biermann Wehmeyer (Libraries Unlimited, Inc., P.O. Box 263, Littleton, Colorado 80160. 1975. 122pp. $7.50). State Departments of Education often can provide a manual of procedure for the clerical aspects of running a library/media center.

MB Nubook Cards (P.O. Box 166, Western Springs, Illinois 60558) provides summaries of reviews of children's and young adult books from many of the major reviewing journals. For audio-visual materials, Educational Film Library Association, 43 West 61st Street, New York, New York 10023, has a similar service.

Appendix 1
Organizing and Running the
Library/Media Center

The past few years have seen a great increase in the number of books devoted to the planning, staffing, and day-to-day operations of the library/media center. This topic is not directly related to sources of information about children's books and media and the answering of reference questions, except insofar as physical facilities and personnel, as well as the collection, certainly have a direct relationship to how well children's needs are served. The following are merely a few suggestions of some recent books for those wishing to pursue the matter of equipping and operating their libraries and the philosophy of their existence and use. They are not by any means a definitive listing of all possible sources. A few books to help teach children how to use the library are also included.

For a list of inexpensive materials on school media centers and related matters, many of them reprints from *School Media Quarterly*, write for the *Checklist of Materials*, American Association of School Librarians, 1201 16th Street, N.W., Washington, D.C. 20036. Many of these publications cost only $.25 or $.50.

SCHOOL

Blueprint for Better Reading, School Programs for Promoting Skill and Interest in Reading, by Florence Damon Cleary. Wilson, 1972.

Certification Model for Professional School Media Personnel, by the American Association on School Librarians. American Library Association, 1976.

Creating a School Media Program, by John T. Gillespie and Diana L. Sprit. Bowker, 1973.

Developing a Successful Elementary School Media Center, by Lillian Glogau, Edmund Krause, and Miriam Wexler. Parker Publishing, 1972.

Developing Methods of Inquiry: A Source Book for Elementary Media Personnel, by Nancy Polette. Scarecrow, 1973.

Elementary School Libraries, by Jean E. Lowrie. Scarecrow, 1970.

The Elementary School Library, by Margaret L. Brewer and Sharon O. Willis. Shoe String, 1970.

Instructional Design and the Media Program, by William E. Hug. American Library Association, 1975.

The Instructional Media Center: Bold New Venture, edited by Harold S. Davis. Indiana University Press, 1971.

Library Instruction in the Elementary School, by Melvyn K. Bowers. Scarecrow, 1971.

Library Media Center Problems: Case Studies, by Louis Coburn. Oceana, 1973.

Media Personnel in Education: A Competency Approach, by Margaret E. Chisholm and Donald P. Ely. Prentice-Hall, 1976.

The Media Program in the Elementary and Middle School: Its Organization and Administration, by Jack J. Delaney. Linnet Books, 1976.

Media Programs, District and School, by the American Association of School Librarians and the Association for Educational Communications and Technology. American Library Association, 1975. (Replaces *Standards for School Media Programs,* 1969.)

A Model School District Media Program, by John T. Gillespie. American Library Association, Summer 1977.

The Modern School Library, by Helen E. Saunders, 2d edition completely revised by Nancy Polette. Scarecrow, 1975.

Pathfinder: An Occupational Guide for the School Librarian, by Patricia Freeman. Harper and Row, 1975.

Problems in School Media Management, by Peggy Sullivan. Bowker, 1971.

The School Librarian as Educator, by Lillian Biermann Wehmeyer. Libraries Unlimited, 1976.

School Libraries Worth Their Keep, A Philosophy Plus Tricks, by Caroline Leopold. Scarecrow, 1972.

The School Library and Educational Change, by M. Rossoff. Libraries Unlimited, 1971.

The School Library at Work, Acquisition, Organization, Use and Maintenance of Materials in the School Library, by Azile Woffard. Wilson, 1959.

The School Library Media Center, by Emanuel T. Prostano and Joyce S. Prostano. Libraries Unlimited, 1971.

The School Library Media Center: A Force for Educational Excellence, 2d edition, by Ruth Ann Davies. Bowker, 1974.

School Library Media Center Procedures, by A. M. Tillin. Demco Educational Corporation, 1973.

The School Media Center: A Book of Readings, compiled by Pearl L. Ward and Robert Beacon. Scarecrow, 1973.

School Media Programs, Case Studies in Management, by Emanuel T. Prostano. Scarecrow, 1970.

Steps to Service, A Handbook of Procedures for the School Library Media Center, by Mildred L. Nickel. American Library Association, 1975.

A Systematic Process for Planning Media Programs, by James W. Leisener. American Library Association, 1976.

Teaching for Better Use of Libraries (Contributions to Library Literature no. 9), selected by Charles L. Tunkner. Shoe String, 1969.

The Vodka in the Punch, and Other Notes from a Library Supervisor, by Nancy Polette. Linnet Books, 1975.

PUBLIC

Children Are People, the Librarian in the Community, by Janet Hill. Crowell, 1973.

An Introduction to Children's Work in Public Libraries, by Dorothy M. Broderick. Wilson, 1965.

Public Libraries and School Libraries, Their Roles and Functions, by the Kitchener Public Library, 1970.

Public Library Service to Children, by Elizabeth Henry Gross. Oceana, 1967.

Public Library Service to Children: Foundation and Development, by Harriet G. Long. Scarecrow, 1969.

Standards for Children's Services in Public Libraries, by the Subcommittee on Standards for Children's Services, Public Library Association. American Library Association, 1964.

The Right to Read and the Nation's Libraries, by the American Association of School Librarians. American Library Association, 1974.

Appendix 2
Criteria for Evaluating a
Children's Book

Often the question arises: How are children's books selected for inclusion in an aid, for a favorable review in a journal, or for purchase for a children's library? Some of the ways a child's book may be evaluated are listed below. These criteria are quite common and are found in many textbooks on children's literature and in the aids themselves. All the criteria would not likely apply to any one book.

LITERARY QUALITY

Does the book have a good plot? Usually for children this will mean a plot with some action.

Is there good characterization, with real-seeming, believable characters and no stereotyping of any group or peoples? This is true of fantasy as well as of realism—the characters may be fantastic and do impossible things, but their essential personalities must "ring true." The dialogue should be natural and appropriate for the characters who are speaking. This may vary a great deal from one book to another, even from one character to another.

If there is a theme, it should be substantial and of some interest to children; be careful in this regard—not all books have a theme and it is not necessary that they do. There should be a distinctive as opposed to a pedestrian style.

ARTISTIC QUALITY

Almost any kind of art may be appropriate for a children's book; the *quality* of the artwork is what is important. Full color, partial color, black and white, and combinations of these are all acceptable. Photographs are sometimes used, more often in nonfiction than in fiction. A few recent children's books have no words at all, only illustrations.

APPEAL TO CHILDREN

A book of outstanding literary and artistic quality will do little good for a child who never reads, hears, or sees it. Forced reading is not always a good answer to this problem, as it may foster a dislike of reading.

FORMAT (PHYSICAL MAKEUP)

The physical appearance of a book should be appropriate to its content and to the age of the child reading it. The size of a book for a small child may vary from the larger size of a good many picture books, perhaps 10" by 12" to something as small as Beatrix Potter's "Tale" books (4" by 5 1/2"); a few are even smaller. Of course, there are all sizes in between. Be careful of a book that is too heavy for a small child to hold unaided. (Very small children, however, may be looking at books only with an adult's assistance, so Mother Goose books, for example, may be quite heavy, since the child will not use them alone.) Older children, on the other hand, are embarrassed to be seen with a "baby book" and prefer books that more closely approximate adult books in size. The same is true of picture book format for older readers, no matter how poorly they read. The size of type, its placement on the page, and the size, style, and placement of illustrations must be taken into consideration in regard to the age of the child. Durability of paper and binding must be suitable for library use.

USEFULNESS IN LIBRARIES

Today there are a few topics that children are not interested in or might not be studying in school. Nevertheless, it is necessary to make judgments as to which books will be the most useful in a library situation, since there is rarely money or shelf space to buy everything. Treatment of the subject matter may do as much as anything to make a book useful for a children's library.

CONCEPTS AND SUBJECTS

These must be understandable and suitable to a child of the age for which the book is intended. However, no rigid age or grade levels are usually assigned to library books, only a broad indication.

NONFICTION BOOKS

Accuracy is the most important criterion. Also, the books should have a logical organization and be clearly written with no contrived conversation. The illustrations should be appropriate, in the right place, and correctly identified. The right amount of detail is important, so that children are neither overwhelmed nor bored. Headings and subheadings, a table of contents, a bibliography, and an index are important features.

SPECIAL CASES

An easy vocabulary and simple sentence structure may be necessary for children who are having difficulty reading; this does not, however, mean a rigidly controlled vocabulary. Ordinarily, library books are not written for a specific age or grade, or from a controlled list of words.

Appendix 3
Further Reading

FOR THE SCHOLAR, STUDENT, OR ADULT
(INCLUDING HISTORICAL ASPECTS)

Annotations are provided for those of particular interest.

Adventures in Understanding, Talks to Parents, Teachers, Librarians, by Lois Lenski. Friends of Florida State University, 1968.

Afro-American History: An Annotated, Selected Bibliography, by Beryle Banfield. New York City Board of Education, 1969.

All Mirrors Are Magic Mirrors, Reflections on Pictures Found in Children's Books, by Welleran Poltarnees. Green Tiger, 1973.

American Children Through Their books, 1700-1835, by Monica Kiefer. University of Pennsylvania Press, 1970

American Diversity: A Bibliography of Resources on Racial and Ethnic Minorities for Pennsylvania Schools, Pennsylvania Department of Education, 1969.

American Picturebooks, From Noah's Ark to the Beast Within, by Barbara Bader. Macmillan, 1976.

Animal Books (formerly *Animal Books for Children*), by the American Humane Association. This is an annotated listing of animal books reviewed and recommended by the association; it is currently out of print but some copies are still available. It may be revived if interest warrants.

An Annotated Bibliography of Books and Short Stories on Childhood and Youth, by the Council of Social Work Education, 1968.

An Annotated Checklist of Children's Stories with Settings in Cities Outside the United States, 1960-1971, by Deane C. Dierksen. Unpublished research paper. Catholic University of America, 1972. This is a good source but was omitted from the text because of its unavailability to many librarians. It has paragraphs, sometimes long, of descriptive and sometimes critical annotations of 104 recent books from twenty-eight countries, including forty-three cities. Each book is in English, either originally or in translation. It has no nonfiction and no fantasy — realistic fiction only. The books were selected mainly from *Children's Catalog, Books for Elementary School Libraries, Horn Book. Booklist, School Library Journal, What Is a City?* (by Rose Moorachian), *Books to Build World Friendship,* and *The World in Children's Picture Books* and included on the basis of good literary quality and an accurate portrayal of ordinary life in the particular city. Those that met all criteria have asterisks. Some that did not are also included. Grade levels are given. There are few, if any, similar publications this recent.

Anthology of Children's Literature, 5th edition, by Edna Johnson, Evelyn R. Sickels, Frances Clarke Sayers, and Carolyn Horovitz. Houghton Mifflin, 1977.

The Art of Art for Children's Books, by Diana Klemin. Clarkson N. Potter, 1966.

Artists of a Certain Line, A Selection of Illustrations for Children's Books, by John Ryder. Bodley Head, 1960. The artists are mostly British but many are well-known in the United States. This is more for the scholar or student than the average children's library.

Authors and Illustrators of Children's Books, Writings on Their Lives and Works, compiled by Miriam Hoffman and Eva Samuels. Bowker, 1972. Articles on fifty contemporary children's authors and illustrators which originally appeared in various sources, written by different authors are included. There are mostly American authors and artists. A combination of biographical and literary criticism, it could be used by older children.

A Basic Book Collection for Elementary Grades, compiled by Miriam Snow Mathes. American Library Association, 1960. This tool consists of annotations of one thousand books for grades K-8. The compiler was assisted by fifteen consultants from the American Library Association, the Association for Childhood Education International, the Association for Supervision and Curriculum Development, and the Department of Classroom Teachers of the National Science Teachers Association, as well as fifteen other consultants who are knowledgeable about children and books. Primarily, the list is designed to be a beginning collection for a small elementary school, or as the basis for a collection in a larger school. It is intended to supply curriculum and "reading interest" needs. Each entry has bibliographic information and a short paragraph, often only a sentence or two, of annotation. Arrangement is by DDC (65.5 percent of the titles), fiction (21.5 percent), and picture books and easy books (13 percent). To ensure good balance, the compiler and consultants predetermined the number of books they felt should be included for each subject. Also, some of the annotations have references to other books on the topic, either to extend the collection in that area or to meet special needs. There is a short section at the beginning of the book, Tools for the School Librarian, which consists of about twenty professional books; a section near the end lists and describes a few magazines for children, subject to qualifications in the review.

Behavior Patterns in Children's Books, by Clara J. Kircher. Kircher, 1966.

Between Family and Fantasy, by Joan Aiken. Library of Congress, 1972.

Beyond Words: Mystical Fancy in Children's Literature, by James E. Higgins. Teachers College Press, 1970.

Bibliographic Survey: The Negro in Print, Five Year Subject Index, 1965-1970, compiled by Dolores C. Leffall. Negro Bibliographic and Research Center, 1971.

A Bibliography of Materials by and about Negro Americans for Young Readers, by Miles M. Jackson, Mary W. Cleaves, and Alma L. Gray. Office of Education, 1967.

A Bibliography of Negro History and Culture for Young Readers, by Miles M. Jackson. University of Pittsburgh Press, 1968.

A Bibliography of American Children's Books Printed Prior to 1821, by D'Alte

Welch. University Press of Virginia, 1972.

A Bibliography of Australian Children's Books, by Marcie Muir. Academy, 1971.

Bibliophile in the Nursery: A Bookman's Treasury of Collectors' Lore on Old and Rare Children's Books, edited by William Targ. Scarecrow, 1957.

Biennale of Illustrations Bratslavia, 1971, 1973, edited by Anna Urblikova. The Horn Book, 1976.

Black Children and Their Families: A Bibliography, by Charlotte J. Dunmore. R and E Research Association, 1976.

Bokbladet (Book Leaf). This is a Norwegian school library publication with articles on children's literature and school libraries.

The Black Man in America, An Overview of Negro History and Bibliography and Basic Booklist for K-12, by Maria Mercedes Lannon. Afro-American Curriculum Studies Project, Philadelphia Public and Parochial Schools, 1969.

The Black Story: An Annotated Multi-Media List for Secondary Schools. Montgomery County Public Schools, Department of Educational Media and Technology, Rockville, Maryland, 1969.

Blowing in the Wind, Books on Black History and Life in America, by Effie Lee Morris. Children's Services, San Francisco Public Library, 1969.

Book for Children's Literature, 3rd edition, selected and edited by Lillian Hollowell. Holt, Rinehart, and Winston, 1966.

A Book of Nursery Songs and Rhymes, edited by S. Baring-Gould. Singing Tree, 1969.

Books, Children, and Men, by Paul Hazard. The Horn Book, 1960.

Books for Beginning Readers, by Elizabeth Guilfoile. National Council of Teachers of English, 1962.

Books in Search of Children, Speeches and Essays, by Louise Seaman Bechtel. Macmillan, 1940.

Books Related to Compensatory Education, by Lois B. Watt and Myra H. Thomas. Library of Congress, 1966.

Books Related to English Language and Literature in the Elementary and Secondary Schools, by Lois B. Watt and Delia Goetz. Library of Congress, 1970.

Books Related to the Social Studies in the Elementary and Secondary Schools, by Lois B. Watt and Delia Goetz. Library of Congress, 1969.

Books to Build World Friendship: An Annotated Bibliography, by Judith W. Chase. Oceana, 1964.

A Bridge of Children's Books, by Jella Lepman. American Library Association, 1969.

Books, Young Children, and Reading Guidance, 2d edition, by Geneva H. Pilgrim and Marian K. McAllister. Harper and Row, 1968.

Canadian Children's Literature. Quarterly.

Caroline M. Hewins: Her Book, by Caroline M. Hewins. The Horn Book, 1954.

The Child and His Book, by Louise F. Field. Gordon. 1892. (Reprinted by Gale Research Company, 1968.)

The Child and His Picture Book, by LaVerne Freeman and Ruth Sunderline Freeman. Century House, 1967.

Children's Books and Reading, by Montrose J. Moses. 1907. (Reprinted by Gale Research Company, 1975.)

The Child's First Books, A Critical Study of Pictures and Texts, by Donnarae MacCann and Olga Richard. Wilson, 1973.

Children and Fiction: A Critical Study of the Artistic and Psychological Factors Involved in Writing Fiction for and about Children, by Wallace Hildick. World, 1970.

Children Are Centers for Understanding Media, by Monroe D. Cohen and Susan Rice. Association for Childhood Education International, 1973.

Children Experience Literature, by Bernard Lonsdale and Helen K. Mackintosh. Random House, 1973.

Children and Their Literature, by Constance Georgiou. Prentice-Hall, 1969.

Children's Books in English in an African Setting, 1914-1964, by Maureen B. Sewtiz. University of Witwatersrand, Johannesburg, 1965.

Children's Books in England: Five Centuries of Social Life, by F. J. Darton, R. West, 1932.

Children's Books of Yesterday, by Phillip James. 1933. (Reprinted by Gale Research Company, 1976.)

Children's Books of Yesterday, edited by Percy H. Muir. 1946. (Reprinted by Gale Research Company, 1970.)

Children's Books to Enrich the Social Studies for the Elementary Grades, by Helen Huus. National Council for the Social Studies, 1966.

Children's Books, Views and Values, revised edition, by Fritz J. Luecke. Xerox, 1973.

Children's Bookshelf, by the Child Study Association of America, 1965.

Children's Classics, by Paul Heins, 5th edition updated by Alice M. Jordan. The Horn Book, 1976.

Children's Interracial Fiction, An Unselective Bibliography, by Barbara Jean Glancy. American Federation of Teachers, 1969.

Children's Literature in Education. Four times a year. This journal consists of articles on British children's literature, some on American.

Children's Literature in the Elementary School, 3rd edition, by Charlotte S. Huck. Holt, Rinehart, and Winston, 1976.

Children's Literature, Old and New, by Virginia M. Reid. National Council of Teachers of English, 1964.

Children's Literature: Views and Reviews, by Virginia Haviland. Lothrop, Lee and Shepard, 1973.

Children's Literature (formerly *Children's Literature: The Great Excluded*). Annual by Temple University Press.

Children's Periodicals of the Nineteenth Century, by Sheila Egoff. Library Association, 1951.

Children's Picture Books, Yesterday and Today, An Analysis, by Rush S. Freeman. Century House, 1967.

Children's Reading in the Home, by May Hill Arbuthnot. Scott, Foresman, 1969.

The Classic Fairy Tales, by Iona and Peter Opie. Oxford University Press, 1974.

A Comparative Anthology of Children's Literature, by Mary Ann Nelson. Holt, Rinehart and Winston, 1972.

Creative Growth through Literature for Children and Adolescents, by Margaret C. Gillespie and John W. Connor. Merrill, 1975.

A Critical Approach to Children's Literature, by James Steel Smith. McGraw-Hill, 1967.

A Critical Handbook of Children's Literature, by Rebecca J. Lukens. Scott, Foresman, 1976.

A Critical History of Children's Literature, revised edition, by Cornelia Meigs, et al. Macmillan, 1969.

Cumulative Book Index, A World List of Books in the English Language. Monthly. H. W. Wilson Company. This tool is a title, author, and subject approach to bibliographic information.

A Descriptive Study of the Literature for Children and Adolescents of Mexico, by Isabel Schon. Ph.D. dissertation, University of Colorado, 1974.

Down the Rabbit Hole, Adventures and Misadventures in the Realm of Children's Literature, by Selma G. Lanes. Atheneum, 1971.

Early American Children's Books, by A. S. W. Rosenbach. 1933. (Reprinted by Kraus, 1966.)

Early Children's Books and Their Illustrations, by D. R. Godine. Pierpont Morgan Library, 1975. This book is beautiful and fascinating; it has many illustrations, some in color.

Education Index. Monthly. H. W. Wilson Company. This index has citations by author and subject to articles about education.

Fables from Incunabula to Modern Picture Books, by Barbara Quinnan. Library of Congress, 1966.

Fifty Years of Children's Books, by Dora V. Smith. National Council of Teachers of English, 1963.

Films in Children's Programs, A Bibliography, by the Film Committee of the Children's and Young People's Services Section of the Wisconsin Library Association, 1972. 39p. OP. This consists of rather lengthy annotations, including suggestions for use, of about one hundred films for children in grades three to six. In addition to the bibliographic information there is a well-written description that usually refers to several other films as well. Both producers and distributors are given as well as title, length, color or black and white, and price. It is somewhat geared to Wisconsin since ordering or borrowing information is given for that state, but it can be useful elsewhere. It has a simple alphabetical arrangement and includes both fiction and nonfiction films. A few of the films, however, seem difficult even for sixth graders. There are also appendixes on Aids for Library Use (a bibliography of books and articles on using films with children), Sources for the Selection of Films—Basic Aids, and Periodicals. These may all suggest further readings for anyone interested in more information about films for children. A small section at the end has some films for adults who are interested in using books with children. It was omitted from the section on audio-visual materials because it is out-of-print and no longer available, but it should be helpful in those libraries that already have, or have access to, a copy, as it is not particularly dated. Plans for a revision are presently indefinite.

Forgotten Children's Books, by Andrew W. Tuer. 1898. (Reprinted by Arno Press, 1969.)

From Childhood to Childhood, Children's Books and Their Creators, by Jean Karl. John Day, 1970.

From Primer to Pleasure in Reading, 2d edition, by Mary F. Thwaite. The Horn Book,

1972.

From Rollo to Tom Sawyer and Other Papers, by Alice M. Jordon. The Horn Book, 1948.

The Girl Sleuth: A Feminist Guide, by Bobbie A. Mason. Feminist Press, 1975.

The Green and Burning Tree: On the Writing and Enjoyment of Children's Books, by Eleanor Cameron. Atlantic Monthly Press, 1969.

Guidelines for Improving the Image of Women in Textbooks. Scott, Foresman, 1972.

Guidelines for Nonsexist Use of Language. National Council of Teachers of English, 1976.

The Hewins Lectures, 1947-1962, edited by Siri Andrews. The Horn Book, 1963.

History in Children's Books, by Zena Sutherland. McKinley, 1967.

Honey for a Child's Heart, the Imaginative Use of Books in Family Life, by Gladys Hunt. Zondervan, 1969.

Horn Book Reflections: On Children's Books and Reading; edited by Elinor W. Field. The Horn Book, 1969.

Horn Book Sampler: On Children's Books and Reading, edited by Norma R. Fryatt. The Horn Book 1959.

I Can Read It Myself; Some Books for Independent Reading in the Primary Grades, by Frieda M. Heller. Ohio State University, 1965.

I Could a Tale Unfold: Violence, Horror and Sensationalism in Stories for Children, by P. M. Pickard. Humanities Press, 1961.

Illustrating Children's Books, by Henry Pitz. Watson-Guptill, 1963.

Integrated School Books, by the NAACP Education Department, 1967.

Introducing Books to Children, by Aidan Chambers. The Horn Book, 1975.

An Introduction to Children's Literature, by Mary J. Lickteig. Merrill, 1975.

Junior Bookshelf. Bimonthly. British journal which carries reviews of children's books and articles about children's literature.

Library Literature: An Author and Subject Index to Selected Material on Library Science and Librarianship. H. W. Wilson Company. Bimonthly with cumulation every two years. Similar in format to *Reader's Guide to Periodical Literature,* it indexes articles from nearly two hundred journals. Look under Children's Literature for extensive citations or under the name of a particular children's book for citations to specific reviews.

Literature for Children: Enrichment Ideas, 2d edition, by Ruth K. Carlson. William C. Brown, 1976.

Literature for Children: History and Trends, by Margaret Gillespie. William C. Brown, 1970.

Literature for Children: Illustrations in Children's Books, 2d edition, by Patricia J. Cianciolo. William C. Brown, 1976.

Literature for Children: Its Discipline and Content, by Bernice E. Cullinan. William C. Brown, 1971.

Literature for Children: Poetry in the Elementary School, by Virginia Wituche. William C. Brown, 1970.

Literature for Disadvantaged Children, compiled by Lois B. Watt. Department of Health, Education, and Welfare, 1968.

Literature for Thursday's Child, by Sam Sebasta. Science Research Associates,

1975.

A Little History of the Horn-Book, by Beulah Folmsbee. The Horn Book, 1942.

Louisa May Alcott, A Centennial for Little Women, compiled by Judith C. Ullom. Library of Congress, 1969.

Margin for Surprise, About Books, Children, and Librarians, by Ruth Hill Viguers. Little, Brown, 1964.

A Moral Tale: Children's Fiction and American Culture, 1820-1960, by Anne Scott McLeod. Shoe String, 1975.

My Roads to Childhood, by Anne Carroll Moore. The Horn Book, 1961.

The Negro Teacher in Schoolroom Literature, Resource Materials for the Teacher of Kindergarten through the Sixth Grade, by Minnie W. Koblitz. Center for Urban Education, 1966.

Negroes in American Life, An Annotated Bibliography of Books for Elementary Schools, by the Department of Educational Media and Technology, Montgomery Public Schools, 1968.

A New Look at Children's Literature, by William Anderson, et al. Wadsworth, 1972.

Nonbook Materials, A Bibliography of Recent Publications, edited by Hans Wellisch. University of Maryland, 1975.

Non-Sexist Education for Young Children: A Practical Guide, by Barbara Sprung. Women's Action, 1976.

On Children's Literature, by Isabelle Jan. Schocken Books, 1974

Only Connect: Readings on Children's Literature, by Sheila Egoff, G. T. Stubbs, and L. F. Ashley. Oxford University Press, 1969.

The Origin and Development of the ABC Book in English from the Middle Ages through the Nineteenth Century, by Susan Steinfirst. Ph.D. dissertation, University of Pittsburgh, 1975.

The Osborne Collection of Early Children's Books, 1566-1910. Toronto Public Library, 1958.

The Oxford Nursery Rhyme Book, by Peter and Iona Opie. Oxford University Press, 1967.

Pages and Pictures from Forgotten Children's Books Brought Together and Introduced to the Reader, by Andrew W. Tuer. 1899. (Reprinted by Gale Research Company, 1969.)

The Paperback Goes to School, A Basic Resource Paperback Guide for Teachers, Librarians, and School Administrators, edited by Dominic Salvatore. Bureau of Independent Publishers and Distributors, 1972. This is a collection of articles by various people about how paperbacks can be used in library or classroom programs. Not all are for use with children—"school" is used to mean high school and college as well as elementary school. The "Selected Bibliography of Periodical Articles, Pamphlets, Booklists, and Books about Paperbacks of Special Interest for Schools, 1965-72" has some books for children.

Paperbacks in the Elementary School: Their Place, Use, and Future, by Mary Lou Kennedy. Weekly Reader, 1969.

Phaedrus: A Newsletter of Children's Literature Research. Twice a year by Fairleigh Dickinson University. *Phaedrus* provides abstracts of theses, dissertations, and articles about children's literature but does not duplicate material abstracted in *Children's Literature Abstracts.*

Picture-Book World, Modern Picture-Books for Children from Twenty-Four Countries with a Bio-Bibliographical Supplement by Elisabeth Waldman, by Bettina Hurlimann, translated by Brian W. Alderson. World, 1969. (First published in 1965.) This is a copiously illustrated discussion of picture books in twenty-four countries, including American and British. Also by the author, *Three Centuries of Children's Books in Europe.*

The Pied Pipers, Interviews with the Influential Creators of Children's Literature, by Justin Wintle and Emma Fisher. Paddington Press, 1975. The title consists of interviews with twenty-three twentieth-century authors and/or illustrators of children's and young adult fiction. Each interview begins with a page or two of introduction to the person's work, written by the interviewer, followed by questions and answers. The approach is autobiographical combined with literary criticism. Many of the interviewees discuss childhood—their own, their children's, or in general. Often the person's work is shown in its relationship to the mainstream of American and British literature. (The interviewees are both American and British.) There is a list of titles for each author/illustrator at the end of each article, not inclusive, and occasional illustrations from a person's work in black and white.

Poetic Composition through the Grades: A Language Sensitivity Program for Teachers, by Robert A. Wolsch. Teachers College Press, 1970.

Preliminary Bibliography of Selected Children's Books about American Indians, by the Association on American Indian Affairs. 1961.

Problems Encountered by Characters in Children's Fiction, 1945-1965, by Zara Natali. University of Witwatersrand, Johannesburg, 1967.

Proof of the Pudding, by Phyllis Fenner. John Day, 1957. This lists popular (as of 1957) as well as good books; the chapters are arranged by children's interests, and the style is anecdotal.

Questions to an Artist Who Is also an Author, by Virginia Haviland. Library of Congress, 1971.

Radio Plays for Children, selected and arranged by Katherine Williams Watson. Wilson, 1947.

Reading about Children's Literature, by Evelyn R. Robinson. McKay, 1965.

Reading Interests of Young Children, by George W. Norwell. Michigan State University Press, 1974.

Reading with Children, by Anne Thaxter Eaton. Viking, 1940.

Real Negroes, Honest Settings, Children's and Young People's Books about Negro Life and History, by Darathula H. Millender. American Federation of Teachers, 1967.

Realms of Gold in Children's Books, by Bertha Mahony Miller and Elinor Whitney. Doubleday, Doran, 1929.

Recipe for a Magic Childhood, by Mary Ellen Chase. Macmillan, 1952

Recommended Materials for a Professional Library in the School, revised edition, compiled by the Committee on Professional Materials. Michigan Association of School Librarians, 1969.

Recommended Reading about Children and Family Life. Annual publication of the Child Study Association of America.

Reference Materials for Young People, revised and enlarged edition, by Muriel

Lock. Linnet Books and Clive Bingley, 1971. This work discusses mostly British children and young adult reference books.

The Reluctant Reader, by Aidan Chambers. Pergamon, 1969.

Resources for Environmental Ecological Education in Elementary and Secondary Schools, by Lois D. Watt and Myra H. Thomas. Library of Congress, 1971.

Rise of Children's Reviewing in America, 1865-1881, by Richard L. Darling. Bowker, 1968.

Science and Mathematics Books for Elementary and Secondary Schools, by Lois B. Watt and Delia Goetz. Library of Congress, 1970.

Science for Youth: An Annotated Bibliography for Children and Young Adults, by Hannah Logasa. McKinley, 1967.

A Sense of Story: Essays on Contemporary Writers for Children, by John Rowe Townsend. Lippincott, 1971. This book is comprised of essays on nineteen children's authors—American, British, and Australian. The articles are more critical than biographical—somewhat similar to *Who's Who of Children's Literature* which, however, is somewhat more biographical in tone. All the people included are living authors of children's fiction. There is a brief biographical paragraph at the start of each essay, then the literary criticism, which covers all the author's major works, not just a single title. There are remarks by the author at the end of each essay and a bibliography for that author. Overall, there are more British authors than any other nationality. This is a good work for the student or scholar of children's literature, but is not suitable for children's use. Children's libraries should consider having it, however, so that the librarian, teachers, and other adults can see, if they do not already know, the high level literary criticism for children's literature can obtain, and can consult it as well for information about the authors.

Serving Those Who Serve Children, by Virginia Haviland. Library of Congress, 1966.

The Spirited Life: Bertha Mahony Miller and Children's Books, by Eulalie Steinmetz Ross. The Horn Book, 1974.

A Study of the Portrayal of the American Indian in Selected Children's Fiction, by Lenore Dusold. Unpublished master's report. Long Island University, 1970. Unfortunately, this is not readily available.

Subject and Title Index to Short Stories for Children, by the American Library Association, 1955.

Subject Collections in Children's Literature, edited by Carolyn Field. Bowker (for the American Library Association), 1969.

Summoned by Books, by Frances Clarke Sayers. Viking, 1965.

Teachers' Guide to Children's Books, by Nancy Larrick. Merrill, 1960.

Teaching the Reading of Fiction: A Manual for Elementary School Teachers, by Elizabeth Parker. Teachers College Press, 1969.

That Eager Zest, First Discoveries in the Magic World of Books, An Anthology, compiled by Frances Walsh. Lippincott, 1961.

The Teachers Library, How to Organize It and What to Include, by the National Education Association, 1966.

Thirty Mid-Century Children's Books Every Child Should Know, by Ethel Heins. The Horn Book, 1973.

The Thorny Paradise: Writers on Writing for Children, edited by Edward Blishen. The Horn Book, 1975.

Three Centuries of Nursery Rhymes and Poetry for Children, by Peter and Iona Opie. Oxford University Press, 1973.

Time for Biography, compiled by May Hill Arbuthnot and Dorothy M. Broderick. Scott, Foresman, 1969.

Time for New Magic, compiled by May Hill Arbuthnot and Mark Taylor. Scott, Foresman, 1971.

Time for Old Magic, compiled by May Hill Arbuthnot and Mark Taylor. Scott, Foresman, 1970.

Time for Poetry, 3rd edition, compiled by May Hill Arbuthnot and Shelton L. Root. Scott, Foresman, 1968.

Time for Stories of the Past and Present, compiled by May Hill Arbuthnot and Dorothy M. Broderick. Scott, Foresman, 1968.

The Tragic Mode in Children's Literature, by Carolyn T. Kingston. Teachers College Press, 1974.

Translated Children's Books Offered by Publishers in the U.S.A., by Storybook International, 1968.

Understanding Peoples of the Non-Western World, revised edition, by Bernice Helff. University of Northern Iowa, 1968.

The Unreluctant Years, A Critical Approach to Children's Literature, by Lillian H. Smith. American Library Association, 1953.

The Uses of Enchantment: The Meaning and Importance of Fairy Tales, by Bruno Bettelheim. Knopf, 1976.

Using Literature with Young Children, by Leland B. Jacobs. Teachers College Press, 1965.

The Vertical File and Its Satellites: A Handbook of Acquisition, Processing, and Organization, by S. Miller. Libraries Unlimited, 1971.

Vertical File Index. Monthly. H. W. Wilson Company. Not particularly for children's libraries but could be useful; free and inexpensive materials are indexed by subject and title.

We Build Together, A Reader's Guide to Negro Life and Literature for Elementary and High School Use, by Charlemae Rollins. National Council of Teachers of English, 1967.

Who's Who in Children's Books: A Treasury of the Familiar Characters of Childhood, by Margery Fisher. Holt, Rinehart, and Winston, 1975.

The World in Children's Picture Books, by the Association for Childhood Education International, 1968. This is an unannotated bibliography of books from other countries or about other countries, arranged by country.

Writing for Children, by Jane Yolen. The Writer, 1971.

Writing, Illustrating, and Editing Children's Books, by Jean Poindexter Colby. Hastings House, 1967.

Written for Children, An Outline of English Children's Literature, by John R. Townsend. The Horn Book, 1976.

Yankee Doodle's Literary Sampler of Prose, Poetry and Pictures, selected by Virginia Haviland and Margaret N. Coughlan. Library of Congress, 1974.

Your Child's Reading Today, by Josette Frank. Doubleday, 1969.

FOR YOUNG ADULTS

An Ample Field: Books and Young People, by Amelia H. Munson. American Library Association, 1950.

American History, by Bernard Titowsky. McKinley, 1964.

Book Bait: Detailed Notes on Adult Books Popular with Young People, 2d edition, by Elinor Walker. American Library Association, 1969.

Books and the Teen-Age Reader, A Guide for Teachers, Librarians, and Parents, by G. Robert Carlsen. Harper and Row, 1971.

Discovering Books and Libraries, A Handbook for Students in the Middle and Upper Grades, by Florence Damon Cleary. Wilson, 1976.

Choice. Monthly. Association of College and Research Libraries of the American Library Association. *Choice* reviews for the young adult, college student, or adult reader.

The Fair Garden and the Swarm of Beasts, by Margaret A. Edwards. Hawthorn, 1969.

A Guide to Historical Reading: Non-Fiction, for the Use of Schools, Libraries, and the General Reader, compiled by Leonard B. Irwin. McKinley, 1976. Primarily for the adult or high school reader, each section of this book has a short list of young adult books (grades seven to ten), many of which could be used by children. It is a selective list.

High Interest-Easy Reading for Junior and Senior High School Reluctant Readers, revised edition, edited by Marian E. White. National Council of Teachers of English, 1972.

Historical Fiction, by Hannah Logasa, McKinley, 1968.

Hooked on Books: Programs and Proof, by Daniel N. Fader and Elton B. McNeil. Putnam, 1968.

Messages, An Annotated Bibliography of African Literature for Schools, by Gideon-Cyrus M. Mutiso. Montclair State College Press, 1970. Although primarily intended for use in high school, especially ninth and tenth grades, this title has a short list of "Juvenilia" in the front with reading levels in the upper elementary range or even lower.

Reading Round the World, A Set of International Reading Lists, edited by Frank Gardner and M. Joy Lewis. International Federation of Library Associations, 1969. No children's books are included; some could be read by young adults.

Smorgasbord of Books: Titles Junior High Readers Relish, by Betty M. Owen. Citation, 1974.

Words Like Freedom, An Annotated Bibliography of Print and Non-Print Materials, by the California Association of School Librarians. 1975.

Your Reading: A Booklist for Junior High Students, edited by Jerry L. Walker. National Council of Teachers of English, 1975.

SERIALS NO LONGER PUBLISHED

19-- Best Books for Children, A Catalog of 4000 Titles, compiled by Eleanor B. Widdoes. Each year from 1951 to 1972 *Best Books for Children* brought together entries for about four thousand children's books based largely on reviews that had appeared in *School Library Journal* during the past year. Some titles from previous years were retained, and some books recommended from other sources, such as *Booklist, American Booksellers Association Basic Book List, Children's Catalog, Junior High School Library Catalog,* and *Senior High School Library Catalog* were included. Only books in print were listed, and those that were new entries had a dagger symbol before the title.

Book World (formerly, *Book Week*). Once available separately, it can now be obtained only as a supplement to the *Washington Post* or *Chicago Tribune*. Fewer children's books are reviewed than in the past.

Books for Children, Preschool through Junior High School. Based on *Booklist* reviews, this ceased publication in 1970/1971.

Children's Book Show Catalog, American Institute of Graphic Arts. Catalogs were published through 1970.

Good Books for Children, by Mary K. Eakin. Based on reviews from *Bulletin of the Center for Children's Books,* it was superseded by *Best in Children's Books.*

Library Journal/School Library Journal, Bowker. The combination of these two journals is no longer published. Each one is available as a separate publication.

Package Library of Foreign Children's Books, sponsored by the Children's Services Division of the American Library Association. This was discontinued in 1970.

School Libraries, American Association of School Librarians of the American Library Association. *School Libraries* was superseded by *School Media Quarterly.*

SELECTING BOOKS FOR CHILDREN

Aids to Choosing Books for Children, revised edition, compiled by Ingeborg Boudreau. Children's Book Council, 1969.

Aids to Media Selection for Students and Teachers, compiled by Yvonne Carter, et al. Department of Health, Education, and Welfare, 1974.

Book and Non-Book Media, Annotated Guide to Selection Aids for Educational Materials, by Flossie L. Perkins. National Council of Teachers of English, 1972. (A revision of *Book Selection Media.*)

Book Selection for School Libraries, by Azile Woffard. Wilson, 1962.

Multi-Media Indexes, Lists, and Review Sources, A Bibliographical Guide, by Thomas L. Hart, Mary Alice Hunt, and Blanche Woolls. Marcel Dekker, 1975. This is a listing of about five hundred sources of information for the librarian or teacher serving children, young adults, or adults. There is bibliographic information and a brief description of the contents of each entry. Entries are divided into five categories: print only; nonprint; combination of print and nonprint; indexes; and periodicals. Arrangement is alphabetical within each group, and there is no division by age or type of material. The information was in most cases supplied by the author or publisher; there is no attempt at critical evaluation or a delineation of the specific uses of the aids—naturally, the description usually includes indication of usage. The work is very up to date and has some sample pages. There is no indication of what ages the material is suitable for except insofar as the title is descriptive; those not familiar with the aids might not know whether they are primarily for use with children or not. (The intent was to list the various sources in one place, not to provide a detailed analysis.) There is one index by author-title-subject.

Selecting Materials for Media Centers: Guidelines and Selection Sources to Insure Quality Collections, by the American Association of School Librarians. American Library Association, 1971.

TOO RECENT TO EXAMINE

British Children's Authors: Interviews at Home, by Cornelia Jones and Olivia R. Way. American Library Association, 1976.

Children's Authors and Illustrators: An Index to Biographical Dictionaries, edited by Dennis La Beau. Gale Research Company, 1976.

Children's Books and Their Illustrators, by Gleeson White. Gordon Press, 1976.

Children's Prize Books, 2d edition, edited by Walter Scherf. Unipub, 1976.

E is for Everybody: A Manual for Bringing Fine Picture Books into the Hands and Hearts of Children, by Nancy Polette. Scarecrow, 1976.

Elementary School Library Collection, 10th edition, by Phyllis Van Orden. Bro-Dart, 1976.

Handbook for Storytellers, by Caroline Feller Bauer. American Library Association, Spring 1977.

Now Upon a Time: A Contemporary View of Children's Literature, by Myra and David Sadker. Harper and Row, 1977.

Periodicals for School Libraries, A Guide to Magazines, Newspapers, and Periodical Indexes, edited by Selma K. Richardson. American Library Association, Fall 1977.

Selected Books on American Indians, by Mary Jo Lass-Woodfin. American Library Association, 1977.

The Special Child in the Library, edited by Barbara Baskin and Karen Harris. American Library Association, 1976.

Subject Index to Poetry for Young People, 1957-1975, compiled by Dorothy B. Frizzell Smith and Eva L. Andrews. American Library Association, Summer 1977.

Toys to Go: A Guide to the Use of Realia in Public Libraries, edited by Faith H. Hektoen and Jeanne R. Rinehart. American Library Association, 1976.

Index

For names of sources not listed in the index, see Appendix 1 and Appendix 3.

Unless noted, numbers in **boldface** refer to sample pages.

ABOUT THE AUTHOR

Mary Meacham is an instructor in library science at the University of Oklahoma in Norman. The coauthor of *The Library at Mount Vernon,* she has also contributed articles to professional journals.